Besieged

Besieged

Siege Warfare in the Ancient World

DUNCAN B. CAMPBELL

First published in Great Britain in 2006 by Osprey Publishing,
Midland House, West Way, Botley, Oxford OX2 0PH, United Kingdom.
443 Park Avenue South, New York, NY 10016, USA.
Email: info@ospreypublishing.com

Previously published as Elite 121: *Ancient Siege Warfare – Persians, Greeks, Carthaginians and Romans 546–146 BC*,
Elite 126: *Siege Warfare in the Roman World 146 BC–AD 378*, New Vanguard 78: *Greek and Roman Siege Machinery
399 BC–AD 363* and New Vanguard 89: *Greek and Roman Artillery 399 BC–AD363*, all written by Duncan Campbell.

A CIP catalogue record for this book is available from the British Library

ISBN-10: 1-84603-019-6
ISBN-13: 978-1-84603-019-2

Page layout by Ken Vail Graphic Design
Index by Alison Worthington
Originated by United Graphics Pte Ltd, Singapore
Printed in China through World Print Ltd

06 07 08 09 10   10 9 8 7 6 5 4 3 2 1

For a catalogue of all books published by Osprey please contact:

NORTH AMERICA
Osprey Direct c/o Random House Distribution Center, 400 Hahn Road,
Westminster, MD 21157, USA
E-mail: info@ospreydirect.com

ALL OTHER REGIONS
Osprey Direct UK, P.O. Box 140, Wellingborough, Northants, NN8 2FA, UK
E-mail: info@ospreydirect.co.uk

www.ospreypublishing.com

Front cover: Roman Soldiers Besieging a Town, plate 23B, class 5 from Part I of 'The History of the Nations',
engraved by A. Nani (aquatint), Italian School (19th century) / Private collection, The Stapleton Collection /
Bridgeman Art Library
Endpapers: Alexander's Siege of Tyre (Adam Hook © Osprey Publishing Ltd)

Contents

ACKNOWLEDGEMENTS

It is again a pleasure to acknowledge the generosity of colleagues who supplied illustrations for this book, or assisted in their procurement: Moti Aviam, Dietwulf Baatz, Donal Bateson, Mike Bishop, Véronique Brouquier-Reddé, Ross Cowan, Megan Doyon, Dan Gill, René Goguey, Crawford H. Greenewalt, Jr., Chris Haines, B. S. J. Isserlin, David Kennedy, Jona Lendering, Franz Georg Maier, Stephen Mitchell, Poul Pederson, Michel Reddé, Stephen Ressler, Israel Shatzman, Alan Wilkins, and Tamara Winikoff.

Finally, it is only right to acknowledge the two formative influences that long ago opened my eyes to the wonders of the ancient world: Peter Connolly and Dougie Ronald.

DEDICATION

To my wonderful family.

AUTHOR'S NOTE

All ancient sources are referenced using the abbreviations recommended by *The Oxford Classical Dictionary*. All translations are my own.

A NOTE ON MEASUREMENTS

Although the Romans imposed a standard system of weights and measures across their empire, several different systems had existed in the Greek world. For example, the Greek foot, subdivided into 16 daktyls, has been found to vary between 27 and 35cm, depending upon the geographical region. However, an intermediate value of 30.83cm was widely employed, and may be deemed an acceptable average. The standard foot of the Romans, by contrast, measured 29.57cm; it was similarly subdivided into 16ths (called digits, the Latin form of the Greek daktyls), or into 12ths.

Several weight standards were employed in the Greek world, all based on the 60-mina talent. However, the Attic standard used at Athens, with its mina of 436.6g, was pre-eminent. The Roman system was based on the pound (libra) of 327.45g, which was exactly three-quarters of the Attic mina.

Greek weights and measurements:
60 minas = 1 talent = 26.2kg
24 daktyls = 2 spans = 1 cubit = 46.24cm
16 daktyls = 1ft = 30.83cm

Roman weights and measurements:
80 librae = 1 talent = 26.2kg
24 digits = 2 spans = 1 cubit = 44.35cm
16 digits = 12in = 1ft = 29.57cm

Introduction

The history of siege warfare stretches back into the 2nd millennium BC. By that time, the towns of Mesopotamia (the land between the rivers Tigris and Euphrates in present-day Iraq) had become naturally defensive, sitting on the raised base (or 'tell') formed by earlier generations of mud-brick collapse. Tells, often 30 or 60ft (around 10 or 20m) high, were crowned by town walls, and might be additionally defended by an encircling ditch further down the slope. The walls themselves were constructed out of sun-dried brick, often built on a stone plinth (or 'socle') for stability, and were made thick enough to facilitate the movement of troops along the top. Crenellations afforded protection to archers and stone throwers on the wall-walk, and towers allowed for long-range surveillance, as well as providing an elevated shooting platform. The security of such formidable defences was compromised, however, by the need for entrances. Access to minor gateways could be restricted by the width of the path, but the main gateway was usually a monumental structure that required the protection of bastions and towers; it was often contrived as a long passageway with a gate at either end, in order to enhance security.

Of course, as soon as people began to build walls around their possessions, others began to devise the means of appropriating these possessions. Equally, as a succession of Sumerian, Babylonian and Assyrian empires conquered their neighbours, new territory could only be held by controlling the main towns. Thus, it was inevitable that sieges would play a central role in the conflicts that raged throughout the Near East in the 1st millennium BC. For example, biblical evidence reports that, in the 920s BC, when Rehoboam became king of Judah, in the southern part of present-day Israel, he immediately secured the key towns: 'he had them strongly fortified and appointed a commander for each of them, and in each one he placed supplies of food, oil, and wine, and also shields and spears' (2 Chron. 11.5–11). But it seems that Rehoboam's preparations were in vain, for the Egyptian king Shishak was able to capture many of the towns, and only bribery persuaded him to leave Jerusalem intact. Archaeological evidence from Megiddo, for example, suggests that it may have been destroyed at this time.

Assyria's rise to power in the second half of the 8th century BC (the so-called Neo-Assyrian Empire, to differentiate it from an earlier period of Assyrian hegemony) presented a greater threat to the kingdoms of the Near East. In the 730s BC, when Ahaz ruled in Judah, his counterpart in the northern kingdom of Israel clearly intended annexation, and allied himself with the Syrian king; Ahaz in alarm turned to the Assyrians for assistance. It was then that Tiglath-Pileser III, in expansionist mood, swept into Syria, capturing Damascus, before continuing south into Israel. Excavations at Hazor have demonstrated that the town, rebuilt after an earthquake around 760 BC, was engulfed in conflagration shortly afterwards and never recovered; Megiddo, too, appears to have suffered destruction at this time. The Assyrians brought a ruthlessness and organizational diligence to siege warfare. Tiglath-Pileser's successor, Shalmaneser V, may have taken three years to reduce Samaria (2 Kings 17.5), but the archaeological record eloquently testifies to Assyrian thoroughness in obliterating the town; Shalmaneser's successor, Sargon II, 'took the Israelites away to Assyria as prisoners'. Some years later, when Hezekiah of Judah rebelled, it was Sargon's son, Sennacherib, who (in the words of Lord Byron) 'came down like the wolf on

Tiglath-Pileser III (r. 745–727 BC) besieges a town using the characteristic Assyrian siege machine (right), while other troops launch an escalade on the opposite side. Assyrian armies often committed atrocities, such as the impaling of enemy captives (background), in an attempt to dismay the defenders. (Werner Forman Archive / British Museum, London)

the fold'. In the Assyrian annals, he records that 'I laid siege to strong cities, walled forts, and countless small villages, and conquered them by means of well-stamped earthen ramps and battering rams brought near the walls with an attack by foot soldiers, using mines, breeches and trenches'.

The great palace reliefs from Nimrud and Nineveh proudly display the range of siege tactics developed by successive Assyrian monarchs. Towns were systematically isolated, siege-works were thrown up, walls were breached or scaled, and, in the end, the captured populace were deported to provide mass labour in the Assyrian heartland. Amongst the most famous of all the Assyrian reliefs is the depiction of Sennacherib's siege of Lachish, south-west of Jerusalem, in 701 BC. A series of ramps are shown, carrying troops up to the walls. Archers and slingers provide a barrage of missiles, covering the advance of spearmen, but the most intriguing elements are the war machines. These many-wheeled, wicker-covered structures, normally incorporating a domed turret at the front, served to convey an iron-tipped beam up to the wall. Most scholars agree that these were intended to batter the town wall, although some of the machines depicted here have pointed beams, while other reliefs appear to show beams with flat blades. It has recently been suggested that, rather than battering walls, the Assyrians actually drilled them by striking upwards with slender, pointed beams; the aim, it is argued, was to encourage the upper part of a mud-brick wall to shear away and slide forward, causing general alarm and destruction. The case, however, remains subjective. The later Greek writer Diodorus Siculus simply displays his ignorance when he writes that, in Assyria, 'tortoises, battering rams, catapults and the devices for overthrowing walls had not been invented' (2.27.1).

The full repertoire of Assyrian siege warfare is on display in this relief sculpture from Nimrud. Soldiers can be seen breaking through a town wall (left) and undermining it (centre), while the defenders attempt to neutralize a siege machine (right) by catching the ramming head with a chain. (© 2003 Topham Picturepoint / TopFoto)

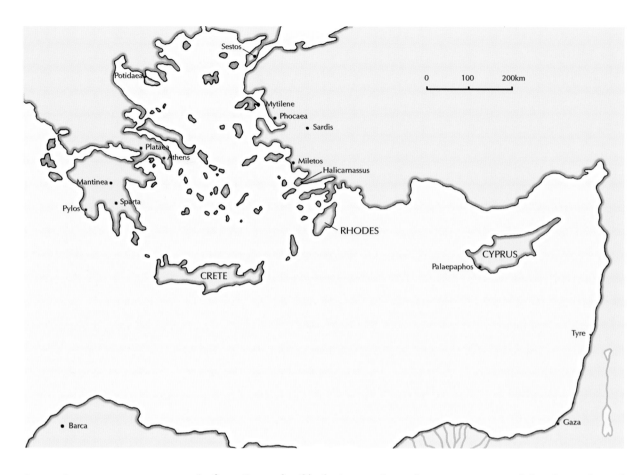

Sites in the eastern Mediterranean mentioned in the text. (© Author)

As far as Sennacherib's designs on Jerusalem were concerned, Isaiah prophesied that 'He shall not come into this city, nor shoot an arrow there, nor come before it with a shield, nor pour out a mound against it' (*Isaiah* 37.33). Lachish was not so fortunate. Archaeological excavations in the 1970s and 1980s revealed a stony, fan-shaped siege ramp, which rose against the defences at the south-west corner of the town, and narrowed towards the summit to create a flat area, some 82ft (25m) wide, where siege machines could be deployed. The Assyrian strategy was clearly to neutralize the massive 50ft-thick (15m) town wall by rising above it and targeting the less substantial battlements above. In response, the defenders had dumped quantities of soil behind their wall, perhaps in a race to heighten the defences. Signs of burning echo the scenes on the Assyrian relief (see page 12), where torches thrown down onto the siege machines are extinguished by crew members, who pour water from large ladles. A fragment of iron chain discovered on the siege ramp recalls the scene from another relief, where defenders attempt to ensnare a ramming beam by lowering such a chain from the wall. The excavations revealed arrowheads and sling stones peppering the area, and a few iron scales of armour were found.

THE FUNDAMENTALS OF SIEGE WARFARE

The siege tactics originally devised by the warlike Assyrians echoed down through the ages, and found employment wherever there was a need to capture strongholds. Towns frequently surrendered in terror at the approach of their enemy; but, more often, the townsfolk barred the gates and hoped that their fortifications would discourage the aggressor. Under these circumstances, five courses of action remained open to the besieger. He could gain entry by crossing over the defences, penetrating through them, or tunnelling under them. If he failed in these, or perhaps lacked the means to attempt them, he might threaten the townsfolk with starvation by blockading their supply routes. The only remaining option was to gain access by treachery or trickery.

The most straightforward route over the defences involved ladders, but this was also the most perilous approach: the apparatus gave no protection, and the climbing individuals were vulnerable to attack from above. The alternative was to pile up an earth embankment high enough to overtop the walls, so that troops could storm up and over. But the construction of these massive ramps was labour intensive, and the process became increasingly risky as the workers drew nearer to the walls.

Breaking through the defences required battering rams, directed either at the wall itself or at a gateway. In theory, the latter represented the weakest point in a defensive circuit, and might even be vulnerable to fire; but for that reason any right-minded defender concentrated his efforts there. Alternatively, walls might be made to collapse by digging away their foundations or undermining long stretches, but both methods carried their own dangers. The third approach, passing beneath the defences, required the excavation of tunnels large enough to deliver an effective strike force into the town. If handled properly, this method had the advantage of secrecy, but this would be lost as soon as the defenders either heard the tunnellers or noticed the accumulation of spoil from the excavation.

The Ishtar Gate at Babylon, reconstructed on its original site. The gate was built during the reign of Nebuchadnezzar II (r. 604–562 BC), with a facing of glazed polychrome bricks over the mudbrick structure. An associated inscription mentions cedar wood gates, reinforced with bronze. (© Author)

A series of reliefs from the palace of Sennacherib (r. 704–681 BC) at Nineveh depict the siege of Lachish (Israel) in 701 BC. Here, the Assyrians advance a war-machine up a specially built ramp, and are met with a hail of burning torches from the battlements. (Werner Forman Archive / British Museum, London)

These methods, singly or in combination, offered the besieger a chance to rapidly seize a fortified town. However, he might suffer heavy casualties in the process. Far less dangerous from the besieger's perspective was the blockade: in theory, by sealing off the townsfolk from the outside world, he could let privation force them to surrender. It is true that sieges usually brought great hardships: when Sennacherib's representatives brought the Assyrian ultimatum to Hezekiah at Jerusalem, they urged him to think of the townsfolk 'who will have to eat their excrement and drink their urine' (2 *Kings* 18.27). However, depending upon the resources of the town and the totality of the blockade, such an operation might drag on indefinitely. This could be as disadvantageous to the besieger as to the besieged, because an army encamped in one location for a protracted period brought its own problems of supply and sanitation.

Of course, if political rivalry existed within the town, one or other faction might be persuaded to grant the besieger access, thus saving time and avoiding unnecessary losses. The besieger's only other option was to trick his way in. The

The Assyrian troops of Ashurbanipal (r. 668–627 BC) assault a town in Egypt. Soldiers storm up ladders while their comrades dig at the walls, and others lead a stream of prisoners away. (Werner Forman Archive / British Museum, London)

standard form of trickery involved the conspicuous departure of the besieging forces, in apparent abandonment of the operation. The relieved townsfolk could then be caught off guard by a strike force that had been left behind in concealment; ideally, the latter's infiltration of the unsuspecting town was timed to coincide with the return of the main besieging force. The legendary capture of Troy was accomplished by just such a ruse.

Siege Warfare of the Achaemenid Persians

Assyrian dominance had passed back to the Babylonians by around 600 BC. They, in turn, were eclipsed by the rise of the Achaemenid dynasty of Persians, with the accession of Cyrus the Great around 560 BC. His son Cambyses (r. 530–522 BC) was succeeded by Darius (r. 522–486 BC), whose designs on Greece were famously thwarted at Marathon in 490 BC. A second invasion of Greece, launched ten years later by Darius' son and successor Xerxes (r. 486–465 BC), similarly failed when the Persians were defeated at Plataea in 479 BC. The armies fielded by these Achaemenid kings seem to have been just as vigorous in siegecraft as their Assyrian forebears. The historical sources carry reports of siege equipment, undermining operations, and the construction of earth embankments to dominate town walls; trickery was also employed on occasion.

THE CONQUESTS OF CYRUS THE GREAT

The Greek writer Xenophon took an interest in Persian affairs following his military service as a mercenary in the region in 401 BC. According to him, in 546 BC, when Cyrus annexed Lydia, the kingdom of Croesus in present-day Turkey, he ordered the construction of battering rams for an assault on the fabulously rich capital city

of Sardis (Xen., *Cyr.* 7.2.2). However, after two weeks of fruitless siege, Cyrus offered to reward the first man to scale the walls. Many tried without success, until a certain Hyroeades led the way up the steep slope to an unguarded section of the acropolis. The Greek historian Herodotus, who composed his *History* around 430 BC, tells the story. According to him, Hyroeades had observed one of Croesus' soldiers climbing down the cliff to retrieve his fallen helmet; he duly led a party of Persians up the same route, and the city was taken (Hdt. 1.84–86). The Roman writer Polyaenus, who published a collection of stratagems (*Stratēgēmata*) around AD 160, claimed that Cyrus had taken the town by trickery, feigning retreat before mounting a nocturnal escalade (*Strat.* 7.6.2); furthermore, he recorded that the Lydians sheltering on the acropolis were moved to surrender when Cyrus threatened to kill their captured relatives (*Strat.* 7.6.3). Although Polyaenus is an erratic source whose testimony should not be allowed to contradict a reliable authority like Herodotus, the latter mentions only the capture of the acropolis; it may be that, prior to this, the main fortification was taken by a ruse.

Herodotus and Xenophon both suggest that Cyrus was troubled by the choice between satisfying his men with plunder, and saving Sardis from destruction. When Croesus was captured during the siege, he asked Cyrus what the Persians were doing, to which the king allegedly replied, 'sacking your city and carrying off your property'; but Croesus retorted, 'it is your property they

The acropolis at Sardis, looking west across the ancient site towards the sanctuary of Artemis. The site of the Lydian city's west gate lies off to the right of the photo, and is obscured by the acropolis. (© Crawford H. Greenewalt, Jr. / Archaeological Exploration of Sardis / Harvard University)

The skeleton of a young man, discovered in 1987/8, amid the 6th-century debris in front of the town wall of Sardis. An apricot-sized stone is clasped in his right hand. Skeletal development, along with the nature of several previous injuries, suggested to the excavators that the man was a warrior. He had been stabbed in the middle of the back, but whether he had fallen, or his corpse had been dumped, is unknown. Another skeleton was later found in a nearby destruction layer. (© Archaeological Exploration of Sardis / Harvard University)

are plundering' (Hdt. 1.88). According to Herodotus, Croesus then advised Cyrus not to allow indiscriminate looting, but to gather all the booty on the pretext that one-tenth had to be dedicated to the gods; Xenophon tells a similar tale. Whether true or not, it neatly highlights a problem that every siege commander eventually had to face.

During excavations at the site, the Harvard-led archaeological exploration of Sardis unearthed a 560ft (170m) length of the Lydian town's mud-brick walls. The massive 65ft-thick (20m) barrier, buttressed in front by a sloping earthwork glacis and still standing 50ft (15m) high at some points, exhibits several peculiarities of design. For example, the stone 'socle', or plinth upon which the mud-brick walls were built, varies in height from 3ft (around a metre) up to 15ft (4.5m). In places, there was evidence that the wall had been violently destroyed, though whether during an assault or in the subsequent sack of the city remains unclear; perhaps the Persians adopted the standard Assyrian practice of slighting the walls of their defeated enemies. The forward tumble of mud-bricks showed signs of burning, and the debris sealed a 4in-thick (10cm) layer of burnt timber. Amid this dramatic evidence of destruction lay the skeleton of a young warrior, apparently poised to throw a stone. Aged in his mid-20s, he may have been a slinger or stone-thrower defending the walls to the last. An unusually ornate helmet found in fragments nearby need not have been his; however, medical autopsy showed that he had already sustained head wounds some years prior to death, which may have persuaded him to invest in a helmet.

THE PERSIANS IN IONIA

Following his annexation of Lydia, Cyrus turned his attention to the Ionian Greek towns along the coast of Turkey, and entrusted their conquest to his generals. First, Mazares plundered Priene and Miletus, then Harpagus extended the operations to the remaining Greek communities; Herodotus explains that 'he enclosed them in their towns, and by piling up embankments against the walls he captured them' (Hdt. 1.162). Xenophon claims that Cyrus had prepared machinery and rams to batter the walls of anyone who refused to acknowledge his supremacy (Cyr. 7.4.1). But Herodotus mentions no siege equipment, and it is possible that the embankments were simply designed to elevate foot soldiers to rampart level, so that they could storm into the town.

At Phocaea in Turkey, Harpagus promised to restrain his troops, provided the townsfolk tore down one of their towers. But, taking advantage of their temporary reprieve, the Phocaeans evacuated their coastal town by sea, carrying off much of their property as well (Hdt. 1.164). Here, in the 1990s, archaeology brought to light a massively built wall, surviving to a height of around 16ft (5m) where it had been preserved within a later tumulus, or burial mound. The wall was externally buttressed by a 10ft-high (3m) stone-built glacis, perhaps to stabilize it against undermining. An attack had evidently been launched at the south gate, where there were signs of a conflagration: on the floor of the entrance lay carbonized fragments of the wooden uprights that once flanked the gate passage, and the excavator, Ömer Özyiğit, believed that a smashed amphora found there had been used to extinguish the fire. Certainly, the entrance way, originally of beaten earth, had been turned to mud, and in the process had preserved two boot prints. Signs of conflict included Persian arrowheads littering the area and a single 48lb (22kg) stone, which had probably been tumbled onto the attackers from the battlements above.

Cyrus' subsequent activities included the capture of Babylon, near present-day Baghdad (Iraq), in 539 BC. The Babylonian text known as the Nabonidus Chronicle claims that Babylon surrendered after Cyrus' brutal destruction of nearby Opis. Similarly, the Persian inscription known as the Cyrus Cylinder tells how the Babylonian god Marduk allowed Cyrus to capture the city peacefully: 'without battle or fighting, Marduk let him enter Babylon'. But Herodotus has a different story. According to him, the Persians lowered the level of the River Euphrates so that they could wade along it where it entered the city; the inhabitants were celebrating a local festival and had no warning of the Persian infiltration until it was too late (Hdt. 1.191). Polyaenus preserves a similar version, perhaps taken from Herodotus (Strat. 7.6.5), but in a later passage he claims that the Persians drew off the Euphrates to deny drinking water to the townsfolk (Strat.

The site of Babylon near Baghdad (Iraq), during excavation and reconstruction work in 1984. The Greek philosopher Aristotle claimed that the city was so big that, two days after it was captured by Cyrus, the news still had not reached all the inhabitants. (© Author)

7.6.8). The story is a good one, but scholars are in general agreement that it must be an invention. It is possible that the Persians engineered the lowering of the river so as to be fordable by the army, but it is just as likely that the ancient writers were confused by a later irrigation project to connect the Tigris and Euphrates.

DARIUS AND THE IONIAN REVOLT

Soon after Darius came to power in 522 BC, Babylon again revolted. But having besieged the town for 19 months, the Persians could make no headway until a certain Zopyrus hatched a desperate scheme. First, he mutilated his own face to convince the Babylonians that he had fallen from Darius' favour; then, by staging a couple of victories over Persian troops, he gained the Babylonians' trust and admiration; and finally, having tricked his way into becoming guardian of Babylon, he threw open the gates to Darius (Hdt. 3.151–9).

Some years later, the Persian governor of Egypt launched an attack on the town of Barca in Libya. Over the course of nine months, the Persians attempted to tunnel into the town, but a Barcan metalworker devised an effective countermeasure. By placing the bronze facing of a shield on the ground at various points around the town circuit, he could detect where the Persians were tunnelling because the underground vibrations caused the bronze to resonate; countermines could then be dug to intercept the enemy (Hdt. 4.200). The stratagem became so well known that it was included in a compendium of advice for besieged towns, written almost 200 years later (Aeneas Tact. 37.6–7). In the end, unable to take the town by military assault, the Persian commander, Amasis, resorted to trickery. He invited a Barcan delegation to meet him in no man's land to make a pact. The Barcans agreed to pay tribute to the Persians, and in return Amasis swore that he would never do them harm for as long as the earth beneath their feet remained firm. However, unknown to the Barcans, they were standing, not on solid ground, but above a concealed trench that the Persians had dug during the previous night. The oath was thus void, and when the unsuspecting Barcans opened their gates the Persians seized the town. The townsfolk were enslaved and sent to Persia.

At the time of the Ionian Revolt, the townsfolk of Lindos on Rhodes took refuge from Persian aggression on their rocky acropolis. The Persian plan to deny them sustenance was thwarted by a timely shower of rain, for which the local cult of Athena duly took the credit. (TopFoto / HIP)

Of course, siege operations were not always successful. In 499 BC, the prosperous island of Naxos revolted against Persian rule, but the subsequent siege was abandoned after four months owing to the islanders' plentiful provisions (Hdt. 5.34). As a result of the Naxians' success, Aristagoras, the disaffected ruler of Miletus, roused other Greek towns along the coast of Asia Minor to join the so-called Ionian Revolt, which rumbled on for six years. He requested aid from mainland Greece, but only Athens and Eretria responded, contributing contingents to the army which sacked Sardis in 498 BC (Hdt. 5.99–102). However, Herodotus records that, not only were they unable to capture the acropolis, but they were also denied loot from the lower town; this was because the thatched houses easily caught fire, and the conflagration soon engulfed the whole city.

In the same year, the revolt spread to Cyprus, where a Persian army defeated the combined Cypriote forces in a pitched battle and besieged the island's towns one by one. Soloi was the last to fall, when its walls were undermined in a five-month operation (Hdt. 5.115). At the town of Palaepaphos (modern Kouklia),

Bronze cauldrons were used to fire the timber props at the end of each Cypriote tunnel. This one is depicted in situ in the sap. Above each cauldron, the extreme heat had calcined the embankment material into a cone-shaped mass of lime. (© F. G. Maier/ Swiss–German Archaeological Expedition Palaepaphos)

archaeological work in the 1950s identified a large siege embankment near the north-east gate, filling the 12ft (3.7m) defensive ditch and rising at least another 8ft (2.5m) against the town wall. In a later remodelling of the defences, long after the siege, the embankment was landscaped into a projecting bastion encompassed by a retaining wall. It must originally have been longer, wider and higher than the surviving mound, but none of its original dimensions can be proven.

The attacking Persians used all available materials for its construction (see illustration p. 22). In addition to earth, field stones and tree trunks, there were more than 1,000 architectural and sculptural fragments; these pieces, which included statues, sphinxes, lions and altars, are thought to have come from a religious precinct demolished by the Persians. Some 500 arrowheads and spear points, and over 400 roughly chiselled stone missiles, show that the construction work came under heavy bombardment from defenders on the town wall. In addition, traces of burnt bone among the embankment material, and the finds of a bronze helmet and fragments of an iron one, give an indication that desperate fighting must have occurred.

The excavations also revealed extensive remains of elaborate counter-siege operations. Using skills gained in local copper mining, the townsfolk attempted to destabilize the Persian embankment by driving a series of large tunnels underneath. In total, five tunnels were dug, one of which was technically a sap; this 5ft-deep (1.5m) trench breached the town wall at its base and ran out for a further 40ft (12m), where it met the edge of the town's defensive ditch. Wooden props along both sides of the 6½ ft-wide (2m) passage must have supported a planked roof, and towards the end of the sap the roof gained additional support from three squat piers of mud-brick, arranged in a row along the centre. The other tunnels began immediately inside the town wall, dropping in roughly cut steps to a depth of about 8ft (2.4m) to get beneath the wall's foundations, and running for a distance of about 66ft (20m) to reach the town ditch. Emerging from the bedrock into the debris-filled ditch, the tunnellers no doubt boarded

The Persian siege embankment at Palaepaphos during excavation. The town ditch can be seen in the centre, where it has been filled by the embankment material. The town wall lies off the photo to the left. The cuttings on the left follow the paths of two tunnels, dug by the defenders in order to destabilize the Persian works. (© F. G. Maier / Swiss–German Archaeological Expedition Palaepaphos)

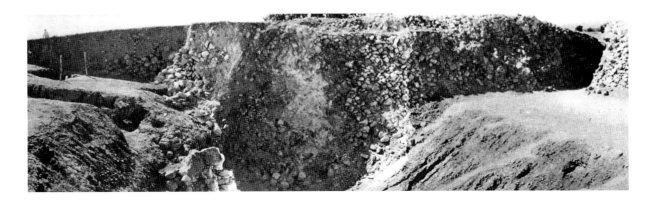

the walls and roof with timber. The width of each tunnel varied from 3½ft to 5½ft (1.1m to 1.7m), and the headroom from 5½ft to 7½ft (1.7m to 2.3m); niches were cut into the walls to hold clay lamps for illumination. The excavated rock was dragged back into the town and dumped at each tunnel mouth, along with material from the Persian embankment.

At the ends of Tunnels 1 and 3, and the sap, archaeologists found the remains of a large bronze cauldron, fire-damaged and filled with carbonized wood and ash. Above each cauldron, the intense heat had fused the embankment material into a large cone of lime. It seems that, rather than steadily extracting the embankment material through the tunnels (as was later attempted at Plataea in 429 BC), the townsfolk hoped to cause sudden and unexpected slumping at the head of each mine by firing its wooden roof and causing internal collapse. The excavator, Franz Georg Maier, reasoned that this kind of localized destabilizing meant that the targets were Persian siege towers on the embankment. Certainly, there was perhaps too little timber and brushwood within the mound for the Cypriotes to have created a general conflagration, with the hope of causing wholesale destruction.

The Persian siege of Palaepaphos, 498 BC. No description of the Persian siege of Palaepaphos exists, but the archaeological remains give a good indication of the course of events. The Persian strategy was based on the construction of an earthen embankment, which the defenders sought to counter by digging tunnels underneath. The excavator believed that the embankment was designed to bring a siege tower against the town wall. (Adam Hook © Osprey Publishing Ltd)

The easternmost tunnel, Tunnel 2, remained unfinished after about 50ft (15m), apparently owing to a roof collapse. Tunnels 1 and 3 headed directly north-east beneath the wall curtain and out to the town ditch. But the western tunnel, Tunnel 4, took a winding course under the town gateway, finally linking up with a lateral spur from Tunnel 3. Investigation showed that, at some point, the access to Tunnel 3 was completely blocked where it passed beneath the town wall. Consequently, it has been suggested that Tunnel 4 was dug in order to rescue miners trapped deep in Tunnel 3; certainly, the spur (designated Tunnel 3A) had headroom of only 2ft (0.6m) for long stretches, perhaps implying that it was an emergency measure. Nevertheless, there is no certainty that Tunnel 3 was blocked during the siege, and an alternative explanation may be advanced for the reduced dimensions of 3A. This may have been designed to control the draught to the fire-chamber at the end of Tunnel 3, making it a more sophisticated version of Tunnel 1.

North-east gate and town wall at Palaepaphos, looking east. The remains of the Persian siege embankment (left) were later incorporated into the town defences as a bastion. (© F. G. Maier / Swiss–German Archaeological Expedition Palaepaphos)

Tunnel 4 at Palaepaphos has headroom of 4½–5ft (1.4–1.8m) and a width of 3½–5ft (1.1–1.5m); the scale at the entrance is 19¾in (50cm). (© F. G. Maier / Swiss–German Archaeological Expedition Palaepaphos)

Unfortunately, the mines seem not to have had the desired effect. None of the fire-chambers was large enough to create major subsidence in the embankment, and the Persians must eventually have broken into the town, if not over the walls then certainly through the gateway, where excavation uncovered burnt debris containing arrowheads, javelin points and stone missiles. Herodotus records that 'the Cypriotes, after a year of freedom, were reduced once more to slavery' (Hdt. 5.116). There were still towns on the mainland to be subdued, and the Ionian Revolt ended only with the fall of Miletus in 494 BC. Apparently, the Persians tried several stratagems here, including tunnelling; the town was plundered and the people were carted off to the Persian capital at Susa (Hdt. 6.6, 18).

PERSIAN SIEGE MACHINES

Little is known of the kind of siege apparatus employed by the Persians. Unlike their Assyrian forebears, the Achaemenids did not surround themselves with sculptural depictions of war, and none of their literary sources describes a siege. By contrast, in his idealized 'Education of Cyrus' (*Cyropaedia*), Xenophon represents the Great King ordering the manufacture of machinery (*Cyr.* 6.1.20–2), which he placed in the care of an engineering corps (*Cyr.* 6.3.8). However, we are not sure what these machines looked like. Xenophon's references to 'machines and ladders' (*Cyr.* 7.2.2) and 'machines and battering rams' (*Cyr.* 7.4.1) are too vague to help matters, but the French scholar Yvon Garlan assumed that they must be siege towers of some description. Cyrus certainly appears to have had such devices. Xenophon (*Cyr.* 6.1.52–54) describes one whose 'lowest storey including the wheels' stood about three *orguiai* (18 Greek feet, or 5.6m) high. It had 'both walkways and battlements' and was crewed by 20 men. The total weight of 120 talents (a little over 3 tonnes) was easily drawn by eight yoke of oxen. However, although such machines apparently accompanied each division of Cyrus' army, they seem not to have been intended for sieges, but to support the army on the battlefield.

It has recently been suggested that the Persians lacked battering technology. The mud-brick fortifications of the Near East, it is argued, were more effectively attacked by sharp, upward-angled beams; the resulting row of parallel borings would cause the upper section of wall to slide away from the base. However,

The Oxford historian George Rawlinson, brother of the Assyriologist Sir Henry Rawlinson, believed that the tall uprights at the right-hand edge of this Assyrian relief from Nimrud represented stone-throwing machines, but this identification is unconvincing. (Drawing by A. H. Layard of a wall relief, originally from the NW Palace of Ashurnasirpal II. © The British Museum)

there is no evidence that this ingenious scheme was ever put into practice. Its proponents emphasize that, since such drilling was useless against the stone-built defences on Cyprus, the Persians resorted to mound-building there. But it seems rather more likely that the embankment at Palaepaphos was designed to facilitate the approach of a battering ram, and that such battering was, in any case, normally aimed at the more vulnerable battlements.

Periodically, scholars have suggested that the Persians must have had some form of artillery. Early speculations were based on biblical evidence. In Ezekiel's prophesy concerning the siege of Jerusalem in around 580 BC, the Greek version of the text (the so-called Septuagint) mentions *belostaseis*, or 'artillery positions' (*Ezek.* 4.2; 21.22). However, the original Hebrew text actually has the word *karim*, meaning battering rams, so the reference to artillery seems to have been an

The Assyrian army of Ashurnasirpal II (r. 883–859 BC) besieges a town using a combination of escalade and undermining. (Ancient Art & Architecture Collection)

THE 'BORER'

The Roman writers Athenaeus and Vitruvius claim that the Macedonian engineer Diades developed a specialized kind of battering ram, called a 'borer' (*trypanon*, or *terebra*), although it did not use the same drilling action as the carpentry tool of the same name. In outward appearance, it resembled a ram-tortoise. Internally, it would have been based upon a rectangular, wheeled undercarriage, of the sort familiar from the other tortoises, but the long, iron-pointed beam, which gave the machine its name, employed a different mechanism from the 'ram-holder' (*kriodochē*) of the ram-tortoise (see below, p. 77).

The ramming-beam ran along a grooved timber (*syrinx*, or *canalis*), which, Vitruvius adds, was 50 cubits (75ft or 22m) long and 1 cubit (0.44m) high and was mounted on supports (*De arch.* 10.13.7). As both authors point out, the same word is also used for the groove of a catapult, in which the arrow is laid in order to guarantee a straight shot; incorporated in this machine, it ensured that the ramming-beam hit the same spot, time after time. In addition, it was equipped with a winch at the rear, again as on a catapult. However, unlike the catapult, the borer's groove was fitted with a series of rollers along the bottom, so that the ramming-beam would easily roll backwards and forwards.

It will have been a simple matter to winch the beam backwards. Driving it forwards with enough energy to break through a wall is quite a different matter. However, for this purpose, another two rollers were positioned towards the front end of the groove, one on either side. Traction ropes, attached to the rear of the ramming-beam, were perhaps run forward around these rollers and back towards the rear, so that hauling-crews inside the shed, positioned to the left and right of the groove, could pull the beam forwards with a violent tug.

It has recently been suggested that this machine was only intended for use against mud-brick.

According to this theory, it was designed to deliver short, sharp upward strikes, cutting through the mud-brick and eventually causing the top part of the wall to shear away and slide forwards. It is true that punching through a mud-brick wall would not require the fierce energy of a battering ram, and the drill could simply be winched forwards and backwards, slowly and deliberately. However, Athenaeus and Vitruvius have preserved insufficient detail to make this identification certain.

Both authors add that the beam 'and the arches' were covered with rawhide, just like the tortoise. The clue to the possible identity of these arches comes when we compare the length of the groove with the length of Diades' tortoise, because it is clear that the former will have projected up to 10 cubits (15ft or 4.4m) beyond the latter. This exposed section must have been arched over to give it some protection from above, but even then it would have been particularly vulnerable to missiles dropped from above. Thus, covering fire would have been essential in order to keep the battlements clear of defenders and ensure that no countermeasures could be launched.

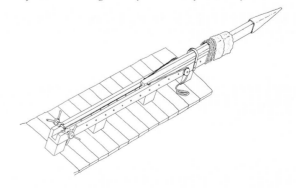

At some point, the Greeks developed a variation on the battering ram, in which the beam terminated in a pointed iron head. The device, known as a trypanon ('borer'), is briefly mentioned by Aeneas under battering rams, and by Polyaenus in a stratagem of uncertain date. The design illustrated here is attributed to Diades, one of Alexander's engineers. (© Author, after Lendle)

error made by the ancient Greek translators. In a different passage of scripture, King Uzziah of Judah is said to have defended Jerusalem around 760 BC with machines for shooting missiles and great stones (2 *Chron.* 26.15), but this is likely to be an anachronism. The chronicler was writing around 300 BC, by which time catapults were becoming common in the Near East, and it is easy to see how he might have elaborated his description with details from his own day. None of this biblical evidence would encourage a departure from the traditional date of 399 BC for the development of artillery (see p. 48, below).

More recently, supporters of an earlier date for the catapult's introduction have been encouraged by archaeological finds from two Persian siege sites. At Palaepaphos on Cyprus, 422 roughly rounded limestone blocks were found, varying in diameter from 4¾in to 11in (12cm to 28cm) and weighing from 4½ lb to 48lb (2kg to 22kg); by far the majority weighed 9–13lb (4–6kg). These came exclusively from outside the town defences, in the layer of debris associated with the Persian siege, which initially led the excavator to suggest that they derived from Persian catapults. This view was tentatively advanced in Elisabeth Erdmann's final report, although she admitted that equipping the Persians with a primitive form of catapult was not an ideal explanation, and the stones could equally well have been dropped from the battlements.

Town wall at Palaepaphos, besieged by the Persians in 498 BC. (© F. G. Maier / Swiss–German Archaeological Expedition Palaepaphos)

A selection of the stone missiles from Palaepaphos. It is often suggested that these represent ammunition for stone-throwing machines, but it appears to have been common practice for defenders to heave boulders from the battlements onto the attackers below. (© F. G. Maier / Swiss–German Archaeological Expedition Palaepaphos)

The discovery of a stone missile during excavations at Phocaea in the 1990s re-opened the debate. The lump of tufa, found on the threshold of the gateway, was roughly worked into a sphere, 11½ in (29cm) in diameter and weighing 48lb (22kg). The Achaemenid specialist Pierre Briant was convinced that the weight of the stone argued against its use as a hand-thrown weapon and proposed that the Persian besiegers had used catapults. That the stone belonged to the besiegers, and not to the defenders, was assumed both by Briant and by the excavator, Özyiğit, on the grounds that it had been hastily manufactured; Briant added the argument that, if the Phocaeans had owned catapults, we would surely have heard about it. Unfortunately, the only author who records catapults at this early date is Polyaenus, whose collected *Stratēgēmata* veer wildly between plausibility and fiction depending on the source of the particular stratagem. According to him, when Cambyses, the son of Cyrus the Great, besieged Pelusium (Egypt) in 525 BC, the Egyptian defenders used 'catapults for sharp missiles, stones and fire' (*Strat.* 7.9); the story is probably false.

Of course, the hasty workmanship of the Phocaean missile does not prove a Persian origin; it could just as easily signify the emergency preparations of the defenders. But, contrary to common assumptions, a stone ball need not imply catapults at all. Certainly, a distance throw with such a missile would be out of the question, but a 48lb (22kg) stone could easily have been dropped from the battlements onto the attackers below. Such a heavy stone might be difficult to manoeuvre into position, but smoothing the edges to make a rough sphere would allow it to be rolled. It seems that the case for Persian artillery at such an early date is far from proven.

Siege Warfare in Classical Greece

The fortifications around Mediterranean cities and towns in the 5th and early 4th centuries BC largely took the form of a 'great circuit'. The entire urban area was enclosed by a wall, taking maximum advantage of the terrain by following high ground or coastlines; towers reinforced potentially weak points, such as angles and gateways. Such a perimeter often ran to extreme length, but this posed no drawback, as it was not intended to be continuously manned. If sentries identified enemy forces massing for an attack, the relatively short lines of communication within the circuit meant that defensive efforts could quickly be concentrated at the threatened sector. In addition, by utilizing natural defences as far as possible, the 'great circuit' denied the attacker the use of overwhelming numbers and forced him to negotiate difficult terrain. Properly defended, such a fortification was impregnable in the absence of siege technology.

Classical Greek warfare was based on the punitive raid, designed to provoke the adversary into pitched battle; the accepted code of conduct obliged the two sides to meet in the ritualized clash of hoplite armies. Herodotus explains this in a speech that he puts into the mouth of the Persian Mardonius on the eve of Xerxes' invasion of Greece (Hdt. 7.9). By and large, there was no question of capturing towns or enslaving enemy populations. Of course, many Greeks would have been familiar with besieging techniques: their cousins in Asia Minor had seen Persian siegecraft at first hand during the Ionian Revolt, and Greek mercenaries had served with the Great King's army. But the resources of the average city-state would not have stretched to supporting the siege of a walled town.

Consequently, Greek armies lacked practice in this branch of warfare. This is illustrated by the Spartan attempt, around 525 BC, to overthrow the tyranny of Polycrates on the island of Samos. The Spartans initially gained a foothold on the town's seaward wall, perhaps by escalade, but were ejected from the town by overwhelming forces. In the mêlée, two of their number rushed through the open gates, but were killed inside the town. The Spartans had reached the limit of their besieging skills and departed after 40 days (Hdt. 3.54–6). An event in 489 BC shows that contemporary Athenian siegecraft was just as rudimentary. In the aftermath of the Greek victory at Marathon, the Athenian general Miltiades tried to punish the island town of Paros for having aided the Persians. But, with the Parians safe within their walls, the only tactic available to the Athenians was to devastate the island, and after 26 days they gave up and left (Hdt. 6.133–5). The Spartan-led coalition outside Thebes in 479 BC found themselves in a similar predicament. The Persian invaders had just been defeated at nearby Plataea, ending their aspirations of Greek conquest, but Thebes was harbouring Persian sympathizers. Fortunately for the Spartans, the traitors gave themselves up after only 20 days of siege (Hdt. 9.86–7).

The western fortifications of Messene. The rambling 'great circuit', dating to 369 BC, encloses the heights of Mount Ithome (to left), and follows ridges of high ground to discourage attackers. (A. W. Lawrence; © Courtauld Institute of Art)

ATHENIAN SIEGECRAFT

At some point, the Athenians acquired a reputation for siegecraft. The historian Thucydides says as much (1.102), although as an Athenian and a soldier he is perhaps a biased source. It is true that, following the battle of Plataea in 479 BC, the Spartans were unable to break into the Persian stockade, where the survivors were rallying, until the Athenian forces arrived (Hdt. 9.70). But when the Roman biographer Plutarch came to retell the story, it seems as though the Spartans were simply inexperienced in storming walls (Plut., *Aristides* 19). A comparison may be drawn with an incident from the battle at Mycale, allegedly fought on the same day as Plataea; during the rout of the Persian forces by the allied Greeks, it was the Athenian contingent that led the assault on the enemy stockade (Hdt. 9.102). As Garlan rightly observed, the supposed Athenian expertise was tested only against wooden palisades, not real fortifications.

Another event from 479 BC illustrates this contrast. The Persian bridgehead on the European side of the Hellespont was based at Sestos, which remained in Persian hands even after Xerxes' withdrawal from Greece. This strongly fortified town was strategically placed to challenge Athenian trade with the Black Sea region, so Xanthippus, the father of Pericles, led an Athenian fleet to capture it. The Persian governor Artayctes was unprepared for siege, so starvation quickly set in. Yet, despite this fact, the Athenians made little headway and complained to their officers, requesting to be taken home. It was only with the escape of Artayctes that the townsfolk were free to open their gates to the Athenians (Hdt. 9.114–121; Diod. Sic. 11.37.4–5). Similarly, the blockade of Persian-garrisoned Eion by Cimon, the son of Miltiades, was only brought to a conclusion when the Persian general Butes set fire to the place, preferring to perish than to be starved into submission (Plut., *Cimon* 7); the method of capture is not recorded by Thucydides (1.98), but a note by the Hadrianic traveller and writer Pausanias suggests that Cimon had diverted the town's water supply (Paus. 8.8.9).

It is clear that the Athenians had developed no revolutionary besieging tactics. During the 470s and 460s BC, in the course of building their maritime empire under the guise of the Delian League, they often found it necessary to bring recalcitrant towns into line, but this was done not with an aggressive assault but by employing the costly method of blockade. Thasos provides a case in point. When the island revolted in around 465 BC, the ensuing Athenian siege dragged on into a third year before the Thasians surrendered; their walls were slighted, their navy was confiscated, and an annual tax was imposed (Thuc. 1.101). At Samos in 440 BC, Pericles is said to have erected blockading walls on three sides of the town (Thuc. 1.116), while Athenian ships patrolled the fourth side, which lay on the coast. When the ships briefly departed, the Samians took the opportunity to raid their oppressor's fleet base and bring in supplies; but, on the return of the Athenian ships, the blockade was once more complete, and the Samians finally capitulated after nine months (Thuc. 1.117).

BLOCKADING WALLS

Athens dealt similarly with Potidaea, which refused the unreasonable Athenian demands to dismantle its fortifications late in 432 BC. Sited on the westernmost finger of Chalcidice at the narrowest point, its walls ran from sea to sea, dividing the southern peninsula from the land mass to the north. The Persians had failed to storm the town during their retreat from Greece in 479 BC, but this was largely down to the incompetence of their commander (Hdt. 8.126–9). The Athenians adopted a different tack: two blockading walls were constructed, one to the north of the town and one to the south, completely barring the isthmus, and naval patrols watched both coasts (Thuc. 1.64). Unfortunately, the town proved surprisingly stubborn; in the second year of the siege, fresh forces from Athens made a vain attempt to storm the place using 'machines' (a word which Thucydides often uses to mean ladders), but their failure was compounded by an outbreak of plague and, after 40 days, they withdrew again (Thuc. 2.58). By this time, the Potidaeans had reportedly been reduced to cannibalism, and finally surrendered after a siege of over two years (Thuc. 2.70; Diod. Sic. 12.46.2–6).

Relief sculpture from the Nereid Monument (Block 878). On the left, the towered wall of a citadel can be seen, occupied by soldiers, one of whom raises his hand to throw a stone. The scene to the right is thought to depict besiegers requesting the defenders' capitulation. Behind the horse, there may be traces of a siege embankment carrying soldiers over the wall. (© The British Museum / GR 1848, 1020.67)

The Athenian siege of Syracuse, 415–413 BC. The scene is from 414 BC, when the Athenians had established a fort at Syca ('the fig tree') on the Epipolae plateau above Syracuse, and embarked upon their usual strategy of periteichismos. Specialist masons and carpenters appear to have accompanied the army to Sicily, and tools for construction work were a normal part of their equipment. (Adam Hook © Osprey Publishing Ltd)

During the Peloponnesian War (431–404 BC), Athens used the technique of encirclement (*periteichismos*) several times, for example in 428 BC, when its erstwhile ally Mytilene on the island of Lesbos revolted. Here, the surrounding siege wall incorporated strongpoints for the Athenian garrison, but their blockade failed to prevent a Spartan agent from slipping into the town by way of a dry river bed. Fortunately for Athens, the Spartan plan to relieve Mytilene backfired when arms distributed among the townsfolk were used in a popular uprising. The town was handed over to the Athenians, who at first resolved to exterminate everyone, but were subsequently satisfied with the deaths of the 1,000 males who had taken part in the revolt (Thuc. 3.18, 25, 27–8, 36, 50). The Athenians were more ruthless at Melos, which they placed under siege in 416 BC for refusing to pay tribute. Different troop contingents vied with one another in building the encircling siege wall, and vigilance was increased after the townsfolk twice managed to bring in supplies through a weak sector. In the following year, when the town finally surrendered, all of the men were put to death, and the women and children were sold into slavery (Thuc. 5.114.1–2, 115.4, 116.2–3).

By that time, the *periteichismos* had become an Athenian hallmark. In 426 BC, the Acarnanian troops accompanying Demosthenes' Athenian army at Leucas urged him to surround the town with walls, in order to speed the townsfolk's surrender (Thuc. 3.94). Sieges occasionally took a different course, as at Mende, south of Potidaea, where internal squabbling between the townsfolk and the Peloponnesian garrison installed by Sparta gave the Athenians an ideal opportunity to burst into the town and subject it to wholesale plundering (423 BC); but the acropolis proved impregnable, so they resorted to constructing siege walls (Thuc. 4.130). Shortly afterwards, Mende's neighbour, Scione, was surrounded with Athenian siege-works; but before the encirclement was complete, troops from Mende managed to break out and slip into Scione (Thuc. 4.131, 133). It did them little good, for they finally succumbed two years later and were put to death; the women and children were enslaved and the land given over to Athenian allies (Thuc. 5.32). As late as 409 BC, the technique was still in favour when the Athenians forced the surrender of Chalcedon by surrounding the town with a palisade (Diod. Sic. 13.66.1–3; Xen., *Hell.* 1.3.4–7); a similar strategy failed at Byzantium, until the town was betrayed from within (Diod. Sic. 13.66.3–67.7; Xen., *Hell.* 1.3.14–22).

The Athenian attack on the little island of Minoa in 428 BC demonstrates that, occasionally, a more direct approach was tried. The city-state of Megara, on the adjacent coast, had built a fort there, but the Athenian general Nicias captured it by landing 'machines' from the sea (Thuc. 3.51). The classicist Eric Marsden, best known for his work on ancient artillery, thought that these machines might have been ship-mounted siege towers. He was perhaps thinking of the transport vessel that the Athenians equipped with wooden towers for fighting in the harbour at Syracuse (Thuc. 7.25), but this could never have been used for an amphibious assault. It seems more likely that Nicias' machines were simply assault ladders. The Athenians planned to use the island as a springboard for an attempt on the coastal town of Nisaea, which had been garrisoned by the Spartans' Peloponnesian allies, but the attack, when it came, took the form of the familiar blockade.

At Syracuse, the Athenian blockade ended in failure. Having established the 'circle' fort as a strongpoint on the Epipolae plateau, the Athenians secured their links to the harbour by driving twin siege walls southwards, breaking through successive Syracusan counterworks. However, the northward extension of the siege-works was delayed, and was finally thwarted by the Syracusans. (© Author)

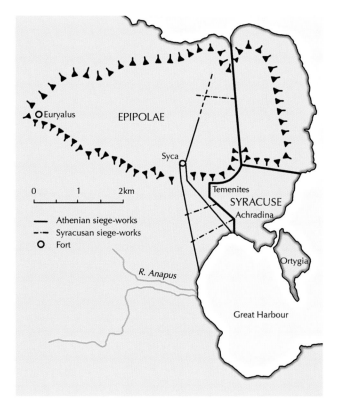

Euryalus   *EPIPOLAE*

Syca

Temenites   *SYRACUSE*   *Achradina*

Ortygia

0   1   2km

—— Athenian siege-works
–·– Syracusan siege-works
O Fort

R. Anapus

Great Harbour

The Megarians had built a pair of 'long walls' linking their town to Nisaea, in order to safeguard the route to the harbour there. However, in 424 BC, 600 Athenian troops crossed by night from Minoa and managed to infiltrate these walls, severing Nisaea's link to Megara. Reinforced by 4,000 hoplites and gangs of stonemasons, they built a wall and ditch around the town, utilizing materials salvaged from the suburbs and even incorporating entire buildings into their work; in two days, the *periteichismos* was complete and the Peloponnesian garrison surrendered (Thuc. 4.66–69).

The Chevalier de Folard's engraving depicts the disabling of a battering ram using a stratagem employed by the Plataeans. First, they suspended a large beam by chains fastened to the ends of two poles which projected horizontally from the top of the wall; then, having drawn the beam upwards, the chains were suddenly slackened, so that the beam crashed down onto the enemy machine. (Author's collection)

Only at Syracuse did the Athenian strategy of *periteichismos* prove disastrous (see illustration p. 34), but this can largely be blamed on poor leadership. In 415 BC, when Athens decided to extend its influence to Sicily by capturing this prosperous port city, an entire year was squandered in minor skirmishing, giving the Syracusans time to organize their defence and enlist Spartan assistance. Early in 414 BC, the Athenians took control of the Epipolae plateau overlooking the city, and built a fort at Syca as the pivotal point of the inevitable siege wall. By midsummer, a double wall extended south from the plateau to the harbour, despite Syracusan attempts to intercept it with palisades (Thuc. 6.97–101), but the Athenians delayed completion of the siege-works to the north. This fundamental blunder was quickly exploited by the Syracusans, under the leadership of the newly arrived Spartan general Gylippus. They intercepted the line of the siege wall with their own cross wall, which, adding insult to injury, was built with the stones already laid out for the Athenian wall (Thuc. 7.4–6). With one action, they had turned the tables on the Athenians, thwarting their blockade of the city.

The Oxford scholar G. B. Grundy memorably summed up the Athenians' fame in siegecraft as 'the reputation of the one-eyed among the blind'. But if their reputation was not based on conspicuous success, it perhaps arose from their ability to organize and finance the labour required to prosecute such an operation. Certainly, of the allied army besieging Miletus in 411 BC, it was the Athenian contingent that contemplated building siege walls (Thuc. 8.25). Of course, a blockade could be maintained without siege-works, but the Athenian predilection for constructing them suggests that real benefits were perceived. Quite apart from the protection of the besieging forces, and the concealment of their movements from the besieged, there were perhaps psychological factors involved, for the visual impact of a siege wall sent the message to the defenders that their plight was hopeless.

Spartan siegecraft

The Spartans' incapacity for siegecraft has become notorious, but is easily explained by the practicalities of hoplite warfare. The Spartans had dominated the Peloponnese by their success on the battlefield. When their army threatened the farmland of neighbouring city-states, the inhabitants could not afford the luxury of remaining behind their walls, allowing their annual produce to be ravaged; economic necessity forced them to take to the field, and this was where the Spartan army excelled. Consequently, where there was little need for siegecraft, there was no opportunity to learn.

The Spartan invasion of Acarnania in 429 BC demonstrates this. The unfortified village of Limnaea was easily sacked, but the walls of Stratus were a more daunting prospect; the Spartans seem to have had no other strategy than the hope that the overawed townsfolk would open their gates (Thuc. 2.80–1). Similarly, in an attack on Naupactus in 426 BC, the Spartans seized the unwalled sector of the town without any trouble, but when they saw that the walled sector was fully garrisoned they departed (Thuc. 3.102). Some years earlier, they had attempted to attack Oenoe 'using machines and other means' (Thuc. 2.18), but every attempt failed. So daunted by walls were they that, in their attack on Mantinea in 385 BC, the Spartans dammed the river Ophis, which flowed through the town, in order to raise the water level and dissolve the mud-brick walls (Paus. 8.8.7; Diod. Sic. 15.12.1–2; Xen., Hell. 5.2.4–6).

Such tactical limitations were not confined to Sparta. When the Thebans decided to attack their hated neighbour, Plataea, in 431 BC, it was treachery that gained them entry to the town; but the advance guard of 300 men failed to subjugate the townsfolk and ended up dead or captured (Thuc. 2.2–4). In 428 BC, the Mytilenians' attempt on neighbouring Methymna came to nothing when the hoped-for betrayal failed to materialize (Thuc. 3.18). Thucydides reports that the Argives, who failed to storm Epidaurus by escalade early in 418 BC, only made the attempt because they thought the place was undefended (Thuc. 5.56). Later the same year, a combined force of Mantineans and Eleans successfully cowed the town of Orchomenus by making repeated assaults on a weak fortification; fearing that the large allied army would eventually break in, the town surrendered (Thuc. 5.61). Speedy capitulation was evidently preferable to resistance, which might aggravate resentment among the besieging forces and result in atrocities should the town fall.

The events at Pylos in 425 BC resulted in siegecraft of a sort. When Demosthenes fortified the headland as a thorn in Sparta's side, the ensuing combined land and sea assault by Spartan troops was badly mismanaged. By striking before the Athenian fleet arrived, they hoped to capture the place easily, 'because it was unprovisioned, since it had been seized in haste' (Thuc. 4.8). However, although on the landward side there was a stand-off with the Peloponnesian besiegers, on the seaward side Demosthenes' palisade frustrated the Spartan attacks there on two consecutive days. Meanwhile, as a fail-safe, the Spartans also landed 420 hoplites on the offshore island of Sphacteria, in case the Athenians planned to use it to dominate the bay around Pylos. But when the

At Pylos, the Athenians spent six days fortifying the headland, but with only one spring and no harbour the position was poor from a logistical standpoint. However, Sphacteria was even worse; the Spartans stranded there had to rely on swimmers to bring foodstuffs across. But it was only when the forest cover on the island was accidentally torched that the Spartan position became vulnerable. (© Author)

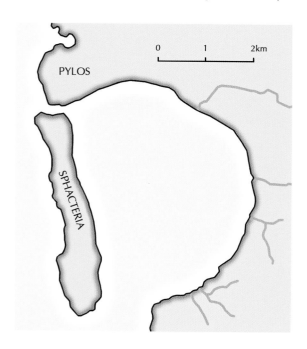

Athenian fleet finally arrived, the Spartan ships were put to flight, marooning their comrades on the island. The Spartan siege of Pylos therefore became an Athenian siege of Sphacteria, run along the familiar lines of the blockade. It was only when it became apparent that the besieged Spartans were being provisioned by blockade runners, that Demosthenes was obliged to take more active measures: landing a force of 800 hoplites, 800 archers and 2,000 light troops, he surrounded and overwhelmed the Spartans (Thuc. 4.31–9).

In view of this history of ineptitude, it is all the more surprising to find that the Spartans were responsible for the first reliably recorded Greek assault on a town wall using the scientific methods of the Persians. In 429 BC, the Spartan king Archidamus arrived before Plataea at the head of a Peloponnesian army, intent on avenging the slight suffered by his Theban allies two years earlier; the little town's allegiance to Athens was a further incentive for the attack. The standard request for the town's surrender was rejected, so Archidamus ordered the ravaging of the countryside, and the Peloponnesians planted a palisade all around the town 'to prevent any sorties' (Thuc. 2.75).

It is the next stage that has mystified scholars, for the Peloponnesians proceeded to raise a siege embankment against the town wall. Exactly why they decided upon this tactic is a mystery, but Archidamus is known to have been in contact with the Persians, and may have benefited from their advice on siegecraft. Timber was felled on nearby Mount Cithaeron and assembled into twin buttresses, arranged perpendicular to the town wall; between these, earth, stones and brushwood were piled up to create a giant ramp. In the meantime, the

Relief sculpture from the Nereid Monument (Block 872). Three soldiers are depicted scaling an assault ladder, while crouching archers provide covering fire. Note that the hoplites appear to be climbing one-handed, in order to maintain a grip on their shields. (TopFoto / HIP)

The Chevalier de Folard's interpretation of the Spartan periteichismos at Plataea. Thucydides describes two concentric walls, with a 16-foot (4.8m) space in between for the garrison; his observation, that the entire work looked like a single thick wall battlemented on either side, is usually taken to mean that the space was roofed over, as shown here. (Author's collection)

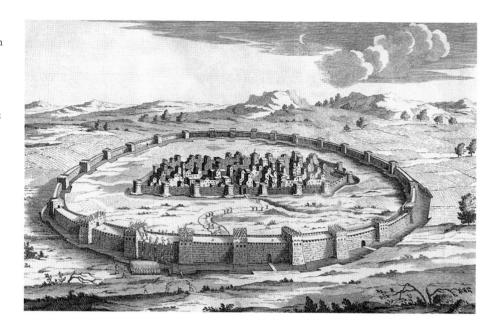

Plataeans did not stand idle, but raised the height of their town wall where it was threatened by the embankment, and erected screens of rawhide as a protection against fire. Then they secretly broke through their own wall where it abutted the embankment, and began extracting soil into the town; although their scheme was soon exposed and the gap stopped up, the Plataeans nevertheless persevered by tunnelling farther underneath the embankment. Simultaneously, they began the construction of a crescent-shaped wall as a second line of defence if the main wall should fail. At this point, the Peloponnesians brought up battering rams, but were frustrated by the defenders' countermeasures, which involved lassoing the ramming beams or snapping off their heads by dropping heavy timbers (Thuc. 2.75–6).

Having failed in their Persian-style attack, the Peloponnesians resorted to the tactic favoured by their Athenian enemies, namely *periteichismos*. They surrounded Plataea with a double wall of mud-brick, battlemented and provided with towers like a town wall; ditches ran around the inner and outer lines, where the material for the bricks had been extracted. The blockade dragged on for 18 months before the Plataeans finally mounted a desperate escape; on a dark and stormy night, 212 men used ladders to cross the wall unseen, and fled. The remaining 200 defenders held out six months longer before finally surrendering, whereupon the Spartans executed all of the males and enslaved the women (Thuc. 2.78; 3.20–24; 3.52; 3.68).

The technique of encirclement was not attempted by Spartan armies for another 40 years; but, having thrown a wall and ditch around Mantinea (385 BC), they decided upon other tactics (Xen., *Hell.* 5.2.4–6). Nor did the technique catch on with other city-states. Another 20 years passed before the Arcadians used a double palisade to encircle the Spartan-garrisoned town of Cromnus (365 BC); a relieving force failed to extricate the besieged, and they were subsequently distributed as prisoners among the Arcadian allies (Xen., *Hell.* 7.4.21–7).

GREEK SIEGE MACHINES

We have seen that, in the ancient Near East, the Assyrians had been adept in the use of siege machinery, and there is some evidence that their Persian descendants made use of the battering ram. Of course, it is very likely that enterprising Western warriors soon would have discovered the value of a stout tree trunk in bursting open a gate. The historian Diodorus Siculus, writing in the 1st century BC, believed that Pericles had been the first Greek to use a battering ram, during the siege of Samos in 440 BC (Diod. Sic. 12.28.3). His engineer, a certain Artemon, hailed from Clazomenae in present-day Turkey, where he may have had experience of Persian machines.

Other writers occasionally claimed that the Greeks used siege machinery, but they were perhaps deceived by the exaggerated tradition of Athenian expertise. For example, at Paros in 489 BC, Miltiades clearly hoped to entice the defenders out from behind their walls, as he lacked the means of breaking into the town. However, when Cornelius Nepos came to write his *Life of Miltiades* in the 30s BC, he added 'shelters and sheds' (*vineis ac testudinibus*) of the sort employed by his Roman contemporaries when they were engaged in aggressive siegecraft (Nep., *Milt.* 7). We have seen that Diodorus Siculus, writing around the same time as Nepos, claimed that it was actually in 440 BC, long after Miltiades had died, that the Greeks first used sheds and battering rams. The story was repeated a century later by Plutarch, who said that he had got it from Ephorus (Plut., *Pericles* 27). But this historian's work, which survives only in fragments, was written fully 100 years after the siege of Samos, by which time siege machines were commonplace; in any case, Plutarch adds that not everyone believed the tale.

In fact, besides the Spartan use of battering rams at Plataea in 429 BC, which were effectively countered by the defenders, the Greeks of the later 5th century showed no

Bronze head of a battering ram, found at Olympia, where it was probably dedicated amongst the spoils of war; the decoration suggests a late 5th-century date. It would have fitted a ramming-beam approximately 9in (22cm) high and 3in (8cm) thick. The vertical blade flanked on either side by five triangular teeth was perhaps designed to cut into mud-brick. (© Deutsches Archäologisches Institut, Athens; neg. no. Olympia 2800)

The battering ram in its simplest form was a beam carried by many men, such as this example depicted on Trajan's Column in the hands of Dacians attacking a Roman fort. It seems to have been conventional to fashion the head in the shape of a ram. (C. Cichorius, Die Reliefs der Traianssäule, *Berlin 1900)*

interest in siege machinery. Thus, amid the general catalogue of besieging incompetence, Pausanias' report of the siege of Oeniadae has understandably been doubted by scholars. According to him, the Messenians undermined the walls and brought up machinery (*mēchanēmata*) for battering down the fortifications (Paus. 4.25.2), whereupon the townsfolk withdrew under truce, to avoid the horrors of a storming assault. However, it is most likely that Pausanias added details familiar to him from Roman imperial siegecraft, but alien to the 5th century BC.

In general, Greek writers used the term 'machines' (*mēchanai*) to refer to a whole range of devices. Thucydides twice refers to the Spartan machines battering the walls at Plataea; from the context (and from Thucydides' use of the word *embolē*, which usually denotes the ram on a ship), these are clearly battering rams, though presumably of a fairly rudimentary design, given the ease with which the Plataeans neutralized them. On another two occasions, Thucydides uses the word 'machine' in reference to the crude but ingenious flame-throwers that enemy forces used against Athenian timber fortifications at Delium and Lecythus in 424 BC. And, in 403 BC, the Athenians so feared the arrival of 'machines' from Piraeus that, on the advice of a *mēchanopoios* ('engineer'), they unloaded boulders onto the road to hinder their progress (Xen., *Hell.* 2.4.27); unfortunately, we cannot say what kind of wheeled contraptions these were. Nevertheless, the remaining eight appearances of the word in Thucydides' *History* seem to refer to assault ladders, and there is no reason to suppose that anything more elaborate was used, under normal circumstances, by the Greeks.

Siege Warfare in the Time of Dionysius I

In the years following the Peloponnesian War, western siege technology made a great leap forward on Sicily, when the Carthaginians of north Africa renewed their claim to the island. A previous attempt in 480 BC by General Hamilcar had been confounded by Gelon, whose kingdom centred around the city of Syracuse and represented the major power on the island. On that occasion, he inflicted a massive defeat on the Carthaginians, while they were occupied in blockading the town of Himera. Diodorus records that Gelon's Syracusan cavalry were able to infiltrate Hamilcar's camp by a ruse, and cut down the Carthaginian general as he sacrificed to Poseidon (Diod. Sic. 11.20–22). Herodotus, by contrast, favoured the remarkable tale that Hamilcar vanished during the final battle with the Syracusans and was never seen again. By a coincidence of the sort that fascinated Greek historians, Hamilcar was defeated on the very day that Xerxes and the Persians were repulsed at Salamis (Hdt. 7.166–7).

For several generations afterwards, the Carthaginians remained disinclined to dabble in Sicilian affairs, although they maintained an interest in the north-west corner of the island, around the towns of Motya and Panormus. However, in 410 BC, the town of Segesta petitioned their aid against Selinus, an overbearing ally of Syracuse. The Carthaginian sovereign at that time was Hannibal, grandson of the Hamilcar who had died at Himera in 480 BC; according to the historian Diodorus, he was burning for revenge (Diod. Sic. 13.43.6).

Thus, the stage was set for the first appearance of sophisticated siege machinery in the classical world, for the Carthaginian people traced their

ancestry back to the Middle East, and were entirely familiar with the use of wheeled siege towers and battering rams.

CARTHAGINIAN SIEGES

Hannibal brought 'machinery for sieges, missiles, and all the other equipment' (Diod. Sic. 13.54.2), which he unleashed onto the unsuspecting Greek towns of Sicily in the style of his Persian forebears. First, at Selinus, he divided his forces into two, probably deployed on opposite sides of the town; then 'he set up six towers of excessive height, and thrust forward against the walls an equal number of iron-braced battering rams' (Diod. Sic. 13.54.7). His machinery towered over the defences, which had in any case fallen into disrepair, and his archers and slingers easily picked off the defenders as they manned the walls (Diod. Sic. 13.55.6–7). A similar strategy was followed at Himera, where 'he camped around the city' (Diod. Sic. 13.59.6) before setting his machines to shake the walls at several different locations. Although no siege towers were deployed, 'he also undermined the wall and put wood under as a support, and when this was set on fire a long section of the walls suddenly fell down' (Diod. Sic. 13.59.8); such chilling efficiency contrasts with Hamilcar's failed siege of the same town in 480 BC. At Akragas in 406 BC, Hannibal opened the attack with two enormous siege towers (Diod. Sic. 13.85.5), but when the defenders burned them down, he resorted to piling up embankments in the Persian manner. His men demolished monuments and tombs outside the town to provide the building materials (Diod. Sic. 13.86.1), in a striking replay of events at Palaepaphos 90 years earlier. Finally, at Gela, Hannibal's successor, Himilcon, battered the walls with rams, but the townsfolk repeatedly repaired the breaches by night (Diod. Sic. 13.108.8), and the Carthaginians only managed to break in when the inhabitants finally fled the town.

Carthaginian warfare was characterized by its cruelty. It is not unlikely that the frustration of a protracted besieging assault was usually vented on the townsfolk. The Athenian playwright Aeschylus, who had famously fought at Marathon in 490 BC, lamented that 'many and wretched are the miseries when a city is taken' (Aesch., *Sept.* 339). It is true that Greek armies of the 5th century had been known to commit atrocities; the treatment of Plataea by the Spartans and of Melos by the Athenians are just two examples. However, Diodorus expresses particular revulsion for the behaviour of Hannibal's mercenaries as they sacked Selinus. Some of the townsfolk were burned alive in their homes, others were slaughtered defenceless in the streets, women were raped, and religious precincts violated (Diod. Sic. 13.57.2–5, 58.1–2; cf. 111.4).

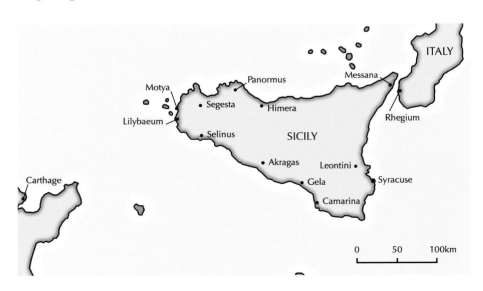

Broadly speaking, the towns in the eastern half of Sicily were Greek foundations, which exercised control over the native Sicel population; Carthage had colonized the western tip. Besides dominating affairs on Sicily, Syracuse extended her control into southern Italy. (© Author)

45

CARTHAGINIAN SIEGE MACHINES

The Carthaginians traced their descent from Phoenicia, in particular the city of Tyre, and they seem to have followed the Persian tradition of siege warfare. The Roman architect-engineer Vitruvius, and his contemporary, the Greek philosopher Athenaeus, both attributed the invention of the battering ram to the Carthaginians (Vitr., *De arch.* 10.13.1–2; Ath., *Mech.* 9.4–10.4). The story goes that, while besieging Gades (Cadiz in Spain) possibly around 500 BC, the Carthaginians were unable to demolish the town walls, until they realized that a wooden beam could be used to gradually batter the wall from the top downwards, course by course. Similarly, the same two writers credited a Tyrian shipwright named Pephrasmenos with being the first to suspend the ramming beam from a frame, rather than having men carry it. For this rudimentary contraption, 'he set up a mast and hung from it another horizontal beam, like the arms of a balance, and struck the wall by drawing the horizontal beam with a pulley' (Ath., *Mech.* 9.9–13). Finally, the distinction of raising the whole machine on wheels was granted to a Carthaginian named Geras, who allegedly 'made a wheeled platform and fixed the ram horizontally, and did not draw it by pulleys but made it move forwards by a large number of men' (Ath., *Mech.* 9.15–10.2).

The tradition that Carthaginians had been the agents of invention was evidently well established. In AD 209, the Carthaginian priest Tertullian wrote the following:

> the ram (and not the backward-horned, wool-skinned, testicle-dragging animal, but the timber machine which serves to break walls), never previously balanced by man, is said to have been mobilized first of all by Carthage, most savage in warfare, for the swing of the pendulous attack, having appreciated the power of the machine like the anger of the beast that asserts itself with its head (Tert., *De pallio* 1.3).

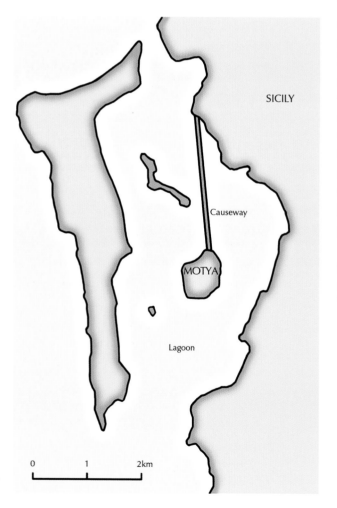

The island of Motya is situated in a lagoon. The remains of an artificial causeway, by which it was linked to the Sicilian mainland in antiquity, are still visible beneath the water. (© Author)

SICILY

Causeway

MOTYA

Lagoon

0   1   2km

Another Roman writer, the elder Pliny, thought that the *ballista* and the sling were Phoenician inventions (Pliny, *HN* 7.201), and even though the attribution is almost certainly wrong it was obviously considered plausible by the ancients. Of course, the Carthaginians cannot have been the inventors of battering technology, as the Assyrians were already using mobile rams around 850 BC. Nevertheless, it is quite likely that Carthage first brought siege machinery to the West, and, if nothing else, these stories demonstrate that they were perceived as a besieging nation.

DIONYSIUS I OF SYRACUSE

Carthaginian successes against the towns of Sicily had alarmed Dionysius, the tyrant of Syracuse (r. 406–367 BC). While extending his control over eastern Sicily, he experienced an initial setback at Leontini because he lacked siege

Dionysius' siege of Motya, 397 BC. In his assault on the offshore town of Motya, Dionysius probably utilized the existing causeway as a track for his siege machines, and concentrated his assault on the north gateway. His machinery included six-storey wheeled towers. This siege represents the first historical mention of the catapult, which at this early date probably means the gastraphetēs, or 'belly bow'. (Adam Hook © Osprey Publishing Ltd)

machinery (Diod. Sic. 14.14.3–4); the inhabitants were soon cowed by the sight of their neighbours falling under Syracusan influence, but the experience must have taught Dionysius a lesson. As well as strengthening his city's fortifications, which now encompassed the exposed Epipolae plateau, he assembled craftsmen from all over the Mediterranean world to equip his arsenal; attracted by the promise of high wages, men came from Italy, Greece and even Carthage. All kinds of armaments were manufactured, including 'unfamiliar machinery that was capable of offering great advantages' (Diod. Sic. 14.42.2). Long afterwards, it was remembered that 'the whole area of mechanical invention developed during the tyranny of Dionysius the Sicilian' (Ath., *Mech.* 10.5–7). By the year 399 BC, he possessed siege towers and battering rams, along with another weapon destined to play an important role in siege warfare: the catapult.

However, although Diodorus Siculus records that the catapult (which he calls the *katapeltikon*) was invented under Dionysius' patronage (Diod. Sic. 14.42.1; cf. 50.4), the weapon did not suddenly arrive out of the blue. In a work entitled *Ctesibius' Manufacture of Missile Weapons* (*Ktēsibiou Belopoiika*), the Roman engineer Heron of Alexandria, writing around AD 60, explains that the

The north gate at Motya, viewed from inside the town. (© Jona Lendering)

catapult was inspired by an earlier mechanical weapon, the 'belly shooter' (*gastraphetēs*). In its original form, this weapon consisted of a powerful composite bow, mounted transversely on a stock so that it vaguely resembled the later crossbow. It took its name, 'belly shooter', from the concave rest at its rear end, against which the archer braced his stomach while drawing (or 'spanning') the bow. Another author, Biton, who is often unjustly discredited as a fraud, describes two advanced forms of the *gastraphetēs*; he credits these to Zopyrus, an engineer from Tarentum in southern Italy who may have been active towards the end of the 5th century BC.

The classicist Sir William Tarn believed that it was this weapon that Dionysius' engineers had invented, an assumption with which the British scholar Eric Marsden underpinned his study of ancient artillery. However, the German artillery officer Major General Erwin Schramm preferred to take Diodorus at his word when he placed the 'invention of the catapult' in the opening years of the 4th century. For Schramm, this was the full-blown torsion catapult, not its composite bow-based predecessor. There is a third possibility, though. Biton

(Continued p.52)

The excavation of the south gate at Motya in 1962. (B. S. J. Isserlin & J. du Plat Taylor, Motya. A Phoenician and Carthaginian City in Sicily, Leiden: Brill, 1974. Plate 13. Reprinted with the permission of B. S. J. Isserlin)

BOW-MACHINES

It certainly seems that bow-machines were known prior to 399 BC. Biton describes two machines designed by Zopyrus, one at Cumae, perhaps in connection with the Sabellian conquest of 421 BC, and the other at Miletus, probably prior to the Persian annexation of the town in 401 BC. The first, the so-called mountain *gastraphetēs* (below, left), had a 5ft (1.5m) stock and a 7ft (2.2m) bow; the second (below, right) had a 7ft (2.2m) stock attached to a 9ft (2.8m) bow, and could apparently shoot two missiles at once. Such unwieldy machines could never have been used as hand weapons. Quite apart from the

large dimensions and increased weight, the bows would have been far too powerful for spanning by body weight alone. However, Zopyrus incorporated two elements that would eventually enable the leap to the torsion catapult: the winched pull-back system, necessitated by increasingly powerful bows, and the stand, which made heavier machines practicable.

In general, Biton's text is seldom clear enough to support unequivocal interpretation. The design of the bow-machine's stand is a case in point. The Miletus machine allegedly sat on a 1ft-high (0.3m) 'pedestal' (*basis*), 9ft (2.7m) long by 3ft (0.9m) wide, surmounted by a 'trestle with a height of five feet [1.5m]', but Biton later states that the trestle

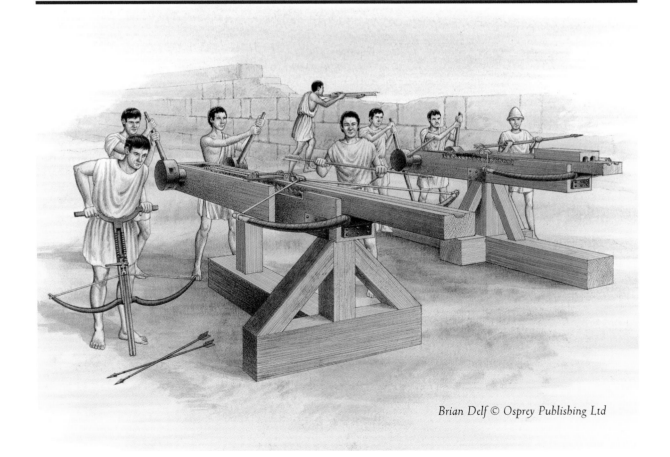

Brian Delf © Osprey Publishing Ltd

measured 3ft (0.9m). Schramm believed that this statement was an error introduced by copyists, rewriting the Greek text down through the ages, and that Biton had originally specified a 5ft trestle with three feet; in other words, a tripod. But a 5ft tripod sitting on a 1ft pedestal would have made the machine over 2m high, placing the trigger out of reach above the gunner's head. Schramm reasoned that Biton must simply have meant a tripod high enough to raise the *gastraphetēs* 5ft above ground level.

Besides the pedestal and the trestle, Biton mentions another element in his description of the Miletus stand: a 2ft-high (0.6m) vertical pillar, placed centrally on the pedestal. Schramm had already departed from Biton's description, visualizing the trestle with a tilt-and-swivel bracket on top, which he fixed to the *gastraphetēs* just behind the bow. This arrangement left the rear of the weapon unsupported, so Biton's pillar was shifted back along the pedestal.

When Marsden came to analyse the same text, he attempted to rationalize Biton's measurements by suggesting that the tripod's legs were each 5ft long, but were excessively splayed on a peculiar Y-shaped base. He restored the vertical pillar to the mid-point of the base, where it functioned as a central support for the tripod, but he retained Schramm's tilt-and-swivel bracket, which he, too, attached to the front of the *gastraphetēs*, near the bow. This was essentially Schramm's design, minus the rear pillar. But, having removed this rear pillar, Marsden was obliged to invent a strut to fulfil the same function.

It is worth noting that Biton does not mention a tilt-and-swivel bracket in connection with the Miletus machine, nor does he mention a rear strut. However, his instructions for the Cumae machine (the so-called mountain *gastraphetēs*) add an interesting item. Here, from the outset, he refers to two trestles – a 5-footer (1.5m), equipped with a 'bowl-shaped bracket' (*agkōna kratēra*), and a 3-footer (0.9m) – both sitting

on a 1ft-thick (0.3m) pedestal. As with the Miletus machine, Schramm reasoned that the main trestle of the mountain *gastraphetēs* should be high enough to raise the stock 5ft above ground level. Similarly, he envisaged the second trestle holding the rear of the weapon 3ft off the ground, thus imposing a peculiar angle of rest on the stock, which he claimed was beneficial to the winch operator. Finally, he interpreted the enigmatic 'bowl-shaped bracket' as the same tilt-and-swivel joint that he had added to the Miletus machine. Again, he fastened this bracket to the *gastraphetēs* near the front of its stock, although Biton specifies a position 4ft (1.2m) 'from the face [*prosōpon*]' (Biton 65.10).

Marsden seized on the 'bowl-shaped bracket' as a precursor to the torsion catapult's *karchēsion*, which he translated as 'universal joint'. This was a tilt-and-swivel mechanism, which Heron expressly linked with the elevation and traversing of the catapult. But Biton gives no indication that his bow-machines were intended to perform in the same way. Marsden also believed that the two bow-machines' stands were more or less the same. For example, he interpreted the rear 'trestle' of the Cumae mountain machine as a strut, like the one he had added to the Miletus machine; but he could not fashion a Y-shaped base-platform out of the shorter Cumae measurements (5ft by 3½ft or 1.5m by 1.1m).

There is no neat solution to these problems. Although Schramm's reconstructions have an elegant functionality, this has been achieved at the expense of accuracy. Equally, Marsden's frequent departures from the text were criticized as 'high-handed' by the Danish scholar Aage Drachmann. The addition of the tilt-and-swivel joint is particularly problematic, as it may not be the same as Biton's 'cup-shaped bracket' and, even if it is, should apply only to the mountain *gastraphetēs*.

The northern defences of the Attic border fort at Gyphtokastro. The difficult approach would have hindered wheeled siege machinery. (© Deutsches Archäologisches Institut, Athens; neg. no. Attika 238)

actually calls the *gastraphetēs*-type machine a *katapeltikon*, which is the very word that Diodorus uses to describe Dionysius' weapons; if Zopyrus or his colleagues had presented this little-known weapon to the tyrant of Syracuse in 399 BC, we can forgive ill-informed witnesses for imagining that it had just been invented.

Having declared war on Carthage, Dionysius marched west, launching assaults on Panormus, Segesta and Entella; but the main focus was the offshore town of Motya, a colony of Carthage and its main supply base on Sicily (see illustration p. 47). As a defensive measure, the townsfolk had severed the artificial causeway linking the island town to the shore, so Dionysius' first task was to repair it for the advance of his heavy machinery (Diod. Sic. 14.48.2; 49.3). When the Carthaginian navy attempted to intervene, they were repulsed by shipborne missile troops and by 'catapults for sharp missiles' lining the shore (Diod. Sic. 14.50.1–4). Scholars continue to debate whether these *katapeltai* were torsion catapults of the sort used by Alexander the Great and his successors. But it seems more likely that Dionysius relied upon the *gastraphetēs* and its larger cousins, which drew their power from oversized composite bows; such weapons were unfamiliar at the time, and would easily have taken the Carthaginians by surprise.

THE SIEGE MACHINERY OF DIONYSIUS I

Diodorus' reference to 'machines of every kind' (14.51.1) advancing along the causeway at Motya is characteristic hyperbole. (He also frequently refers to 'missiles of every kind'.) Besides the catapults, only battering rams and six-storey wheeled towers are specifically mentioned. Machines were also used at Caulonia in 389 BC (Diod. Sic. 14.103.3); and for his siege of Rhegium in the following year, Dionysius 'prepared a great quantity of machinery of incredible size, with which he shook the walls, striving to capture the town by force' (Diod. Sic. 14.108.3). At Motya, the townsfolk countered Dionysius' assault with the age-old defence of fire: 'they raised up men in crow's nests resting on yard-arms suspended from the highest possible masts, and these from their high positions hurled lit fire-brands and burning tow and pitch onto the enemies' machines' (Diod. Sic. 14.51.2). The Syracusans evidently had not yet devised an effective means of fire-proofing, for they were obliged to quench the flames wherever they caught hold (Diod. Sic. 14.51.1–3); perhaps teams of water carriers were detailed to pass buckets hand-to-hand from the surrounding lagoon.

Once the Syracusans had broken into Motya, Dionysius actually inserted his siege towers into the town, where their design allowed

Aeneas (33.2) suggests that combustible material should be attached to poles, bristling with iron points 'like an engraving of a thunderbolt'. Like Philon's incendiary caltrops (Pol. 3.41), these could then be embedded in enemy machinery to guarantee fire damage. The standard Greek and Roman image of a thunderbolt, with spikes at both ends, is depicted on this Spartan coin. (© Hunterian Museum and Art Gallery, University of Glasgow)

Soldiers man the battlements in this scene from the Heroon at Trysa, where the seated couple perhaps represent the town's ruling elite. Outside the walls, more soldiers shelter beneath their shields, while others infiltrate the town through an open postern. (© Kunsthistorisches Museum, Vienna)

drawbridges to be lowered onto the house rooftops, and prolonged hand-to-hand fighting ensued, until the attackers prevailed by sheer weight of numbers. In the chaos, only those who had taken refuge in the temples were spared, and the town was plundered. It was a different story at Rhegium, which held out for almost a year before starvation forced its surrender; the 6,000 who survived were sent to Syracuse as slaves (Diod. Sic. 14.111.1–4).

However, siege machinery was not the universal key to capturing fortified towns. As Dionysius realized at Motya, heavy machines required a smooth, flat running surface, but even then they did not guarantee rapid success, as the case of Rhegium shows. In an earlier attempt on the town, in 393 BC, Dionysius sprang a nocturnal escalade, no doubt hoping to avoid the toil of bringing up machinery; part of his strategy was to burn the gates down, but the townsfolk deliberately fed the conflagration, so that the flames prevented the Syracusans from entering (Diod. Sic. 14.90.5–6). On other occasions, machinery simply could not be deployed. The mountain town of Tauromenium, for example, was scarcely accessible to infantry, far less wheeled machines. In 394 BC, when Dionysius launched a daring mid-winter assault on the rocky snow-clad citadel, his men were wrong-footed by the defenders and routed (Diod. Sic. 14.87.5–88.4).

EARLY ARTILLERY FORTIFICATIONS?

Prior to his death in 367 BC, Dionysius of Syracuse had enjoyed over 30 years of friendship with Sparta, and had latterly made overtures to Athens. There are a few hints that, perhaps as a result of these links, news of the bow-machine had travelled to mainland Greece. In particular, a 'catapult arrow' (*katapeltikon belos*) was apparently displayed at Sparta around this time, to the general dismay of the observers (Plut., *Mor.* 191E). However, the literary accounts of the period carry no reports of the bow-machine's use. Consequently, scholars have turned to archaeology to fill the void, claiming that fortifications erected in central Greece in the mid-4th century show signs of having been designed for bow-machines.

Marsden had already reasoned that the presence of shuttered windows, as opposed to arrow slits, in the upper storeys of towers indicated that they were designed for catapults. Developing this theme, Ober re-dated several Theban and Athenian towers to the 360s BC, and linked them with the deployment of bow-machines. Basing his theory on small weapons with 6½ft (2.0m) stocks and 5½ft (1.7m) bows, he found that the average chamber size of roughly 59ft² (5.5m²) could accommodate two of these. But, besides making an unimpressive artillery battery, two machines are far fewer than the number of windows would suggest.

The great corner tower of the fort at Aegosthena, dating from 343 BC, is exceptional in this regard; the generous provision of windows in the 81ft² (7.5m²) upper chamber suggested to Marsden that it was designed for artillery. But, if so, it would seem to have been poorly planned, for only two of the three windows on each side can be used by bow-machines, the third window being obstructed by the machines on the neighbouring wall. Equally, deploying catapults some 53ft (16m) above ground level may not have been the best use of such machines, and the tower's extreme height was probably to facilitate long-range surveillance. Of course, when under attack, archers and other missile troops would surely have made full use of the windows.

AENEAS TACTICUS

We gain a picture of broadly contemporary Greek siegecraft from a book by Aeneas 'the Tactician', who was probably the homonymous Arcadian general of the 360s BC. Aeneas tells his readers how to survive under siege, with instructions on defending walls and gates and on neutralizing incendiary attacks, but the bulk of his treatise concerns guarding against treachery. In this, Aeneas simply reflects the realities of contemporary siege warfare. For example,

(Opposite) The Chevalier de Folard's engraving depicts the snaring of a battering ram, in order to stop it working. Instead of a rope noose, as suggested by Aeneas, the crane is equipped with the grabbing device known to the Greeks as a harpax. (Author's collection)

the Spartan army operating in north-west Asia Minor in 399 BC certainly captured a succession of towns by force, but others they took by deceit (Diod. Sic. 14.38.3).

If the attacker could not rely upon betrayal from within, escalade probably remained the most common assaulting strategy. Aeneas recommends keeping assault ladders away from the walls using forked poles, and he describes an elaborate moveable framework to do the same job (36.1–2). He also appreciates that fire could be a powerful ally to both the besieger and the besieged. Besides creating a smoke screen (32.1), the defenders should use fire 'if sheds are brought up' (33.1), adding pitch, tow and sulphur to ensure a blaze. Besiegers working within missile range of the walls must have developed various types of shelters. For example, Xenophon relates how, at Egyptian Larissa in 399 BC, the Spartan general Thibron attempted to siphon off the town's water supply through a tunnel, and protected the access shaft with a wooden shed (Xen., *Hell.* 3.1.7). But the shed was burned down, a danger which Aeneas warns against for any exposed timberwork in the besieged town. He recommends fire-proofing with rawhides or a liberal coating of birdlime, a viscous substance derived from mistletoe berries, and if anything should catch fire, vinegar was the best quenching agent (33.3; 34.1).

When Aeneas mentions 'large machinery' bringing an overwhelming barrage 'from catapults and slings' (32.8), he is perhaps envisaging the kind of mobile tower used by Dionysius on Sicily. Aeneas seems to have been aware of Sicilian history – in a passage on secret messages, he alludes to events there in 357 BC (31.31) – whereas siege towers do not figure largely on the Greek mainland for another decade or so. Similarly, the catapult, by which Aeneas more probably means the *gastraphetēs* or bow-machine, must still have been rare in Greece. But the pairing of the catapult with the sling, as the only other weapon to comfortably outrange the archer, became a continuing feature of siege warfare.

As far as battering rams are concerned, Aeneas' knowledge is clearly drawn from Thucydides' description of the Peloponnesian attack on Plataea. For example, he recommends cushioning the ram's blows with sacks of chaff, bags of wool, or inflated ox-hides, and disabling the machine by lassoing the ram-head or breaking it off entirely by dropping heavy weights (32.3–6). It is true that, in 376 BC, Chabrias the Athenian besieged Naxos by 'bringing machines up to the walls and shaking the wall with them' (Diod. Sic. 15.34.4), and he seems to have used rams in his later siege of Drys (Polyaen., *Strat.* 2.22.3), but these are very much isolated incidents. Nothing similar is recorded until 350 BC, when Greek mercenaries in the service of Persia overthrew the walls of Pelusium using 'machines' (Diod. Sic. 16.49.1). We are left with the

suspicion that battering rams (indeed, siege machines in general) were used only infrequently, perhaps owing to a lack of expertise, combined with the difficulties of manoeuvring heavy, wheeled machinery in the mountainous Greek terrain.

Aeneas' brief section on tunnelling (37.1–9) has led to the suggestion that sieges of this period often involved the undermining of town walls. Of course, the fact that this Persian (and Carthaginian) technique must have been familiar to all readers of Herodotus does not mean that every general would have been anxious to put it into operation. Contemporary Greeks were, of course, familiar with mining technology, but, as the American scholar Josh Ober has observed, citizen soldiers would have taken a very dim view of such work, which was normally carried out by slave labour. And surely, if undermining had been at all widespread in Greek siegecraft, Aeneas would have chosen a more pertinent example than the Persian siege of Barca (37.6–7).

Macedonian Siege Warfare

It seems that the Greeks did not realize the full potential of mechanized siege warfare until the advent of Philip II of Macedon (r. 359–336 BC). This must be due, in part, to the fact that maintaining a siege train was expensive. But also, the possession of such equipment implied the intention to besiege repeatedly, which only arose with Macedonian imperialism. Finally, modern authorities have pointed to the willingness of Philip's full-time professional army to assault walls that would have daunted the citizen militias of the 5th century BC. More importantly, the professional character of the Macedonian army allowed for the incorporation of specialized craftsmen and engineers, without whom Alexander the Great (r. 336–323 BC) would have had no siege train.

PHILIP'S SIEGECRAFT

Demosthenes, the great Athenian orator, railed against the Macedonian style of warfare: fighting was no longer a fair and open contest reserved for a summer's day; on the contrary, Philip might arrive outside a town at any time of year, set up his machinery, and lay siege (Dem., *Third Philippic* 50). Philip, like Dionysius before him, was particularly associated in the ancient consciousness with the development of siege machinery. Indeed, the first Greek military engineer to be mentioned by name, Polyidus of Thessaly, served 'when Philip, son of Amyntas, was besieging Byzantium' in 340 BC (Vitr., *De arch.* 10.13.3; Ath., *Mech.*

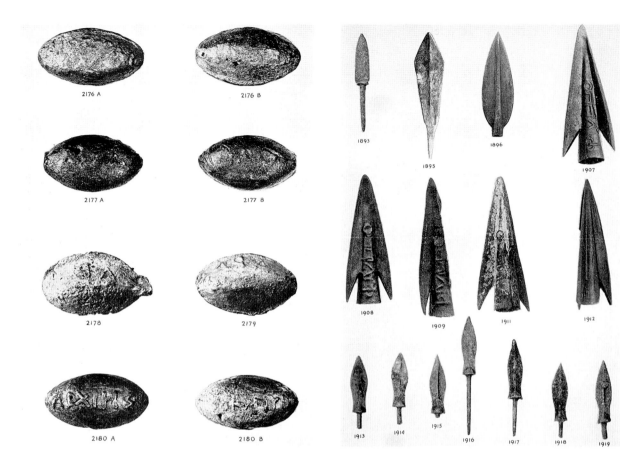

A selection of sling bullets and bronze arrowheads from Olynthus. Some carry inscriptions relating to Philip or his generals: bullet 2180 (bottom row) reads 'Archias the ready'. Others display soldiers' humour, such as bullet 2176 (top row), which reads 'an unpleasant gift'. (D. M. Robinson, Excavations at Olynthus: Part X: Metal and Minor Miscellaneous Finds: An original contribution to Greek life. Plates CXXX and CXX. © 1941 The Johns Hopkins University Press. Reprinted with the permission of The Johns Hopkins University Press.)

10.7–10); Polyidus allegedly developed different types of battering ram, and was also remembered as the builder of a giant siege tower (helepolis).

Ancient writers preserve a long (but by no means exhaustive) list of Philip's conquests: Amphipolis in 357 BC, Pydna and Potidaea in 356 BC, Methone in 355 BC, Pherae and Pagasae in 352 BC, Stageira in 349 BC, Olynthus in 348 BC, Halus in 347 BC, Pandosia, Bucheta and Elataea in 342 BC (Dem., *First Olynthiac* 5, 9, 12; *Halonn.* 32; Diod. Sic. 16.52.9), not to mention the 32 Thracian towns that he razed to the ground (Dem., *Third Philippic* 26). Methone was certainly taken by assault, for it was here that Philip was struck in the eye by an arrow (Diod. Sic. 16.31.6, 34.5; cf. Polyaen., *Strat.* 4.2.15). And we know that, at Amphipolis, 'by advancing machines against the wall, and making vigorous and continuous assaults, he overthrew part of the wall with battering rams, and by entering the town through the breach, striking down many opponents, he gained possession of the town' (Diod. Sic. 16.8.2).

It is interesting that Demosthenes alleges treachery at both Amphipolis and Pydna (Dem., *First Olynthiac* 5), for the king certainly had a reputation for bribery. Mecyberna and Torone, at least, were said to have been taken 'by treachery, without the hazard of battle' (Diod. Sic. 16.53.2), and many other towns were probably taken by the same means. Demosthenes lamented the proliferation, in every Greek state, of traitors willing to treat with Philip (Dem., De cor. 61). There was a tale that, when the inhabitants of a certain town boasted of its impregnable defences, Philip mischievously enquired whether not even gold could climb its walls (Diod. Sic. 16.54.3). And Cicero records that Philip once memorably claimed that any fortress could be taken, if only a little donkey laden with gold could make his way up to it (Cic., Att. 1.16.12).

However, Philip did not always enjoy success. In 340 BC, his siege of Perinthus ended in miserable failure, despite the deployment of a full siege train:

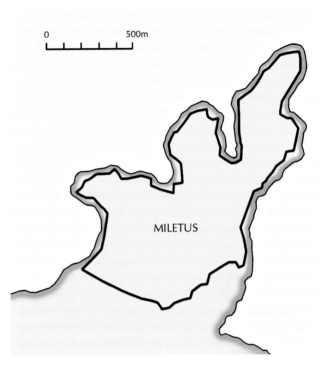

Having built 80-cubit [37m] siege towers, which far overshadowed the towers of Perinthus, he continued to subdue the besieged from his superior height; likewise, he shook the walls with battering rams, and undermined them with tunnels, and threw down a long stretch of the wall. But when the Perinthians warded him off stoutly, quickly erecting a second wall, some extraordinary struggles and wall-fighting took place. Great rivalry was exhibited on both sides; on the one hand, equipped with many and varied arrow-shooting catapults, the king destroyed the men fighting from the battlements; but on the other hand, the Perinthians, losing many every day, received an alliance from the Byzantines, with missiles and catapults (Diod. Sic. 16.74.3–4).

Peninsular towns were vulnerable to being 'walled off' from the mainland. Such a strategy, allegedly contemplated at Miletus both by the Athenians in 411 BC and by Alexander in 334 BC, was properly called apoteichismos, *as distinct from the encircling* periteichismos. *(© Author)*

Nor did the Persian king, Artaxerxes III, wish Philip to gain a foothold on the Hellespont, and he duly sent a force of mercenaries, with 'abundant supplies, sufficient corn, missiles, and everything else of use in war' (Diod. Sic. 16.75.2). With Persian and Byzantine aid bolstering the Perinthian defence, Philip was soon bogged down in an impossible siege. Furthermore, his simultaneous strike on Byzantium, gambling that it had been left undefended, simply stirred up enmity among the neighbouring Greek communities, and Philip had to abandon both sieges (Diod. Sic. 16.76.4, 77.2).

THE MACEDONIAN SIEGE TOWER

During a siege, the simplest way for troops to mount the enemy battlements was by ladder. However, such a manoeuvre was fraught with danger: the apparatus was often flimsy and easily repulsed, and the climbing troops were exposed to attack from above. The development of the siege tower made the process less hazardous, by providing a protected staircase with a gangplank or drawbridge, which could be let down onto the enemy wall. The machine's debut at Motya in 398 BC illustrates more or less this technique, when Dionysius actually inserted his towers into the town through a breached wall, and used them to convey troops by gangplank onto the house-tops.

Of course, by its very nature, the siege tower also presented an elevated platform from which missile troops could target the defenders on the wall-walk. At Perinthus in 340 BC, Philip II's siege towers, perhaps designed by the engineer Polyidus, were almost 130ft (40m) high, allowing an overwhelming barrage of missiles to be directed onto the towers and battlements, and probably the built-up area beyond.

Instructions for building such a machine left by Diades, a pupil of Polyidus, have been preserved for us in three ancient accounts: the works of Athenaeus and Vitruvius, both composed towards the end of the 1st century BC, and an anonymous Byzantine compilation, entitled *Siegecraft instructions* (*Parangelmata poliorkētika*). According to these, Diades prescribed two sizes of tower. The smaller version was 60 cubits (90ft or 26.6m) high, and tapered from a base of 17 cubits (25ft or 7.5m) square to 13½ cubits (20ft or 6.0m) square at the top; it was divided into ten storeys, not in the form of complete platforms, but rather landings to support a system of internal staircases.

The larger version was an incredible 120 cubits (180ft or 53.2m) high and 23½ cubits (35ft or 10.4m) wide, tapering to around 19 cubits (27½ft or 8.4m) wide at the top; again, each of the 20 storeys took the form of a 3-cubit (4½ft or 1.3m) wide walkway around a central opening, through which the staircase rose in stages. The whole machine was covered with rawhide as a defence against fire.

Unfortunately, no details of the undercarriage have been preserved, although the anonymous Byzantine claims that the smaller tower sat on six wheels, and the larger on eight. Nor are there any instructions regarding the gangplank or boarding-bridge (*epibathra*) that must have been extended from the tower to carry the storm troops across to the enemy battlements. It was especially important to ensure that it could bear the weight of the combatants, unlike the first of Alexander's boarding-bridges at Massaga in 327 BC, which broke, spilling the troops onto the ground and exposing them to missiles thrown from the battlements. Equally, the troops crossing the bridge required protection along the flanks, and a waist-height wicker-work fence would have had the added benefit of preventing men from stumbling off the edge. Ironically, the sources note that Diades had promised to write on the subject of boarding-bridges, but never did.

The 18th-century Chevalier de Folard's reconstruction of the siege tower is ingenious, but inaccurate: it would have run on wheels, rather than this overly complex system of rollers, and the external galleries simply add to the machine's vulnerability. (Author's collection)

The Myndus gate at Halicarnassus. (© Jona Lendering)

THE SIEGES OF ALEXANDER THE GREAT

Philip's son and successor, Alexander, had quite a different attitude to siegecraft. As Sir Frank Adcock long ago observed, 'he pressed his sieges home with fiery and resourceful determination', not with treachery and betrayal. Marsden preferred to attribute his success to the possession of superior siege machinery. It is true that, in his attack on Miletus in 334 BC, Alexander 'shook the wall with machines' (Diod. Sic. 17.22.3; Arrian, *Anab.* 1.19.2), creating a breach for his storming attack. And some weeks later, at Halicarnassus, his men filled the 30-cubit (44ft or 13.5m) wide ditch under cover of wheeled sheds, so that machinery could be brought up (Arr., *Anab.* 1.20.8). Again, Alexander 'rocked the towers and the curtain in between with rams' (Diod. Sic. 17.24.4), and the gradual destruction of the fortifications persuaded the Persian garrison to flee.

It is equally clear that Alexander was perfectly willing to launch an assault without the support of heavy machinery. For example, at Thebes in 335 BC, there was a three-day delay while he 'put together the siege machines' (Diod. Sic. 17.9.6). But, when the Thebans marched out against him, they were beaten back by the Macedonian phalanx, which proceeded to rush through the gate at their heels; the machinery was never brought into action. Similarly, the machinery assembled for attacking the main town of the Mallians in 326/5 BC did not arrive quickly enough for Alexander (Diod. Sic. 17.98.4), so he stormed the place without it. And earlier, at Sangala, he 'had his machines assembled and brought up' (Arr., *Anab*. 5.24.4), intending to batter the town wall, but by then his men had undermined it and crossed over the ruins by ladder (Curt. 9.1.18).

Of course, many factors determined whether siege machines should be used, not least the strength and situation of the defences. In 329 BC, on hearing of a revolt in Sogdiana, Alexander ordered only assault ladders to be constructed; the half-dozen towns affected had such low walls that they quickly fell to escalade (Arr., *Anab*. 4.2.3). But other factors might dictate whether machinery was required. During the siege of Halicarnassus, Alexander made a detour to Myndus without his siege train, expecting the town to be betrayed to him; but he was double-crossed, and although his men began undermining the walls, the arrival of a relieving force persuaded them to withdraw (Arr., *Anab*. 1.20.6).

Alexander's siegecraft is often characterized by the spectacular siege of Tyre, an island town off the coast of present-day Lebanon (see illustration pp. 66–67). In order to bring machinery up to the walls, the Macedonians spanned the straits with a long, wide causeway; but after spending around six months building it, Alexander must have realized that, by attacking the town on such a narrow front, he had given the advantage to the defenders. Consequently, he ordered the adaptation of ships to carry 'machines, especially battering rams' (Curt. 4.3.13; cf. Diod. Sic. 17.43.4, 46.1; Arr., *Anab*. 2.23.3), which allowed attacks to be

View of Gaza taken in 1922. The mound on which the village sits represents centuries of occupation dating back to the 2nd millennium BC. It may have been this site that Alexander besieged in 322 BC.
(© École biblique, Jerusalem)

coordinated all around the island. Troops were finally able to enter the town on its seaward side through breaches in the wall, while others crossed on gangways extended from the siege towers on the causeway.

These machines were 'equal in height to the walls' (Diod. Sic. 17.43.7), which Arrian alleges to have been 150ft (45m) high (Arr., *Anab.* 2.21.4). The German scholar Erwin Schramm attempted to rationalize this astonishing claim by suggesting that the battlements ran along a cliff-top, which has since disappeared, but this seems unlikely; most scholars agree that Arrian was exaggerating. 'The king himself climbed the highest siege tower with great courage', writes Curtius (4.4.10), and 'when the Macedonians with Alexander crossed over the gangplanks onto the wall, the city was captured' (Diod. Sic. 17.46.3). Although it had been a long-drawn-out affair, the technical aspects of the siege impressed the ancients.

The subsequent operations at Gaza (332 BC) are more difficult to analyse, because the two surviving descriptions, by Arrian and Quintus Curtius, are not

(Continued p.69)

City wall of Halicarnassus. View from the northernmost tower towards the south-east, showing the ruined wall and the line of the fortification ditch in front of the wall. The ground is comparatively level in this area, and it might very well be here that Alexander managed to break through the fortifications in 334 BC. (© Poul Pedersen)

ALEXANDER'S SIEGE OF TYRE, 332 BC

At Tyre, Alexander allegedly mobilized tens of thousands to construct the causeway, 2 plethra (62m) wide and 4 stades (740m) long. Building materials came from the demolition of the old town on the mainland, and timber was brought from the mountains of Lebanon; entire trees and rocks were heaved in to build up the structure. Wicker screens protected the workmen, and two siege towers were erected so that missile troops could provide a covering barrage. The Tyrians responded with a fire-ship, a large transport vessel filled with combustible material and guided under sail against the causeway; cauldrons slung from the yard-arms were rigged to set the boat ablaze when it reached its goal. In the event, considerable damage was done, including the destruction of the siege towers, but Alexander's engineers set to work again and the causeway was finally completed. Both Diodorus and Curtius indicate that the walls were well furnished with arrow-shooting catapults, and the city engineers had contrived devices to counter the Macedonians. Screens of stretched hides helped to protect the defenders. Also illustrated is an example of the 'iron hand', or *harpax* (right), used to grab individual men or machines. (Adam Hook © Osprey Publishing Ltd)

entirely in agreement. The town's location on a high tell required a siege embankment to be piled up, which necessarily protracted the operation. Both writers mention machinery (Arr., *Anab.* 2.27.2; Curt. 4.6.9), Curtius adding the detail that the sandy ground subsided, damaging the undercarriages of the siege towers. But where Arrian concentrates on the embankment, claiming that it was 2 stades wide (about 1215ft or 370m) and 55ft high (17m), it is clear from Curtius that the main thrust of the assault involved undermining the walls (Arr., *Anab.* 2.27.4; Curt. 4.6.23).

The sieges of Tyre and Gaza highlight Alexander's ability to visualize large-scale operations, and his willingness to carry them through to completion. Similarly, at Massaga in 327 BC, there was a nine-day delay while the 'ditch of massive proportions' (Curt. 8.10.24, 30–31) was filled; the wall was soon breached by 'machines' (Arr., *Anab.* 4.26.5), but Alexander met stiff resistance, and the townsfolk only surrendered after their chieftain was killed by a catapult arrow. In the following year, more earth-moving was required at the Rock of Aornus, where Alexander's Macedonians spent seven days filling a vertiginous ravine to allow access to the impregnable stronghold (Arr., *Anab.* 4.29.7–30.1; Curt. 8.11.8–9; Diod. Sic. 17.85.6–7).

Some months earlier, a completely different strategy had been adopted at the Sogdian Rock, where the inhabitants not only refused to acknowledge Alexander's authority, but arrogantly claimed that their stronghold was impregnable: 'they told Alexander to seek soldiers with wings' (Arr., *Anab.* 4.18.6). In fact, the rock rose sheer on every side, and deep snow made it difficult to approach; furthermore, the Sogdians had laid up plentiful provisions to match their unlimited water supply. Any traditional siegecraft was out of the question, so Alexander sent 300 mountaineers to make the hazardous ascent. When they appeared unexpectedly on the summit, the defenders surrendered in amazement.

There was no place for the passive blockade in Alexander's dynamic style of siege warfare. Although we find him occasionally adopting the old Athenian strategy of *periteichismos*, or 'encirclement', this was never an end in itself. For example, during the campaign against the rebel Sogdian towns in 329 BC, Alexander instructed his general Craterus to encircle the strongest one, Cyropolis, with a ditch and palisade (Arr., *Anab.* 4.2.2). However, his intention was to contain the rebels there, while he himself recovered the other towns. Returning to Cyropolis, he began a battering attack and, while the defenders were fully occupied, infiltrated the town along a dry watercourse, repeating a stratagem used by the Persians at Babylon, 300 years before. The gates were thrown open from within and, after a fierce struggle, the town was captured.

(Opposite) The river Indus and the Rock of Aornus at Pir-sar, viewed from the north-west. (Marco Prins; © Jona Lendering)

The explorer Sir Aurel Stein identified the site of Aornus with Pir-sar, the flat-topped ridge to the left of the photograph. Alexander approached from the west (right) where the 500ft-(150m) deep Burimar-kandao ravine had to be bridged by a timber-framed embankment. (J. F. C. Fuller, The Generalship of Alexander the Great, Eyre & Spottiswoode, London, 1958. Plate 4)

MACEDONIAN SIEGE MACHINES

Large and complex machines would have been costly to construct and maintain, and almost by definition were only required by expansionist powers. So it is not surprising that they virtually disappeared for 50 years, following the campaigns of Dionysius I on Sicily, before re-emerging in the Macedonian armies of Philip II and his son, Alexander the Great. Philip's place in the development of siege warfare is secure, but Marsden was intrigued by his failure at Perinthus. He suggested that, around 350 BC, Philip established permanent workshops for mechanical engineering, but that inadequacies were shown up during the campaign of 340 BC, and a new chief engineer had to be appointed for the siege of Byzantium. This was the context into which Marsden placed Polyidus, whose service he dated to the years 340–335 BC. Of course, this is all conjectural. Polyidus' name was certainly linked with the building of a giant siege tower at Byzantium (*Lat. Alex.* 8.5–8: 'the man who built the *helepolis* at Byzantium and the *tetrakuklon* at Rhodes'), but we cannot say whether this event stood at the beginning of his career or at the end.

Marsden's scheme perhaps gains support from the fact that Polyidus' pupils, Diades and Charias, 'campaigned with Alexander' (Vitr., *De arch.* 10.13.3; Ath., *Mech.* 10.9–10), probably from the very start. They were perhaps responsible for developing the wheeled shed or 'tortoise' (*chelōnē*, or *testudo*), which thereafter became increasingly common in siegecraft, particularly for carrying battering rams up to the wall. In antiquity, Diades became famous as 'the man who captured Tyre with Alexander' (*Lat. Alex.* 8.12–15), and it was perhaps during that siege that he developed his famous boarding-bridges; later writers lamented the fact that his instructions for assembling these were never written down (Vitr., *De arch.* 10.13.8; Ath., *Mech.* 15.5–7).

The massive and complex machinery often deployed by Macedonian armies must have been expensive to manufacture. Faced with failure at Pherae, Philip was determined to withdraw his machinery intact, so he set his engineers the task of dismantling it by night. Such an operation left his men vulnerable to counter-attack, so they made it sound as if they were constructing new machines; the terrified townsfolk spent the night strengthening their defences, and were in no position to contest Philip's surreptitious departure (Polyaen., *Strat.* 4.2.20). Such large machines were also troublesome to transport. After the fall of Miletus, Alexander had his siege train carried to Halicarnassus by sea (Diod. Sic. 17.24.1), and the artillery used at Gaza was shipped from Tyre (Arr., *Anab.* 2.27.3). Transfer by land must have been more difficult, but we know that Diades designed his siege towers to be disassembled (Vitr., *De arch.* 10.13.3; Ath., *Mech.* 10.11), and it was presumably this innovation that permitted Alexander to use machinery in the mountainous terrain of the Hindu Kush.

MACEDONIAN ARTILLERY

Marsden believed that Alexander's frequent deployment of artillery was made possible by the technical advances of his father's engineers. As a hypothesis, this has much to commend it, not least the fact that contemporary Athenian comedy represented Philip as surrounded by catapults (Mnes., *Philip* frg. 7),

THE HELEPOLIS OF POSIDONIUS

The term 'city-taker' (*helepolis*) usually evokes the gigantic artillery-armed towers utilized by Demetrius Poliorcetes at the end of the 4th century BC, but the machine had a long pedigree. Polyidus was known as 'the man who built the *helepolis* at Byzantium', during Philip's unsuccessful siege of 340 BC. Although nothing is known about his machine, it is likely that its purpose was to elevate missile troops to such a height that they commanded not only the battlements, but the towers on the city wall as well, not to mention the interior of the town. The term *helepolis* perhaps came to be applied indiscriminately to any particularly impressive piece of siege machinery. Certainly, in the Roman era, it was briefly used to indicate a battering ram, but is still found associated with siege towers in the 4th century AD.

Posidonius' 'city-taker', described by Biton, was built for Alexander the Great, presumably in the 330s BC. In one of the few remarks on the optimum varieties of timber to use for siege machinery, he recommends fir or pine for the long timbers and the planking, but specifies hard wood like oak or ash for load-bearing components, such as the wheels and axles; and, in addition, the long beams should be reinforced with iron bands.

The brevity of Biton's description has led to confusion amongst modern scholars. In fact, not so long ago, it was customary to dismiss Biton as a worthless fraud. The Danish scholar Aage Drachmann went so far as to state that 'there is no sense in Biton at all', but that is too extreme a position to adopt; there is still much of value in his descriptions of siege machines.

The footprint of Posidonius' tower, at 60ft (18.5m) long by 50ft (15.5m) wide, was considerably larger than the contemporary siege towers of Diades. Biton says that the tower's axles were supported by an iron-strapped joist, 60ft (18.5m) long and 3ft (0.95m) high. Eric Marsden suggested that both sides of the undercarriage comprised two such joists, side by side, sandwiching the wheels in between. Biton's text does not preserve this level of detail, but the suggestion is sensible as the same type of construction is found later, in Roman machines. There must also have been crossbeams.

The bottom floor apparently sat on 2ft-high (0.62m) posts, fixed to the joists above the axles. According to Biton, these posts were just big enough, 'so that the rims of the wheels rubbed [presumably against the floor above] and the men pushing the machine [i.e. standing on the ground between the timbers of the undercarriage] were not

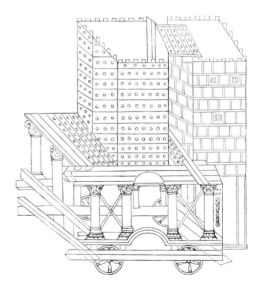

Posidonius' helepolis. It is unlikely that this manuscript illustration, dating to the 11th/12th centuries, is in any way faithful to Biton's original diagram. For one thing, Biton's text presupposes that the main elements of the machine were labelled on the drawing with Greek letters. This Byzantine drawing probably represents the attempt of an early reader to reconstruct the machine from the instructions alone. (C. Wescher, Poliorcétique des Grecs, Paris 1867)

cramped' (Biton 53.9). If we assume that the joists sat on the axles, there will have been a 5ft (1.5m) gap between the axle and the timbers of the first floor. The reference to 'rubbing' implies that the wheels took up much of this space, and must have been a shade less than 10ft (3m) in diameter, which would certainly have given the pushing-crew ample headroom.

However, Biton later states that the wheels were only 3ft (0.92m) in diameter and 9ft (2.8m) in circumference (Biton 55.5–6). Marsden took a somewhat cavalier approach to the text, proposing 6-cubit-high (9ft or 2.8m), 4ft-thick (1.2m), spoked wheels, and claiming that Biton's 3ft diameter applied only to the wheel-hubs. However, the division of the wheel into spokes would have introduced an unnecessary weakness, and it seems unlikely that such a massive machine would have been equipped with anything other than solid wheels. Furthermore, wheels of 3ft in diameter would have made moving the machine excessively difficult – the larger the wheels, the easier the movement. It seems more likely that Biton's figure of 3ft was the width of the wheels, and 9ft was the height.

Biton goes on to describe, in a convoluted fashion, an arrangement of beams and posts that apparently formed the 17ft-high (5.2m) chassis of the *helepolis*. Both long sides of the machine were provided with a central arched doorway (*propylis*), giving access to the interior of the chamber, where the staircase leading to the upper levels would have started.

The rest of the machine is a little vague. At the outset, Biton sensibly advises that siege towers should be tailored to the height of the enemy wall, but he later suggests a 50-cubit (75ft or 23m) superstructure, presumably rising above the 17ft chassis and 9ft undercarriage, resulting more or less in a 100ft (31m) tower. It was not the tower height that was most crucial, but the positioning of the boarding-bridge within, so that when the machine was drawn up at the enemy wall, the troops could storm across onto the battlements. Unfortunately, Biton does not explain how this feature worked, but it clearly required an opening in the front face of the tower in order to provide an exit for the storm troops. As for the boarding-bridge itself, there are two possibilities: first, the bridge could have taken the form of a gangplank, stored horizontally within the tower and slid forward through an opening, perhaps on rollers; or, second, it could have been fitted vertically on the tower's exterior, hinged at the bottom like a drawbridge and lowered by a winch mechanism. The latter seems to be the more practical option, although later Roman towers apparently used both.

Biton states that the exterior was plastered with lime and covered with sheep's wool fleeces. This was just one of many schemes utilized for fireproofing siege machines. Philon of Byzantium recommends that exposed timbers should be daubed with a mixture of ash and birdlime (a sticky substance derived from mistletoe berries) as a protection against fire, and mentions the use of wool fleeces soaked in vinegar or water. No doubt, a fleece layer also helped to absorb the impact of missiles.

and a word-list composed around AD 180 contains an entry for *katapeltai Makedonikoi* ('Macedonian catapults'), suggesting some special relationship with Macedon. The development of the torsion catapult must have been a slow process of trial and error, and the stone-projectors that first appear at Halicarnassus and Tyre cannot have been particularly powerful. Diodorus must be exaggerating when he says that, at Tyre, Alexander 'struck down the walls

(Continued p.79)

THE DITCH-FILLING TORTOISE

Wheeled siege machinery required an approach path that was smooth, level and firm. It would have been difficult enough to set the great *helepoleis* in motion, without having to negotiate humps and bumps in the ground. And, as has been seen, such machines were vulnerable to soft ground. In fact, during the attack on the coastal town of Gaza in 332 BC, the wheels of Alexander's towers sank in the sandy soil, so that the undercarriages were damaged and the machines had to be hauled back. In addition, by the mid-4th century BC, many towns had provided themselves with defensive ditches, which needed to be filled if machinery were to be wheeled up to the walls. In the Greek world, artificial ramps of the sort favoured by the Romans were virtually unheard of, but it became usual for men to level out the terrain in advance of the heavy machinery.

Naturally, they required some form of protection that could be moved forward with them as they advanced, and that would permit them to work unhindered. The solution was the ditch-filling tortoise (*testudo*, or *chelōnē chōstris*), a type of shed resembling a pitched roof on wheels. These machines were cleverly designed so that any projectiles would simply glance off and roll away; they were also protected by a fireproof layer. Diodorus Siculus mentions such machines deployed during Alexander's siege of Halicarnassus in 334 BC, and Demetrius later used eight of them at Rhodes, to prepare the way for his *helepolis*; similar machines were still in use a century later by Macedonian and Seleucid armies.

Athenaeus describes how the machine was built around a 7-cubit-high (10ft or 3.1m) central compartment, sitting on a 14-cubit-square (20ft or 6.2m) undercarriage (*escharion*). The pitched roof,

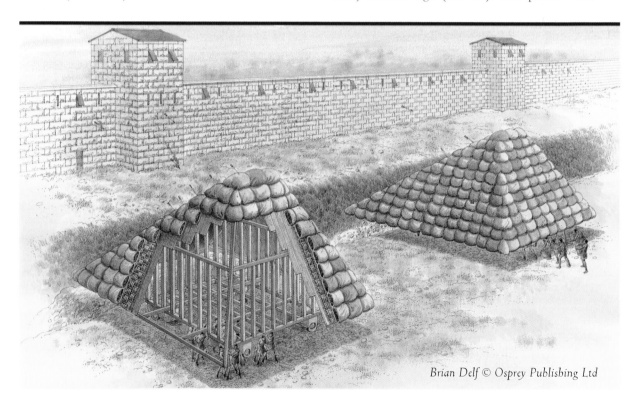

Brian Delf © Osprey Publishing Ltd

which was the machine's main feature, extended a further 4 cubits (6ft or 1.7m) to either side. However, rather than terminating in gable-ends, it seems to have sloped to the front and rear, the four faces meeting in a transverse ridge some 23ft (7m) above ground level.

Athenaeus attributes the design to 'Philon of Athens', which is surely a slip for Philon of Byzantium, whose *Mechanical encyclopedia* (*Mēchanikē syntaxis*), compiled in the later 3rd century BC, included works on artillery and on siegecraft. In the latter, he draws a distinction between the 'wicker-tortoise' (*gerrochelōnē*) and the 'ditch-filling tortoise' (*chelōnē chōstris*). The 'wicker-tortoise' seems to have been a simple, open-ended shelter of the sort that the Romans called the *vinea*, whereas the 'ditch-filling' version was entirely enclosed.

The 'ditch-filling' tortoise also had massive foot-thick (29.5cm), 3-cubit-high (4½ft or 1.33m) wheels, one at each corner of the *escharion*. The individual axles were incorporated into an ingenious steering mechanism, which allowed sideways movement. Vitruvius' version allegedly enabled the machine to travel, not only sideways, but also diagonally; however, it is not clear how this was accomplished. One common theory, that each wheel was designed to swivel independently like a castor, is unlikely; Vitruvius envisages a wheel-assembly that was adjustable in 45° increments, whereas a castor would be able to swivel continuously.

Athenaeus recommends that the roof be boarded with palm wood, because of its resilience, and covered with green wickerwork. The suitability of palm wood was apparently well known; Philon also mentions it for general use in siege machinery, but recommends an outer skin of iron scales and some kind of padding, too. Certainly, Athenaeus prescribes an overall cushion of rawhide, padded with seaweed or vinegar-soaked chaff, both to absorb the impact of missiles and as a defence against fire.

The ditch-filling tortoise covered around 1300 square feet (120 square metres) of ground. Men would have been able to work comfortably over much of that area, on account of the frame's height above ground, but only practical experiment will reveal exact details of how to move the machine.

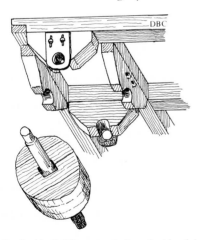

In the 'ditch-filling tortoise', each side of the corner-square has a cradle-like component, which Athenaeus calls a 'wagon-foot' (hamaxipous), and each wheel has its own short axle. At any one time, the axle sits in two opposing 'wagon-feet', so that it either faces forwards or sideways. (© Author, after Sackur)

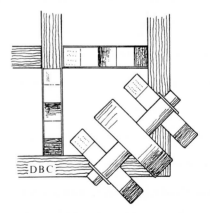

The German scholar Walter Sackur made an ingenious suggestion to allow the diagonal movement which Vitruvius mentions. The two outer 'wagon-feet' are made to pivot in the centre, creating a third position for the axle, midway between the forward and sideways positions. (© Author, after Sackur)

THE RAM-TORTOISE

Besides crossing over the enemy wall by means of ladders or a siege tower, an alternative option was open to the besieger; namely, breaking through the wall. Most ancient sources simply refer to 'battering rams' during such operations, which has occasionally led to the suggestion that the machine consisted simply of a scaffold, set up at the wall, from which a ramming-beam was suspended. Of course, an unprotected timber framework would not have lasted long in such an exposed location, even if a construction crew could have survived long enough to build it there. In fact, it is clear that, from the mid-4th century BC (if not earlier), battering rams were normally concealed within wheeled sheds, and brought up to their action stations just like siege towers.

Originally, the Greek version of the ram-tortoise may even have been the work of Philip's engineer Polyidus, who allegedly developed battering rams that were 'easier to use' (Vitr., *De arch.* 10.13.3). Athenaeus and Vitruvius describe the machine built for Alexander the Great by Diades, a pupil of Polyidus. Like the ditch-filling and digging sheds, it more or less resembled a penthouse on wheels, and was similarly designated as a 'tortoise' (*testudo*, or *chelōnē*).

As with his siege tower, Diades apparently had a small version and a large version, but measurements are given only for the latter. Its overall dimensions were 30 cubits (44ft or 13.3m) wide by 40 cubits (60ft or 17.74m) long, and the apex of the pitched roof stood 16 cubits (24ft or 7.1m) high; the whole structure was covered with rawhide. Unusually for a tortoise, a three-storey turret crowned Diades' machine. That, and an ambiguous reference to an intermediate floor within the shed, has led to much scholarly confusion.

The most likely interpretation of Athenaeus' text (in conjunction with Vitruvius' more summary version) results in a machine very similar to the ditch-filling tortoise. Like it, the ram-tortoise would have

De Folard's reconstruction of the battering ram. It is unlikely that a single suspension point would enable the ram to work effectively. However, the ramming-beam itself is a fairly accurate representation. (Author's collection)

been based upon three key elements: the rectangular, wheeled undercarriage; the main internal compartment; and the familiar hipped roof. The enigmatic 'middle floor' will then have been the area between the main compartment and the roof ridge; no doubt, it was instrumental in allowing access to the turret, which rose through the apex of the roof.

The upper levels of the turret accommodated 'scorpions and catapults', while the lowest level held a reservoir of water to extinguish any fires caused by incendiary missiles. Vitruvius adds the useful detail that the turret was 4 cubits (6ft or 1.77m) wide. The term 'scorpion' usually denotes an arrow-shooting catapult of smaller calibre; the largest catapult still qualifying as a 'scorpion' was perhaps a machine designed to shoot a 70cm arrow (equivalent to 3 spans). The stock of such a machine was about 4ft (1.2m) long, and, although the torsion-frame was only 20in (0.5m) wide, each arm protruded about half as much again, giving an overall width of 1m.

We should not underestimate the amount of working-room required by the artilleryman, particularly at the rear, where the catapult arms were winched back, but also at the sides, where the stock would swing round when the weapon was traversed. It would not be far wrong to assign a 3-span arrow-shooter a minimum floor-space of 5ft by 8ft (1.5m by 2.5m). Consequently, it would have been impossible to station more than one catapult in a room 4 cubits wide. Furthermore, the turret must have been considerably longer than it was wide, to suit the dimensions of a catapult, and it would seem sensible to assume a length of 6, or even 8, cubits (9–12ft or 2.7–3.5m).

Of course, the tortoise was simply a mobile platform for the 'ram-holder' (*kriodochē*, or *arietaria machina*), upon which the battering ram rested. This obscure component apparently took the form of a cylindrical roller, which was probably mounted transversely within the framework of the turret; in fact, it would go some way towards explaining the function of the 'middle floor' if the 'ram-holder' were located there. Vitruvius clearly states that the ramming-beam sat on the 'ram-holder' and was set in motion by pulling and releasing ropes. It seems a somewhat precarious mounting for a heavy ramming-beam, and part of the mechanism is perhaps missing from the description.

Locating the beam 6m above ground level has interesting implications for the ramming process. Clearly, Diades did not intend to breach the enemy wall at its foot, where the foundations could be expected to have been more solid. Nor was he aiming at battlement level, which may have been as high as the 20 cubits (30ft or 9.25m) recommended by Philon, or even higher (though the alleged height of 40 cubits for the walls of Piraeus has been doubted). Rather, the target seems to have been a midway point, guaranteed to weaken the wall-walk above, thus preventing any countermeasures. Defenders commonly disrupted ramming operations by dropping heavy weights onto the ram head or ensnaring it with lassos, both of which required a vantage point directly above the ram. Perhaps Diades incorporated some method of adjusting the angle of the ramming-beam, in order to continue the breach downwards, to a height at which infantry could enter.

The late Eric Marsden with his reconstruction of a three-span arrow-shooter at Maiden Castle (England). This machine, designed to shoot arrows 2¼ft (69cm) long, was probably the standard catapult from the 3rd century BC until the 1st. (P. Johnstone, Buried Treasure, London: Phoenix House, 1957. Plate 61)

The ancient sources mention defenders using grapnels, or 'iron hands', for ensnaring men and siege machinery. Diades is credited with the invention of one of these, the corvus demolitor or 'demolition raven', imaginatively reconstructed here by de Folard. (Author's collection)

with stone-projectors, and with arrow-shooters forced back the men standing on the battlements' (Diod. Sic. 17.42.7). The use of arrow-shooters in this suppressing role is expected, but it is extremely doubtful whether stone-projectors could ever have demolished masonry walls.

Some towns of the eastern Mediterranean were already equipped with catapults. Byzantium loaned some to Perinthus in 340 BC, Halicarnassus had them in 334 BC, and the Tyrians had 'a great abundance of catapults and the other machines needed for sieges' (Diod. Sic. 17.41.3). Even the Persian troops who halted Alexander at the Persian Gates appear to have been equipped with catapults; besides rolling gigantic boulders down from the heights on either side of the pass, Arrian alleges that they fired volleys of arrows from 'machines' (Arr., *Anab*. 3.18.3). In Marsden's opinion, these catapults were of the *gastraphetēs* variety, but the question must remain open; even if torsion technology was funded by Macedon, as seems likely, peripatetic engineers could still have spread it around the eastern Mediterranean.

The wide isthmus that now connects the ancient island of Tyre to the mainland is thought to have resulted from centuries of silting around the remains of the Macedonian causeway. (© IFAPO)

Hellenistic Siege Warfare

The so-called Diadochoi, or successors of Alexander, are better known for their field battles, and it is commonly assumed that little emphasis was placed on siege. Of course, where one side sought refuge behind walls, the other had no recourse but to employ whatever besieging skills were available to them. Directly after Alexander's death, an Athenian army under Leosthenes defeated the Macedonian regent, Antipater, and shut him up in the town of Lamia in central Greece. When assaults on the walls proved fruitless, Leosthenes resorted to a blockading strategy and began surrounding the place with a wall and ditch (Diod. Sic. 18.13.3); only his accidental death in a mêlée around the siege-works brought an end to the operation.

In the winter of 317/16 BC, Antipater's son Cassander similarly surrounded Pydna with a stockade running from sea to sea, intending to assault the walls when better weather arrived. But, in the meantime, the garrison suffered so badly from famine that cavalry horses were slaughtered for food and the townsfolk allegedly resorted to cannibalism (Diod. Sic. 19.49.1–50.1). Much the same strategy had been adopted by Antigonus, the commander in Asia Minor, when he cornered Eumenes in the Armenian fortress of Nora (320 BC). Diodorus records how he surrounded the place with 'double walls and ditches and astonishing palisades' (Diod. Sic. 18.41.6) and continued the blockade for a year. (It was during his captivity that Eumenes evolved a novel method of exercising his cavalry horses using a machine, so that they would remain fit for battle.)

Not every general was so ready to embrace passive siegecraft. When Perdiccas, who had fallen heir to Alexander's grand army, invaded the Egyptian kingdom of Ptolemy, his first objective was the so-called Camel Fort; but, although he combined an escalade with the unusual tactic of assaulting the palisade with elephants, he could not dislodge Ptolemy's troops and was forced to withdraw (Diod. Sic. 18.34.1–5). A different type of assault was tried by Arridaeus against the offshore town of Cyzicus, with 'all sorts of missiles, and both arrow-shooting and stone-projecting catapults, and all the other supplies fit for a siege' (Diod. Sic. 18.51.1); but without naval support his attack failed. Elephants again formed the centrepiece in the attack on Megalopolis by Polyperchon, when he succeeded Antipater as regent of Macedon in 319 BC. Although the townsfolk had repaired their fortifications and constructed new arrow-shooting catapults, Polyperchon's forces managed to undermine a long stretch of wall, under cover of troops shooting from siege towers. The elephants were then directed into the breach, but when they trod on the spiked doors that the Megalopolitans had laid in their path they ran amok, maddened by pain, and created havoc among Polyperchon's troops (Diod. Sic. 18.71.3–6).

DEMETRIUS POLIORCETES

Consolidating his hold on Asia Minor and the Middle East, Antigonus was able to take Joppa and Gaza by storm. But the 15 months he spent reducing Tyre to capitulation (Diod. Sic. 19.61.5) stand in stark contrast to Alexander's dynamic siege of the same town, a generation earlier. By contrast, Antigonus' son Demetrius, known to posterity as Poliorcetes, 'the besieger', is commonly credited with raising siegecraft to the pitch of perfection. Certainly, one of his closest advisors, named Philip, may well have been Alexander's engineer of the same name. And it is true that Demetrius enjoyed a string of successes, for example in 307 BC, when he captured Piraeus, Munychia, Megara, Ourania and Carpasia. In the following year, at Salamis on Cyprus, his combined siege machinery proved to be devastating: 'bringing the machines up to the city, and putting down a barrage of missiles, he tore away the battlements with his stone-projectors and shook the walls with battering rams' (Diod. Sic. 20.48.4). Demetrius captured the town, despite the fact that the townsfolk managed to destroy his siege train in the process. It is all the more curious, then, that he is chiefly remembered for his siege of Rhodes in 305/4 BC, which was a signal failure. As the Greek scholar Arnold Gomme long ago observed, Demetrius was not *ekpoliorketēs*, 'taker of cities', but simply 'besieger of cities'; the nickname seems to have been applied in derision after his failure at Rhodes.

Relief sculpture from the Heroon at Trysa, thought to date from around 370 BC. Three soldiers assault the walls under cover of their shields, while the townsfolk adopt the age-old defence of dropping boulders onto them, and hurling stones and spears. (© Kunsthistorisches Museum, Vienna)

Later generations clearly misconstrued the insult; Diodorus, for one, believed it was due to his 'devising many things beyond the skill of the engineers' (20.92.2). On the contrary, Demetrius' siege tactics show no particular innovations, but he is rightly remembered for the scale and variety of his siege machinery.

At Rhodes, Demetrius initially launched a shipborne attack on the harbour, hoping to isolate the maritime city from its allies:

> He began to prepare two sheds, one for the stone-projectors, the other for the arrow-shooters, each of them fastened astride two freighters, and two four-storey towers, taller than the harbour towers, each of them mounted on two similar ships and fastened so that, as they advanced, the weight was equally balanced on each ship. He also prepared a floating palisade by nailing squared timbers together, so that, as it floated in front, it might prevent the enemy from sailing up to ram the ships carrying the machines. While this was under way, he collected the sturdiest of the boats, reinforcing them with planks and equipping them with shuttered portholes, and put in them those of the three-span arrow-shooters which shot furthest and the men to operate them properly, and also Cretan archers. Then, sending the ships forward within missile range, he shot down the men of the city who were heightening the wall along the harbour (Diod. Sic. 20.85.1–3).

Rough seas and the countermeasures of the defenders repeatedly foiled the besieger's attack, and he was unable to capture the harbour. Shifting his focus to

The citadel at Corinth, known as the Acrocorinth, viewed from the north. When Demetrius assaulted the town in 303 BC, the garrison of the citadel was intimidated into surrender by his military reputation. (© Author)

the landward side, Demetrius ordered the construction of a *helepolis*, along with various tortoises and galleries, but again he was repulsed, and even had to withdraw the *helepolis* when it was set ablaze by the Rhodians. Finally, Antigonus advised his son to make peace with the town. Vitruvius alone records the colourful story that a Rhodian engineer named Diognetus foiled the *helepolis* by pumping water, mud and sewage into its path; the huge machine, he says, 'settled in the quagmire that had been created, unable afterwards to either advance or retreat' (Vitr., *De arch.* 10.16.7).

THE HELEPOLIS OF EPIMACHUS

For Demetrius, the giant siege tower, or *helepolis* ('city-taker'), became something of a hallmark. The largest of these, used during the siege of Rhodes, was built by Epimachus of Athens. Four ancient authors preserve the details: Athenaeus and Vitruvius; the historian Diodorus Siculus; and Demetrius' biographer, Plutarch, writing around AD 100. Of course, all will have consulted earlier sources, perhaps even a lost work by Epimachus himself; Diodorus' account, in particular, has the flavour of having been drawn from a technical manual. He records that the machine's undercarriage, or 'grid-iron' (*escharion*), had sides measuring 'almost 50 cubits' (Diod. Sic. 20.91.2), which squares with the 48 cubits (72ft or 21m)

The helepolis of Epimachus. According to Diodorus, 3,400 of the strongest men were employed to propel the machine, but there can only have been room for, at most, 800 of them to push against the joists of the undercarriage at any one time. This seems inadequate to move such an immense machine; it is possible that draught animals were used, in conjunction with pulleys anchored in the ground beneath the front of the helepolis. (Brian Delf © Osprey Publishing Ltd)

recorded by Plutarch and Athenaeus; Vitruvius' '6oft' (17.75m) is obviously a mistake. Diodorus says that crossbeams partitioned the interior of the undercarriage at one-cubit (46cm) intervals, 'so that there was room for those destined to move the machine forward' (Diod. Sic. 20.91.2); the clear intention was for crowds of men to push against the crossbeams.

The machine rolled on eight wheels, but it is unknown whether they were arranged in two rows, each with four wheels, or four rows of two. The latter arrangement would perhaps tend to create two deep wheel ruts, whereas the former would have distributed the weight of the tower more evenly across the running surface. The wheels were 2 cubits (3ft or 0.92m) thick and plated with iron. We know that a *helepolis* built for Demetrius three years earlier at Salamis, on Cyprus, had only four wheels, each 8 cubits (12ft or 3.7m) high, and larger wheels will generally have made for easier movement, but there is no evidence that the Rhodes machine also had 8-cubit wheels. Diodorus alleges that sideways movement was possible, but it remains a mystery exactly how this would have been accomplished.

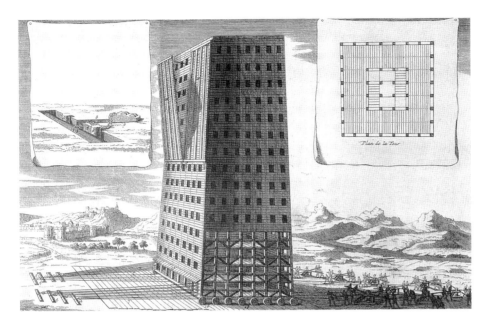

De Folard's reconstruction of the helepolis of Epimachus incorporates several errors, such as the number of wheels, the number of storeys, and the provision of gigantic draw-bridges. But it demonstrates the inventive use of the block-and-tackle for winching the machine forwards. (Author's collection)

The *helepolis* itself was divided into nine storeys, each of which had two stairways, one for men moving upwards through the tower, the other for men climbing down, to avoid congestion. Athenaeus says that it was 90 cubits (134ft or 39.9m) in overall height; Vitruvius' measurement is again short at 125ft (37m), and Plutarch's figure of 66 cubits (98ft or 29m) is presumably a slip for 96 cubits (143ft or 42.6m). Again, Diodorus gives much more information, reporting that the corner timbers were 'almost 100 cubits long' (Diod. Sic. 20.91.4), but instead of standing vertically they tapered in towards the top. Such a structure would have stood around 135ft (40m) high, like Demetrius' previous nine-storey *helepolis* at Salamis.

Each level had shuttered windows opening to the front, through which a variety of missiles could be fired. The shutters were apparently padded with wool-stuffed hides, like mattresses, to absorb the shock of enemy artillery stones, and, although it is likely that they opened outwards, it is not clear whether they were hinged at the top or at the bottom.

The bottom storey of the Salamis tower, which was only marginally smaller than its counterpart at Rhodes, is supposed to have accommodated three-talent stone-projectors; in other words, artillery designed to throw stone balls weighing three talents (171lb or 78kg). Such machines weighed a colossal amount, and were around 33ft (10m) long by 20ft (6m) wide, so there would have been space for only three, side by side; however, the torsion-frame alone was over 13ft (4m) high, so the operational head-room must have been considerably greater than in a standard siege tower.

The intention was clearly to concentrate a heavy bombardment at the battlements, where men and masonry were most vulnerable, but the third storey of the *helepolis* was probably already higher than most town walls. There would have been little point in deploying artillery in the upper storeys, where its limited angle of depression was a handicap to its functionality, but catapults

THE METHOD OF PROPULSION

No ancient author indicates the means by which these heavy machines were moved. A passage by Dionysius' contemporary, the author Xenophon, is often claimed to be relevant here. Xenophon records how the Persian Cyrus, in the mid-6th century BC, utilized eight yokes of oxen to drag a 3-storey, 12-cubit (18ft or 5.55m) tower, with its crew of 20 men. However, this was not a siege tower. It was, in fact, intended for battlefield use, positioned behind, and in support of, the main army; no doubt, after the oxen had hauled the tower into position, they were unhitched and herded out of harm's way. Deploying a siege tower in the heat of combat presented quite a different proposition. An effective argument against the conventional use of draught animals is demonstrated by the Goths' siege of Rome in AD 537. Their leader, Wittigis, decided to advance a siege tower against the wall, but the Roman defenders simply shot the oxen harnessed to it while the machine was still some way off, thus instantly neutralizing it.

Several of the machines sat on an undercarriage (*escharion*), designed to accommodate the axle-assemblies, as well as incorporating crossbeams for men to push against. However, even in the largest machine, there would not have been enough room to accommodate the thousands who are occasionally mentioned as propelling these vast machines. Of course, the ancients were well acquainted with compound pulleys and winches, and it is tempting to assume that they were used to drag wheeled towers forward.

In fact, the tower built by Posidonius seems to have incorporated something of the sort; according to Biton, it was equipped with 'a place for a windlass ... causing the axles to turn more easily' (Biton 55.4–5). Marsden

followed Schramm in assuming that the windlass must have operated directly on the axles, via a kind of continuous belt-drive. But such a concept probably did not arise until the medieval spinning wheel; even then, it is doubtful whether its application to a siege tower would have been practicable, given the tremendous weight that it was expected to move.

There is an alternative use to which Posidonius could have put his winch. It would have been possible (though this is entirely conjectural) for anchor points to be driven into the ground ahead of the machine, and for ropes to run from these back to the on-board winch; men inside the machine could then have winched it forwards as far as the anchor points. Of course, such a scheme did not necessarily require the winching apparatus to be aboard the *helepolis*, and something similar could have been employed to move any heavy, wheeled machine. If the ropes were securely attached to the undercarriage and were run forwards, through pulleys at the anchor points, and back to the rear, a hauling crew (perhaps including draught animals, or utilizing winches) could have dragged the machine forwards. The only danger would have been to the men and tackle exposed ahead of the machine, where they were vulnerable to enemy missiles.

These massive machines must have moved almost imperceptibly, scarcely advancing by the length of their own wheelbase from one day to the next. Under these circumstances, it would have been sufficient to anchor the pulleys in the ground beneath the front of the machine, and secure the ropes to the rearmost beams of the undercarriage. Then the entire system remained concealed beneath the machine throughout. Of course, any hauling arrangement could have been assisted by a multitude simply pushing against the undercarriage and wide wheels.

in the third and fourth storeys could have proved useful at long range. The other floors would have accommodated a variety of missile troops.

The huge quantity of timber used in the machine's construction presented a real fire hazard. Diodorus records that, to offset this, sheets of iron were nailed onto the front and sides. Vitruvius, on the other hand, claims that the machine was protected by padded hides, which would certainly have been a lighter and less costly means of fireproofing. But it seems that Vitruvius is again mistaken, as the Rhodians allegedly managed to knock several of the iron sheets off the tower, exposing the timber beneath to their incendiary missiles, whereupon Demetrius had the machine hauled out of harm's way. The rear of the tower was never in any danger, and it would have been most sensible to leave it not only unarmoured, but also completely unboarded, thus providing the interior with much-needed illumination and ventilation.

Although Diodorus, Athenaeus and Plutarch are obviously describing the same machine, Vitruvius' text, taken at face value, specifies an altogether smaller tower. He also diverges from the other sources in claiming that the machine was fouled in a puddle of sewage which the defenders contrived to pour in its path; apparently, the tower was so heavy that the wheels simply sank in the morass. Is it possible that Vitruvius mistakenly described a different *helepolis*? Certainly, Demetrius is known to have utilized similar machines at Argos in 295 BC and Thebes in 291 BC. Vitruvius' story strikes an interesting chord with Plutarch, who records that the *helepolis* at Thebes was so ponderous that, after two months, the men had managed to drive it forward by only two stades (1200ft or 355m). Was the slow progress caused by Theban sewage?

Workers prepare to use an A-frame to lift the giant BBC ballista onto its stand. This stone-projecting catapult was designed to shoot 26kg (57lb) missiles. (© A. Wilkins)

HEGETOR'S RAM-TORTOISE

Demetrius is often thought to have been the sponsor of another gargantuan machine. This was the enormous ram-carrying tortoise that Athenaeus and Vitruvius attribute to an otherwise unknown engineer named Hegetor of

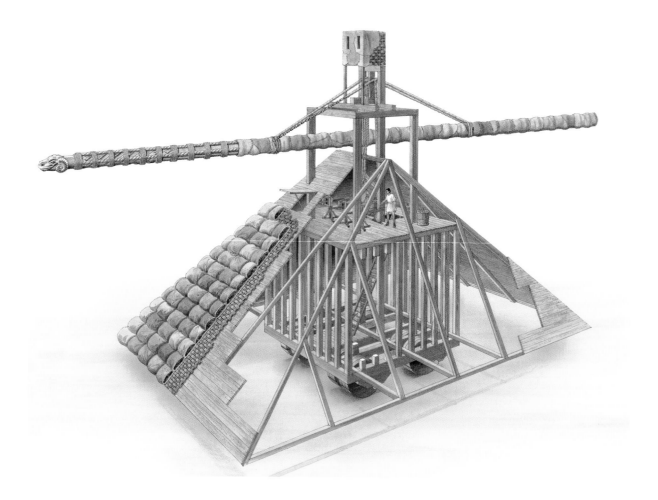

The ram-tortoise of Hegetor. In essence, the machine is a 10-metre-high tortoise with a central turret, but the reconstruction of this key element is controversial. The battering-ram is suspended from a rope cradle high up in the turret, and is stabilized by rawhide-covered chains, running around a pair of rollers. The use of the space above the internal compartment as a 'middle floor' can be seen. (Brian Delf © Osprey Publishing Ltd)

Byzantium. The link has been suggested on the basis of Demetrius' penchant for grandiose machinery, though the connection is more than a little tenuous. The historian Diodorus Siculus records that, during the siege of Salamis, Demetrius 'constructed enormous battering rams and two ram-carrying tortoises' (Diod. Sic. 20.48.1), and that, at Rhodes, his two ram-tortoises were 'many times larger' than the ditch-filling tortoises that preceded them. Their ramming-beams are said to have been 120 cubits (175ft or 53.2m) long (Diod. Sic. 20.95.1), the very length that Athenaeus attributes to Hegetor's battering ram (Ath., Mech. 23.11), but the practicality of such a long beam has been questioned.

Athenaeus claims that Hegetor's ramming-beam was rectangular in cross-section, and tapered from a rear end 2ft (59cm) 'thick' (by which he must mean the 'height' of the beam) and 1¼ft (37cm) broad, to a tip 1ft by ¾ft (29.6cm by 22.2cm). Vitruvius gives a completely different set of dimensions: the length, he says, was 104ft (30.75m), and the rear end was 1¼ft by 1ft (36.9cm by 29.6cm), tapering to 1ft by ¾ft (29.6cm by 22.2cm) at the tip. (The anonymous Byzantine muddies the waters by combining Athenaeus' statement of length, with Vitruvius' dimensions for the thickness of the beam.)

Schramm believed that a 50m beam would buckle, and the ends would drag on the ground, making the whole contraption unusable. He proposed that Athenaeus' text should be emended to read 120ft (35.5m), considerably shorter than 120 cubits, but still some way from Vitruvius' figure. (The alternative approach adopted by the Greek scholar Sir William Tarn, who postulated that a special 'short' cubit of around 34cm was used in Macedon, takes us even further from Vitruvius.)

The German scholar Otto Lendle proposed a better solution, which actually goes some way towards reconciling the two sources; he assumed that the Greek text of Athenaeus had been corrupted during transmission down through the ages, and that an original statement of '70' (*hebdomēkonta*) cubits had been miscopied as '120' (*hekatoneikosi*) cubits. A length of 70 cubits (104ft or 31m) is very close to Vitruvius' measurement. (Precisely how Diodorus Siculus came upon the measurement of 120 cubits for Demetrius' battering rams, however, remains unknown; perhaps both he and Athenaeus drew upon a common source, which had already become corrupted by their day.)

The ramming-beam was capped with an iron tip, like the beak (*embolē*) of a warship. Basically, this was a hollow lump of iron, designed to fit over the end of the beam, but it was secured by four ten-cubit (15ft or 4.4m) iron strips, which trailed back along the beam like streamers and were nailed into position. (Vitruvius calls these streamers *lamminae*, which is the usual term for a strip of metal, but Athenaeus calls them 'iron spirals', implying that they were wound around and along the beam.) The beam was further reinforced with ropes, using a technique well known in the ancient world for bracing the hulls of ships, and was completely wrapped in rawhide, a necessary protection against fire because it was entirely exposed above the level of the tortoise.

The tortoise itself was similar in size to Diades' model (above, p. 76). Athenaeus gives the dimensions as 42 cubits (63ft or 18.62m) long and 28 cubits (42ft or 12.42m) wide (Ath., *Mech.* 21.2–3). Vitruvius' version, at 60ft by 13ft (17.7m by 3.8m), is obviously wrong (Vitr., *De arch.* 10.15.2), and is usually corrected by emending the manuscript 13 (*XIII*) to read 42 (*XLII*); 42ft is the equivalent of 28 cubits, and thus matches the width quoted by Athenaeus. Vitruvius' length of 60ft is 3ft short of Athenaeus' 42 cubits, but this may also be a manuscript error.

The machine ran on eight wheels, 4½ cubits (1.99m) high and 2 cubits (0.88m) thick, which, according to Vitruvius, comprised three layers, each 1ft thick, pegged together with dowels and fastened with iron bands. (Here again, Vitruvius uses the word *lamminae*.) Unfortunately, as with that other

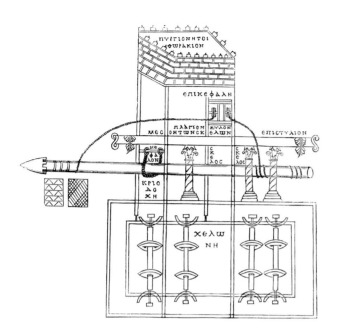

eight-wheeled machine, the *helepolis* of Epimachus, we are not told the configuration of the wheels, but positioning them four abreast would distribute the massive weight of the machine more evenly. Also, a machine built to Athenaeus' dimensions and following the principles of the ditch-filling tortoise would have rested upon an undercarriage some 16 cubits (24ft or 7.1m) square; consequently, there would not have been space for four in-line wheels, and they must have been arranged four abreast.

Like the ditch-filling tortoise, the ram-tortoise would have had a hipped roof meeting at the top in a transverse ridge. The whole machine could then be boarded over and covered with a fireproof layer. As with Diades' ram-tortoise, this style of construction resulted in a 'middle floor' (*mesē stegē*, or *media contabulatio*), which has caused

Hegetor's ram-tortoise. This illustration, dating to the 11th/12th C., combines several viewpoints, demonstrating a convention which is often found in manuscript diagrams. The artist has attempted to show a perspective view of the turret, superimposed on a plan of the undercarriage, while the ramming-beam is shown in a simple side elevation. (C. Wescher, Poliorcétique des Grecs, Paris 1867)

such confusion amongst those attempting to reconstruct the machines. In the case of Hegetor's tortoise, this second storey had floor space of 16 cubits (24ft or 7.1m) square, and headroom of 8 cubits (12ft or 3.55m) up to the roof ridge. Athenaeus says that it accommodated a 'missile position' (*belostasia*), and Vitruvius explains that scorpions and catapults were located there. Firstly, this contrasts with Diades' version, where the artillery occupied a three-storey turret rising above the middle floor; and secondly, it implies that there were windows through which the catapults could shoot. This seems an altogether more practical arrangement than Diades' rather fragile and cramped turret.

But even though Hegetor deployed the necessary supporting artillery in the middle floor, he did not entirely dispense with a central turret. According to both Athenaeus and Vitruvius, the working of the ram somehow depended upon a frame, which rose through the middle floor to project some 13ft (4m) above the roof ridge and incorporated a crow's nest at the top.

The artillery armament of the tortoise can be estimated by comparing the middle floor area with the space requirements of small- to medium-sized catapults, but both the sloping penthouse construction and the timber uprights of the turret must be taken into account. The first would have limited the usable area to the very middle of the floor, and the second divided this area across the middle. The rear was best reserved for ladders, allowing the crew to move from the undercarriage up into the turret, leaving just enough space in front (around 12ft [3.7m] wide by 9ft [2.7m] deep) for three 3-span arrow-shooters, side by side.

The construction of the turret is not explained and we must resort to conjecture. The sources mention four robust, 24-cubit (35ft or 10.64m) uprights, and another two 30-cubit (44ft or 13.3m) uprights. The latter pair supported a device consisting of two rollers, sitting side by side. In the words of Vitruvius, 'the ropes which held up the ram were fastened around these [rollers]' (*De arch.* 10.15.4). He doesn't name the device, but the parallel text of Athenaeus mentions the ram-holder (*kriodochē*, or *arietaria machina*) (Ath., *Mech.* 23.7–8). But whereas Diades' battering ram seems to have rested upon the ram-holder, Hegetor's ram was suspended in the middle by a thick hank of ropes (Ath., *Mech.* 24.6–8). Lendle's interpretation of this enigmatic structure has the ram-holder, as the suspension point for the ramming-beam, located centrally and, in order to distribute the weight most efficiently, fixed between the four uprights of the turret. At this point, there would have been less than 2m clearance above the roof of the tortoise, so the suspension-tackle must have been relatively short, to prevent the ramming-beam from snagging on the roof ridge.

More recently, it has been suggested that Athenaeus' 'cables which hold the ram in the middle' (Ath., *Mech.* 24.6–8) are simply bindings to reinforce the beam itself. And, instead of suspending the beam in the middle, it has been proposed that it rested upon the ram-holder, as in Diades' version. Furthermore, the ram-holder, it is argued, was actually a wheeled trolley that ran backwards and forwards on rails situated above the tortoise's roof. Unfortunately, there is no sign of this ingenious contraption in the descriptions of Athenaeus and Vitruvius; in fact, the reference to 'the cables running out from the rollers on the ram-holder, and holding up the ram' (Ath., *Mech.* 24.9–10) can only indicate a suspended ramming-beam.

It has been conjectured that these cables running from the rollers were in some way instrumental in altering the height of the ram head, and indeed both Athenaeus and Vitruvius suggest that the enemy wall could be battered up to a height of 70 cubits (104ft or 31m). This is an extraordinary claim, given that the battering ram was suspended only about 26 cubits (38ft or 11.5m) above the ground. In any case, 70 cubits greatly exceeds the usual range of fortification heights; even operating horizontally, the beam would have been higher than most town walls. Sadly, neither author gives any idea of how the battering ram was operated. The necessary pendulum motion would have required some means of pulling the beam backwards, and there were perhaps several ropes attached to its rear end, to be pulled by hauling crews on the ground. Furthermore, the length of the beam's suspension would have restricted it to short blows. It is not clear how successful this method would be if the beam were set at any angle other than the horizontal, and it must be admitted that many aspects of Hegetor's ram-tortoise remain a mystery.

Lendle himself was moved to exclaim, 'What an impressive machine!' But still he wondered whether it had ever been built, far less brought into action. The emphasis on scale and grandeur, particularly during the lifetime of Demetrius Poliorcetes, perhaps encouraged engineers like Hegetor to explore the limits of technology within a theoretical framework. In the end, we must acknowledge that Hegetor's ram-tortoise perhaps only ever existed in its designer's fertile imagination.

The BBC ballista was built in 2002 under the direction of Alan Wilkins, following Vitruvius' specifications. The historian Josephus claims a range of 2 stades (about 400yds or 370m) for this size of ballista, but Philon suggests that its effective range was nearer 540ft (160m). The reconstructed machine achieved only 300ft (90m) before teething troubles forced it into retirement. (© A. Wilkins)

ARTILLERY IN THE 3RD CENTURY

It seems that the first torsion catapults were designed to shoot only arrows. The catapults associated with Philip of Macedon were specifically *katapeltai oxybeleis*, 'catapults for sharp missiles'; in other words, arrow-shooters. It was Alexander who pioneered the use of *katapeltai petroboloi*, 'stone-projecting catapults', in siegecraft. At this early stage of development they were probably fairly lightweight machines. Yet, only 30 years later, Demetrius Poliorcetes was able to deploy monstrous machines designed to throw stones weighing 3 talents (172lb or 78kg).

However, we should beware of interpreting every stone-throwing incident as evidence of these complex and expensive machines. In the ancient world, there was a long tradition of combatants throwing stones by hand, but it is usually clear from the context whether men or machines were intended. For example, the Phocian general Onomarchus is said to have deployed stone-throwing troops on a hilltop to pelt Philip's Macedonians on the plain below with rocks. Our source for this anecdote, the Antonine philosopher Polyaenus, uses the word *petroboloi*, 'stone throwers' (Polyaen., *Strat.* 2.38.2), which has frequently led to misinterpretation.

The rules for constructing a serviceable torsion catapult appear to have been standardized by around 280 BC, if not before; engineers refined the ideal proportions and developed complex formulae to calibrate each machine. Philon of Byzantium indicates a lengthy developmental process, which resulted in the codification of a set of rules: 'others later theorized from earlier mistakes and, from subsequent trials, observed a standard element which would represent the basic principle and the method of setting about construction' (*Bel.* 50.21-23). He placed this major breakthrough at Alexandria. Although the crucial date is not given, his reference to research being sponsored

Herod the Great built a fortified palace at Herodium (near Bethlehem, Israel), crowning a conical hill. The place was equipped to withstand siege. Prominent amongst its defensive arsenal were dozens of large worked boulders. Too large to be thrown by catapults, these were designed to be rolled down the hillside onto any attackers. (© Author)

by 'ambitious kings' suggested to Marsden that the period in question spanned the reigns of Ptolemy I (r. 323–283/2 BC) and Ptolemy II (283/2–246 BC).

During the latter's reign, the mechanical genius Ctesibius rose to prominence. Although he left no writings, he is often mentioned by later engineers. Indeed, it was a summary of his work on artillery that Heron published during the reign of Nero (above, p. 48). Philon even claims to have interviewed men who knew Ctesibius and were familiar with his machines. But it would seem that artillery construction had long since been standardized by his day, as he felt at liberty to explore new developments, such as the compressed-air catapult and the bronze-spring catapult (neither of which seems to have been put to military use).

EARLY ROME

While the new developments in machinery and artillery were being explored in the eastern Mediterranean and on Sicily, quite a different style of siege warfare was being practised in Italy. Our main source for early Roman history is Livy, supplemented to some extent by Dionysius of Halicarnassus; both writers

Roman legionaries assault an enemy wall. The famous testudo shield formation gave protection against missiles and objects thrown from above, represented here by a sword, a wheel and a firebrand. (E. Petersen, A. von Domaszewski & G. Calderini, Die Marcus-Säule, Munich, 1896)

were active in Augustan Rome (c.25 BC), long after many of the events they describe, and scholars generally doubt the accuracy of their narrative prior to around 300 BC. For example, both authors describe the siege of Corioli in 493 BC, renowned as the event from which the young Coriolanus took his name. According to Livy, the besieging army was caught between a Volscian relief column and a sortie from within the town, but Coriolanus led a daring charge through the open gates and set fire to the place (Livy 2.33); this is substantially the story later preserved by Plutarch (*Coriolanus* 8). Dionysius, on the other hand, incorporates battering rams, wicker screens and ladders into his account (6.92.1–6), although it is generally acknowledged that this kind of equipment was unknown in Roman warfare of the 5th (or even 4th) century BC. Consequently, Dionysius has been accused of exaggeration, if not complete fabrication.

The most famous of the early Roman sieges was undoubtedly the reduction of the Etruscan town of Veii in 396 BC; the operations allegedly stretched over ten years, but the parallel with the legendary siege of Troy has raised suspicions. Here again, events are tied up with a celebrated Roman hero: in this case, the upright Marcus Furius Camillus, who famously punished a Falerian schoolmaster for offering to betray his town to the Romans. It is likely that, as with Corioli, a kernel of truth was gradually embellished to glorify the central character. Early in the siege, prior to Camillus' arrival, the Romans are supposed to have tried 'towers, shelters, sheds and the other apparatus for besieging a city' (Livy 5.5), to no avail; but these elements were probably a later addition, designed to make Camillus' subsequent success seem all the more impressive. Equally unlikely is the tale that Camillus sent picked troops to tunnel up into the rocky citadel and open the gates from within. Interestingly, the locality is known for its honeycomb of drainage tunnels, which perhaps gave rise to this popular story.

It must be remembered that Rome in the late 4th century was a city-state struggling to dominate its neighbours in the Italian peninsula. It was entirely oblivious to events on nearby Sicily, where Syracuse was again locked in combat with Carthage, and the tyrant Agathocles was employing the full range of besieging tactics, from encirclement and undermining at Croton (295 BC) to the use of machinery at Utica (307 BC); the siege tower at the latter even had enemy prisoners nailed to the sides in a gruesome attempt at psychological warfare (Diod. Sic. 20.54.2–7). By contrast, Roman sieges of the period were relatively unsophisticated affairs. Livy records the storming of Murgantia, Ferentinum and Romulea in 296 BC, the latter at least by escalade (Livy 10.17), and in 293 BC the gates of Aquilonia were broken open by troops who were formed up into the *testudo* formation with shields locked over their heads (Livy 10.41).

FORTIFICATIONS

Unsettled conditions in the Greek world of the later 4th and 3rd centuries BC prompted a renewed interest in town fortifications. The precise dating of these is notoriously difficult. For example, it has been said that the recessed gateway, standing inside an open courtyard flanked by towers, was a response to the development of mechanized siegecraft. This layout is certainly found in the late 3rd-century circuits of Perge and Side, but it was already used at Messene, where it ought to date from the foundation of the town in 369 BC (Diod. Sic. 15.66.1). It is often suggested that the plentiful provision of minor, so-called postern gates indicates a dating in the later 4th century. This was a time, it is argued, when infantry adopted a vigorous strategy of 'aggressive defence', counter-attacking siege machinery outside the walls; however, the gates could equally be intended to cater for the peacetime activities of the local population.

Another diagnostic feature favoured by scholars is the tower. Larger, taller varieties are often taken to imply the presence of defensive artillery, particularly where windows (rather than archers' loop-holes) are evident. However, the study of towers is a complex one, and the existence of a large floor area does not automatically imply that a large catapult was to be accommodated. In general, towers fulfilled a range of functions, which included sheltering sentries and enabling archers to enfilade adjacent stretches of curtain wall, not forgetting the equally important role of surveillance.

When catapults became available for town defence in the later 4th century BC, they were surely stationed under cover, for protection from sun, rain and enemy action; furthermore, the need for a clear operating space, to allow the machine and its crew to work quickly and effectively, would most easily have been met in a tower chamber. However, the Carthaginian defence of Lilybaeum against Pyrrhus in 274 BC demonstrates that, in time of need, catapults could easily be deployed along the walls (Diod. Sic. 22.10.7). Marsden believed that it was crucial to gain an advantage in range by placing catapults as high as possible, but no ancient writer ever expresses this opinion. In fact, the behaviour of torsion artillery rather encourages the opposite belief, that the accuracy of short-range targeting and the direct impact of a low trajectory were preferred.

Siege Warfare During the Roman Republic

The Greek writer Polybius compiled a history of the Roman world from 264 to 146 BC; as a military man, he gives a fairly reliable picture of siege warfare during these years. The First Punic War (264–241 BC), which took Roman troops overseas for the first time, involved a handful of sieges on Sicily, where many of the towns were still held by Carthaginian garrisons. But the Romans lacked the equipment and expertise to besiege effectively, and the war was decided in naval encounters.

The siege of Agrigentum (the Greek Akragas) in 262 BC provides a case in point. The Romans surrounded the town with double ditches, the inner guarding against sorties from the town, the outer against a relieving force, in an effort to starve the garrison into submission (Polyb. 1.18.2–3). But after five months of static blockade, the besiegers themselves were running short of provisions and suffering from dysentery, and although they easily defeated a Carthaginian relief column their negligence permitted the garrison to escape from the town by night. In the following year, a seven-month blockade of Mytistratum failed (Diod. Sic. 23.9.3), and the town was only taken three years later, when the townsfolk willingly opened their gates to the Romans (Zonaras 8.11). Most tellingly, at Lilybaeum, down the coast from the old Carthaginian base at Motya, the Roman siege dragged on for ten years without resolution. Initially adopting an assaulting strategy, the Romans managed to demolish a length of fortifications using machinery perhaps supplied by their ally Hiero, the tyrant of Syracuse; but they were repulsed by vigorous Carthaginian counter-attacks (Polyb. 1.42.8–13; 45.1–14). A storm further thwarted the Romans' efforts, wrecking their machinery:

At Lilybaeum, Polybius records that the Romans built two camps and linked them with a ditch, a palisade, and a wall. De Folard's imaginative reconstruction shows the town surrounded by double earthworks, as at Agrigentum, while Carthaginian ships continue to ply in and out of the harbour unmolested. (Author's collection)

the young townsmen mustered at three points and threw fire onto the siege-works. Since the apparatus had been made easily combustible by its age, and since the wind blew strongly upon the towers and machinery, it so happened that the spreading of the fire was most effective, whereas the salvaging efforts of the Romans, in the long run, were difficult and futile (Polyb. 1.48.5).

The siege soon degenerated into stalemate, largely because the Romans failed to seal the town's harbour, which left the blockade incomplete. When the war ended in 241 BC, the town still had not fallen.

PHILON OF BYZANTIUM

Siege warfare of the period is illuminated by Philon's *Mechanical Encyclopedia*. Besides a section on constructing artillery (*Belopoiika*), the encyclopedia included instructions for both the besieged and the besieger; modern editors usually run these together to form a single book on siegecraft (*Poliorkētika*).

In general, it is clear that Philon expected the attacker to use wheeled machinery. For example, he suggests the use of tunnels to draw away any material with which the attacker has filled the town's defensive ditch (*Pol.* 1.36); the filling of ditches always preceded the advance of machinery (see above, p. 74). In addition, he suggests burying large storage jars outside the defences, upright and with their mouths loosely stopped up with seaweed and concealed by a layer of soil, to trap the wheels of enemy sheds and machinery (*Pol.* 1.76).

He is especially concerned about stone-projecting catapults. It is unlikely that these were ever powerful enough to demolish a wall, but they could wreak havoc along the battlements. Philon says that the merlons ('the topmost blocks of stone', in his words) should be fastened down so that the stone-projector's missiles would glance off and not demolish them (*Pol.* 1.8). He also recommends that the battlements should be padded with palm-wood boards and nets filled with seaweed (*Pol.* 3.3–5), and that window shutters should be iron-plated inside and outside, so that stone-projectors could not shatter them (*Pol.* 1.23).

When he turns to besieging, Philon mentions encirclement almost as an afterthought, and only in connection with a blockade: '[a town can be taken] by starvation, surrounding it with a palisade and fortifying a strong position against the town, and garrisoning it with steadfast guards to prevent anyone bringing in [supplies] by land or by sea' (*Pol.* 4.84). By contrast, almost his first recommendation for capturing a town is to 'secretly approach the wall by night with ladders, in wintry weather or when the townsfolk are drunk at some public festival, and capture some of the towers' (*Pol.* 4.4). The Achaean capture of the Acrocorinth in 243 BC, for example, was achieved by scaling an unusually low section of the defences (Plut., *Aratus* 18.4; 21.2–3). To counter just such an eventuality, Philon recommends building walls at least 20 cubits (9m) high 'so that ladders brought up against them will not reach' (*Pol.* 1.12). And in a frequently misunderstood passage, he reiterates that 'it is necessary, regarding those towers which will face attack by machinery, to build them high and strong, but the others [i.e., where machinery cannot approach] only so that ladders will not reach' (*Pol.* 1.26). Later, he lists various countermeasures for hindering and dislodging ladders, by using beams 'bent like an anchor', forked poles, and caltrops (*Pol.* 1.79), and by throwing fire from above (*Pol.* 3.39).

THE 'SEESAW'

The siege tower was an expensive alternative to the perils of the assault ladder. Engineers attempted to strike a happy medium, by devising a machine that incorporated the simplicity of the ladder, with the superior protection of the siege tower, and the ease of use of the flying drawbridge. The siegecraft writer Athenaeus found one solution in the *Commentaries* written by Ctesibius of Alexandria in the mid-3rd century BC.

The contraption (*mēchanēma*), Athenaeus notes somewhat unflatteringly, has no practical value, but the engineer deserves our admiration for his ingenuity. In essence, a four-wheeled wagon (a *tetrakuklon*) provided the base for an upright frame with a tilting mechanism at the top. Attached to this mechanism at its mid-point was a component that Athenaeus calls the 'pipe' (*syrinx*); the presence of a door at its far end suggests a kind of covered gangway. Athenaeus explains that, when soldiers walked along this gangway they upset its balance, like a seesaw. Clearly, once the machine was wheeled into position, those inside (for it would take more than one man to finely alter the balance) would lower the end onto the enemy wall, throw open the door, and emerge fighting.

It is revealing that Vitruvius does not include this device in his section on siege machines. He simply writes that 'those who are attracted by Ctesibius' cleverness' should consult his *Commentaries* for other devices (Vitr., *De arch.* 10.7.5).

These are much the same methods recommended by Aeneas Tacticus over a century earlier (above, pp. 55–58), and they remained common throughout the period.

HANNIBAL AND CARTHAGINIAN SIEGECRAFT

Hannibal sparked off a new war with Rome in 219 BC when he attacked Saguntum in Spain. The methods he employed hark back to the Carthaginian sieges on Sicily in the 400s BC. First, battering rams were brought forward under the protection of shelters, and the wall was breached. Then, when the townsfolk repulsed the Carthaginian assault and hastily repaired the damaged wall, Hannibal resorted to undermining, with covering fire from artillery in a siege tower. Battering rams were simultaneously reapplied elsewhere around

Siege of Saguntum, 219 BC. (Prisma / Ancient Art & Architecture Collection Ltd)

the town perimeter, but the town's strong fortifications and hilltop location enabled it to hold out for eight months (Livy 21.15.3). Appian, a writer who flourished in the AD 140s but who clearly used earlier sources of information, says that Hannibal had the place surrounded by a closely guarded ditch (App., *Hisp.* 10); although this sounds like a *periteichismos*, it is clear that Hannibal intended no passive blockade. In fact, combining the old technique of encirclement with an active assaulting strategy was not entirely novel, as Antigonus had done something similar at Caunus in 313 BC (Diod. Sic. 19.75.5).

But it was in the use of machinery that Hannibal's siegecraft differed from contemporary Roman efforts. Livy records how, at Nola in 216 BC, the Carthaginians had 'all the equipment for besieging a town' (Livy 23.16.11), and they only resorted to blockading Petelia because the townsfolk persisted in burning their machines. Among the equipment that Hannibal brought up to the walls of Cumae, pride of place went to an immense wheeled tower, but it too was destroyed by fire (Livy 23.37.2–4). Finally, Appian lists Hannibal's equipment at Tarentum as 'towers and catapults and sheds and hooks' (App., *Hann.* 33).

The operations at Tarentum spanned 213–209 BC. Its initial betrayal to Hannibal by disaffected townsfolk forced the Roman garrison to take refuge in the citadel, which lay on a promontory between the sea and the harbour. The garrison were in no danger of starvation, as they were easily supplied (and even reinforced) by sea, but the Carthaginians hemmed them in with a palisade, a ditch and rampart, and a wall (Livy 25.11.7). As at Saguntum, Hannibal clearly intended to assault the position with various kinds of siege equipment; but, when the Romans sallied out and burned it, a stalemate ensued (Polyb. 8.32.3–34.2). In 209 BC, betrayal again delivered the town, this time to the Romans. The Roman consul Fabius Maximus arrived by sea and feigned an assault on the citadel; his fleet was equipped with 'machines and apparatus for attacking walls' and 'artillery, stones, and every sort of missile weapon' (Livy 27.15.4). Meanwhile, Hannibal's Italian mercenaries guarding a particular sector of wall were persuaded to turn a blind eye to a nocturnal escalade, and the Roman assault was coordinated with a break-out from the besieged citadel. Caught in between, the Tarentines were subjected to looting and indiscriminate slaughter.

ROMAN SIEGECRAFT IN THE SECOND PUNIC WAR

In 218 BC, Cnaeus Scipio, uncle of the famous Scipio Africanus, employed blockades against the Carthaginians' allies in Spain: at Atanagrum, his army 'sat down around the town' (Livy 21.61.6), forcing surrender within days, and the same treatment brought the Ausetani to heel after only 30 days. There is no mention of siege-works on those occasions, and Roman armies operating in Greece in the 190s BC sometimes used cordons of troops to cut off and intimidate enemy towns. However, when three Roman armies converged on pro-Carthaginian Capua in 212 BC, they elected to blockade the town with an encirclement of earthworks. Nothing similar had been attempted by a Roman army since Agrigentum, 50 years earlier. There, the town had been encircled by two lines of ditches. This time, according to Appian, they built walls as well:

they dug a ditch around Capua and in addition to the ditch they built a wall in a circle round the whole place. Then the generals built another one outside the encircling wall, using the middle as a camp. There were battlements turned towards the besieged Capuans, and others towards those outside, and the appearance was of a great city with a smaller one in the middle (App., *Hann.* 37).

The choice of strategy perhaps depended as much upon the commanding officer's temperament as upon the available resources and the lie of the land. In 214 BC, Claudius Marcellus and Fabius Maximus, nicknamed Cunctator ('the delayer'), met stiff resistance at Carthaginian-occupied Casilinum. Fabius' instincts were to withdraw, but Marcellus brought up 'shelters and all the other sorts of works and machinery' (Livy 24.19.8); at the sight of this, the townsfolk panicked and fled, and the garrison was captured. However, Roman armies of the day were generally ill-equipped for full-blown mechanized operations. Only during the siege of Utica, up the coast from Carthage, do we hear of machinery on any significant scale. Here, in 204 BC, Scipio requisitioned artillery and machines from Sicily, where it is likely to have been captured from the Carthaginians, and set up field workshops to manufacture more. Although the siege ultimately failed, Appian claims that Scipio raised siege embankments in order to bring his battering rams into play (App., *Pun.* 16).

If this is true, it represents a breakthrough in Roman siegecraft. Until then, most sieges were conducted as straightforward storming operations, for example at the Italian town of Arpi, where a heavy downpour drowned the noise of the assault and kept the guards under cover, where they could not interfere (Front., *Strat.* 3.9.2). In 209 BC, Scipio Africanus' capture of heavily fortified Carthago Nova was achieved by an audacious assault (see illustration overleaf), and three years later, at Ilourgia, he threatened to scale the wall himself, in order to embolden his troops, who were despondent after their initial failure. Ladder length was always critical to the success of an escalade. Plutarch claims that Marcellus himself studied the Epipolae wall at Syracuse to ensure that his ladders would reach (Plut., *Marc.* 18.3), a precaution that Scipio perhaps omitted at Carthago Nova, where many of the ladders were too short (Livy 26.45.2). For the siege of Locri in 205 BC, the Romans persuaded some craftsmen to assist them by letting down ladders over the wall (Livy 29.6–8); local knowledge presumably ensured that they were long enough.

The state of Roman siegecraft in the late 3rd century is encapsulated by the events at Syracuse, which was targeted by Marcellus in 213 BC after it switched allegiance to Carthage. He advocated a two-pronged assault, coordinating his naval attack on the Achradina sea wall with his colleague Claudius Pulcher's land attack on the Epipolae plateau from the north. However, he had reckoned

Scipio's siege of Carthago Nova, 209 BC. When the Romans arrived outside the town, the garrison, bolstered by the townsfolk, rushed out to join battle, but were driven back within their walls. Scipio immediately launched an escalade, but many of the ladders were too short to be useful. Simultaneously, a body of troops, drawn up in a testudo shield formation, attacked the gates. (See map on p. 108.) (Adam Hook © Osprey Publishing Ltd)

without the genius of Archimedes, the renowned Syracusan mathematician. Plutarch claims that Archimedes was disdainful of practical mechanics (Plut., *Marc.* 17.3–4); but he rose to the challenge of defending his native town, chiefly with catapults of various sizes to ensure complete coverage of all the approaches, but also with machines that capsized the Roman ships. The Romans soon resorted to blockading the town, but early in 212 BC, in the midst of celebrations in the town, Marcellus managed to seize the Epipolae plateau in a nocturnal escalade (Front., *Strat.* 3.3.2) which followed the precepts of Philon to the letter (above, p. 99). Although the garrison of the formidable Euryalus fortress soon surrendered, the Achradina fell only after another lengthy blockade. It is said that one of the victims of the final looting, late in 212 BC, was Archimedes; unwilling to leave his current mathematical calculation incomplete, he was killed resisting his Roman captors (Livy 25.31.9).

THE TOLLENO

A simple device, employed by besiegers and besieged alike, consisted of a long, horizontal lever with a hinge in the middle, by which it was fastened to the top of an upright timber; when one end was pulled down, the other end swung up. The besieged had ample scope to adapt such a device for disrupting the activities of the besiegers, either by catching equipment with a hook or grab, or by dropping heavy weights onto machinery. At Syracuse in 213 BC, Archimedes used the device to jerk the Roman besiegers' ships out of the water, and at Cremona in AD 69 the defenders snatched individual combatants and swung them over the town wall to be dealt with inside. In 429 BC, the besieged Plataeans used a similar machine (the historian Thucydides calls it a *keraia*, 'yard-arm') to drop heavy beams onto the Spartan battering rams in an attempt to

De Folard's reconstruction of the defence of Syracuse against the Romans in 214 BC, showing the tolleno devised by Archimedes, the mathematician and engineer. (Author's collection)

snap off the ram heads (above, p. 40); the Ambracians employed the same tactic in 189 BC (below, p. 110).

An interesting variant for use by besiegers is described by Vegetius in his *Summary of military topics* (*Epitoma rei militaris*); although written in the later 4th or early 5th century AD, the information on siegecraft is thought to have been lifted from a lost tactical manual (*Tactica*) by the 1st-century writer Frontinus. In Vegetius' *tolleno*, one end of the crossbeam is equipped with a wickerwork basket, large enough to accommodate a few soldiers. With the upright planted near the enemy wall, the basket of soldiers could be swung up onto the battlements in a workable, if rather perilous, manoeuvre.

105

ROME AND MACEDON

In the late 3rd and early 2nd centuries BC, Roman armies campaigned in Greece, against Macedon, Sparta and the Aetolian League. Artillery was often present, courtesy of Rome's alliance with Pergamon and Rhodes, and machinery became more frequently employed, but sieges remained firmly based on the storming assault. At the same time, there was something of a revival in Macedonian siegecraft under Philip V (r. 221–179 BC) and his son Perseus (r. 179–168 BC), and Macedon's brief alliance with Rome (192–189 BC) perhaps led to some cross-fertilization of ideas.

The Macedonians were always ready to employ undermining tactics, despite the inherent dangers. In 217 BC, the army of Philip V spent nine days tunnelling towards the town of Phthiotic Thebes, and another three days undermining its walls for a distance of 200ft (60m), but the mine collapsed prematurely, and perhaps buried the sappers beneath the ruined wall (Polyb. 5.100.2–5). Similar operations at Palus in the previous year had gone without a hitch: the wall was undermined and propped with wood, the town was invited to surrender, and when it refused the props were fired and the wall collapsed; but Philip's treacherous

The fortifications at Cnidus (Turkey) defend a large area surrounding two harbours, and climb the hills to the acropolis (top right). Philip V attacked the town unsuccessfully in 201 BC. (A. W. McNicoll, Hellenistic Fortifications from the Aegean to the Euphrates, Oxford, 1997. Plate 25. Reprinted by permission of Oxford University Press and Ms T. Winikoff)

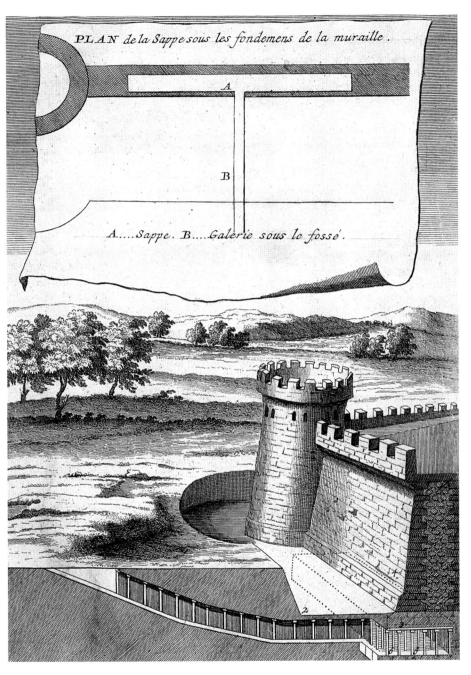

PLAN de la Sappe sous les fondemens de la muraille.

A

B

A....Sappe. B....Galerie sous le fossé.

The 18th-century Chevalier de Folard made a study of ancient military science, accompanied by detailed engravings. This one shows how the fire chamber at the end of a siege mine was intended to work. (Author's collection)

lieutenant Leontius deliberately botched the final assault (Polyb. 5.4.6–13). At Prinassus in 201 BC, and at Lamia ten years later, the bedrock proved too hard for tunnelling. At the latter, Philip's opportunistic cooperation with Rome backfired when his allies ordered him to desist, and he was forced to leave empty-handed

107

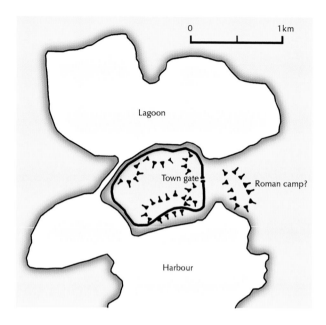

The ancient town of Carthago Nova (modern Cartagena, Spain) was situated on a peninsula; the narrow neck of land to the east provided the only access. The Roman general Scipio launched his main assault from this direction (see illustration p. 104). However, while the defenders were distracted by an all-out assault on the town gate, they failed to notice a Roman escalading party wading across the unexpectedly shallow lagoon to the north of the town. Crossing over the undefended wall, they were able to open the gates from within, and the town was captured. (© Author)

(Livy 36.25.1–2). But at the former, he deceived the townsfolk by a cunning ruse: the Macedonians made the noise of mining by day and heaped up soil brought from elsewhere by night, so that, when Philip claimed to have underpinned nearly 200 feet (60m) of wall, the Prinassians were convinced and surrendered their town (Polyb. 16.11.2–6). The stratagem was so ingenious that it later featured in the works of both Frontinus (*Strat.* 3.8.1) and Polyaenus (*Strat.* 4.18.1).

Philip rarely built his strategy around machinery, perhaps owing to the difficulty of transporting such cumbersome devices around the Greek landscape. A full siege train can be glimpsed only once, at Echinus (see illustration opposite), a town easily approached by sea. Similarly, although Philip clearly had access to artillery, it was used sparingly. More often, he relied on the storming assault, for example at Psophis (219 BC), where three divisions of ladder-carrying troops made simultaneous assaults on the walls; the town was captured when the garrison, charging out through a postern, was repulsed and chased back through the open gate (Polyb. 4.70–72).

Contemporary Roman armies continued to use similar methods. In the decades following the defeat of Hannibal in 202 BC, various conflicts took Roman armies far and wide around the Mediterranean, but the siege warfare that they practised largely took the form of the storming assault. In 200 BC, Claudius Cento mounted a dawn raid on the major Macedonian base at Chalcis. Some troops with ladders seized a tower and the adjacent sector of wall, before quietly making their way to the gates and breaking them open to admit the entire army; in the ensuing chaos, a fire broke out, destroying an arsenal full of artillery (Livy 31.23.1–24.3). But ladders were not the only means to scale a wall. Heracleum was captured in 169 BC by troops who clambered up the walls by standing on top of a *testudo* shield formation (Livy 44.9.1–10).

Rome's acquaintance with Macedon, as both adversary and ally, perhaps opened the eyes of her generals to the possibilities of more sophisticated tactics. P. Sulpicius Galba, attempting to raise Philip V's siege of Echinus in 210 BC, cannot fail to have been impressed by the Macedonian siege train. Machinery was gradually introduced wherever necessary. At Atrax in 198 BC, Quinctius Flamininus threw up a siege embankment to carry rams up to the wall, and although his troops entered the town through the resulting breach they were

repulsed by the Macedonian garrison. The siege tower that Flamininus then deployed almost fell over when one of its wheels sank in the rutted embankment, and the Romans finally gave up (Livy 32.18.3). Their failure can probably be attributed to inexperience in mechanized siege warfare: first, their siege embankment was obviously insufficiently compacted to bear the weight of heavy machinery; and second, they seem rarely to have used a siege tower before. Polybius mentions towers among the equipment destroyed at Lilybaeum 50 years earlier (Polyb. 1.48.2), but these may well have been supplied by Hiero and were hardly a resounding success in any case (above, pp. 97–98).

At Heraclea in 191 BC, M'. Acilius Glabrio divided his forces into four squads and set them a competition to build siege equipment; having erected embankments, for 24 days they persevered with 'siege towers, battering rams, and all the other equipment for besieging a town' (Livy 36.22.9), before they were finally unleashed in a terrifying dawn escalade. Even at Ambracia, which Fulvius Nobilior invested in 189 BC, the Romans pressed the siege actively 'with iron and fire' (Livy 38.6.2), although they had hemmed the town in with a siege

Philip V's siege of Echinus, 210 BC. According to Polybius, Philip's siege-works comprised a battlemented gallery running parallel to the town defences, with a great wheeled ram shed positioned at either end; rearward communications were secured by the provision of covered passages. Three heavy catapults were deployed. In addition, Philip began driving two tunnels towards the town, with the intention of undermining the walls. Philip's assault was never carried through because the town surrendered. (Adam Hook © Osprey Publishing Ltd)

109

For an assault on a town gateway, Roman soldiers were frequently drawn up in the testudo *shield formation, depicted here on Trajan's Column in Rome. (C. M. Dixon / Ancient Art & Architecture Collection Ltd)*

wall. The defenders employed a full range of countermeasures, including dropping heavy weights from the *tolleno* onto the Roman battering rams and using grappling irons to seize Roman siege weapons; wall breaches were quickly repaired, and raids were mounted by day and night to burn Nobilior's machinery. The Romans finally resorted to tunnelling:

> Then a gradually rising pile of earth betrayed the operation to the townsfolk and, fearful lest undermined walls had already opened a route into the city, they began to dig a trench inside the wall, in the region of the siegework covered by shelters … They opened a direct route into the [Roman] tunnel … At first, with the very tools that they were using in their work, then as armed men rapidly approached, they began a hidden battle under the ground. Eventually, it finished with the blocking of the tunnel where they wished, sometimes with stretched out cloaks, sometimes with doors hastily thrown in the way (Livy 38.7.4–13).

THE DIGGING TORTOISE

Both Athenaeus and Vitruvius record a variation of the tortoise (*testudo*, or *chelōnē*), adapted for use in close proximity to the enemy wall. It has recently been suggested that this 'digging tortoise' was simply the ditch-filling tortoise (above, p. 74) turned through 90°, so that it approached the wall side-on. However, it differed from the ditch-filling tortoise in one major respect. Rather than the gently sloping front, designed to deflect missiles, it had a vertical front face, to enable it to abut the enemy wall.

Both authors concur that this front face was triangular, implying a longitudinal roof ridge and giving the machine the form of a simple penthouse. Any missiles dropped from the battlements would have rolled off the broad, sloping sides without causing damage. The roof would have been boarded and covered, either with fresh wickerwork and padded hides, or with clay mixed with hair. Either

De Folard's reconstruction of the 'ditch-filling tortoise' was accepted by generations of scholars. However, several elements of his machine are vulnerable to counter-attack, particularly the exposed wheels. (Author's collection)

method would have provided some degree of fireproofing, and the sloping sides avoided the necessity of cushioning the structure against heavy weights dropped from above.

The machine was specifically designed to enable men to work in safety at the foot of the enemy wall. Of course, the front face of the machine prevented its occupants from attacking the wall directly, as some modern writers have assumed, with pickaxes and crowbars. Rather, its structure was designed to permit the men to dig at the foot of the wall, undermining the foundations and destabilizing the fortification. Unfortunately, the ancient sources preserve no clear description of the machine in action, in marked contrast to its ditch-filling cousin.

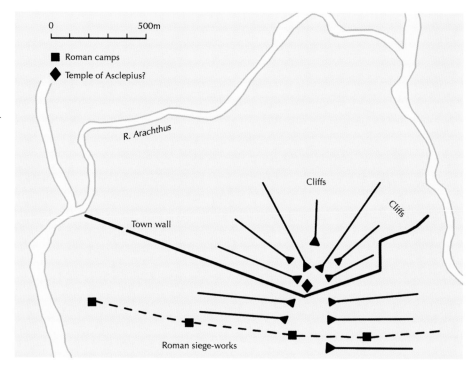

The townsfolk foiled the Roman plan by filling the tunnel with noxious smoke, and Ambracia only surrendered when the siege reached deadlock. However, smaller towns frequently surrendered, not as a last resort, but immediately, from fear of a Roman storming attack. They wished to avoid the fate of towns like Antipatrea: in 200 BC, the Roman general Lucius Apustius 'attacked and took the place by storm, killed all the men of military age, gave all the booty to his troops, demolished the walls, and burned down the town' (Livy 31.27.4). In 199 BC, Celetrum initially refused a Roman request to capitulate, but promptly surrendered at the sight of a *testudo* formation of troops approaching its gates (Livy 31.40.1–3). Similarly, the Roman fleet had scarcely disembarked its siege equipment on the island of Andros, when the islanders abandoned their defences and fled (Livy 31.45.3–8). Gytheum held out a little longer, when under attack in 195 BC, but having seen their walls collapse to a combination of undermining and battering, the townsfolk rapidly surrendered (Livy 34.29.5–13). And in 190 BC, although the Phocaeans put up a spirited defence, they realized they were doomed without the assistance of their Syrian allies, so they surrendered.

Siege Warfare in the Late 2nd Century BC

Carthage herself finally came under siege in 149 BC in the so-called Third Punic War, when she refused to comply with Rome's ruthless demands for the city to be destroyed. Having already surrendered and dutifully disarmed, handing over 2,000 catapults in the process, she began desperately re-arming; hundreds of weapons were manufactured each day and, as an emergency measure, newly built catapults were allegedly sprung with women's hair (App., *Pun.* 93).

Rome's favoured tactic for capturing fortified positions remained the storming assault, which her armies appear to have conducted with particular ferocity. Nevertheless, initial Roman attempts on Carthage and her allies proved incompetent. Nor did the increasingly common employment of machinery guarantee success, a fact that perhaps indicates a general absence of artillery in a suppressing role. In 148 BC, for example, at Hippagreta near Carthage, L. Calpurnius Piso is said to have spent all summer attempting to break into the town, but the defenders persisted in burning his siege machines (App., *Pun.* 110). Wooden machinery was always susceptible to burning; this is a theme that all siegecraft writers return to, again and again. However, in later ages, artillery and missile troops were deployed to provide the continuous bombardment which discouraged such incendiary attacks. At Hippagreta, Piso gave up, where a better general would perhaps have persevered.

In fact, events at Carthage neatly encapsulate Roman siegecraft of the period. The consuls of 149 BC, ignorant of the fact that the demilitarized city was actively re-arming, rashly assumed that she would easily fall to escalade. When

In 146 BC, the Romans captured the harbour area of Carthage, before heading toward the Byrsa citadel, which can be seen in the foreground. (G. Tortoli / Ancient Art & Architecture Collection Ltd)

several attempts failed, they settled down to construct siege machinery. Appian records the construction of 'two enormous ram-carrying machines' (App., *Pun.* 98), allegedly crewed by 6,000 men; their deployment required the consolidation of a pathway along the edge of the stagnant Lake of Tunis, which implies that they were targeted at the city's south wall (see map p.116). The attempt was frustrated, however, when the defenders not only repaired any wall breaches that the Romans managed to make, but also crept out by night and set the machines ablaze. Nothing was achieved in this first year of the siege, and in the second the Romans concentrated on Carthage's allies in the north African hinterland. In the third year, 147 BC, a mishandled escalade resulted in several thousand Romans being pinned down in an area just inside the city; they were extricated only by the timely arrival of P. Cornelius Scipio Aemilianus, who was due to take up the command in 146.

Scipio restored the men's flagging morale by mounting a raid on the leafy Megara district of Carthage. Then, reviving a strategy from past generations, he proceeded to isolate the city by imposing a blockade. None of the great sieges within recent memory had utilized such a strategy. But as the adopted grandson of the great Scipio Africanus, he must have heard the story of Orongis, besieged by Africanus' brother in 207 BC; here, the town had been ringed with a double ditch and rampart, before being subjected to full-scale assault (Livy 28.3.2–16). Scipio had something similar in mind for Carthage.

First, he cut the city's land communications with a huge earthwork that simultaneously sealed the 2¾ mile-wide (4.5km) isthmus and provided shelter for the Roman siege troops; in concept, this was a linear version of the Capuan

View over the harbour area of Carthage. (G. Garvey / Ancient Art & Architecture Collection Ltd)

circumvallation (above, pp. 102–103). Then, he blocked the great harbour, Carthage's lifeline to the Mediterranean, by constructing a mole across the entrance. With the city isolated, the assault could commence, and Scipio brought up battering rams to break down the quay wall. In desperation, some of the Carthaginians swam across the harbour to set fire to the Roman machinery, while others attempted to fortify the quay but were repulsed with horrendous loss of life. Appian (perhaps quoting the eyewitness report of Polybius) claims that 'the walkway was so slippery with blood, freshly and copiously spilled, that [the Romans] reluctantly abandoned the pursuit of those who were fleeing' (App., *Pun.* 125). It only remained to launch the storming assault, which had sealed the fate of so many of Rome's adversaries, and after six days of destruction the city lay in ruins.

THE TREATMENT OF TOWNS

If the Persians and Carthaginians were notorious for their merciless treatment of captured towns, the Romans often matched their excesses. In the final destruction of Carthage, as the Romans entered the city, they became embroiled in street fighting; whole areas of multi-storey housing were set ablaze, with their inhabitants still in residence, and any who survived were unceremoniously despatched by the troops clearing the streets. Appian says that, for six days and nights, the soldiers were rotated, 'so as not to be distressed from want of sleep,

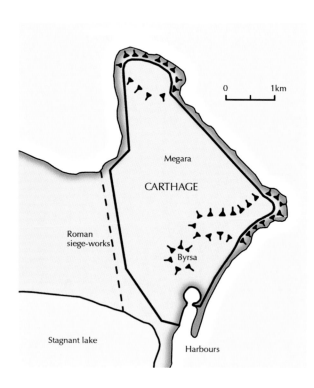

Having cut Carthage off from its hinterland with siege-works, Scipio Aemilianus proceeded to seal the harbour entrance, completing his blockade. His troops then broke into the city from the captured quayside. (© Author)

hard labour, slaughter, and unpleasant sights' (App., *Pun.* 129–130). By extraordinary coincidence, the same year saw the crushing of the Achaean League by the Romans. The wealthy city of Corinth was laid waste by the Roman general Lucius Mummius (Paus. 2.1.2). The Greeks, already defeated in battle, did not attempt to hold the city, and the Romans entered through the open gates; they slaughtered any men who remained, auctioned off the women, children and slaves, and carried off everything of value (Paus. 7.16.5).

The brutal treatment of Carthago Nova in 209 BC was allegedly typical of Roman armies, with the slaughter of all the inhabitants, even including dogs and other animals, and the looting of the town by designated troops, while others stood guard (Polyb. 10.15.4–9). But different generals clearly managed their siege operations in different ways. At the surrender of Gytheum, the undisciplined Roman troops commenced wholesale looting, despite the orders of their general Aemilius Regillus, who asserted that towns that surrendered ought not to be plundered; although he failed to exert his authority, he managed to protect any townsfolk who gathered in the forum (Livy 37.32.1–14). It was presumably to retain some measure of control that Marcellus, during the penultimate phase of the siege of Syracuse, decreed that there should be no bloodshed, only looting (Livy 25.25.5), but in the final sack he was obliged to set guards at any locations he did not want despoiled, such as the royal treasury.

After Cyrus' looting of Babylon in 539 BC, he is portrayed assuring his troops that 'it is a custom amongst all peoples at all times that, whenever a town is conquered in war, the people in the town and their goods belong to the captors' (Xen., *Cyr.* 7.5.73). This was as much the philosophy of Scipio as of Cyrus. And in Classical Greece, plunder belonged, first and foremost, to the general. He seems usually to have reserved the lion's share for the state treasury, after subtracting expenses and awarding prizes to deserving combatants; as a contribution towards defraying the costs of war, the proceeds might be used to provide soldiers' pay. A well-known pronouncement by Philip V shows him closely controlling the goods plundered by his army, in much the same way that contemporary Roman generals did: officers were entrusted with receiving the plunder for equitable division, at the general's discretion (Polyb. 10.16.2–9).

Thus, at Carthage, Scipio Aemilianus rewarded the troops, while reserving the bullion and the contents of the temples. The general could even forgo his own entitlement, as Mummius is said to have done, when he distributed the spoils of Corinth throughout Italy (Front., *Strat.* 4.3.15). But the principle was clear: the decision rested with the conquering general, following a precedent set 400 years earlier by Cyrus at Sardis (Hdt. 1.89).

THE EASTERN MEDITERRANEAN, 163–133 BC

From Rome's involvement in the affairs of Macedon and Greece, it was a short step to Asia Minor; but, for the time being, the Romans studiously avoided military involvement farther east. However, warfare continued in her absence, notably in Judaea, where Judas Maccabaeus led the Hasmonean revolt against

The Mediterranean world, showing some sites besieged during the period 146–31 BC. (© Author)

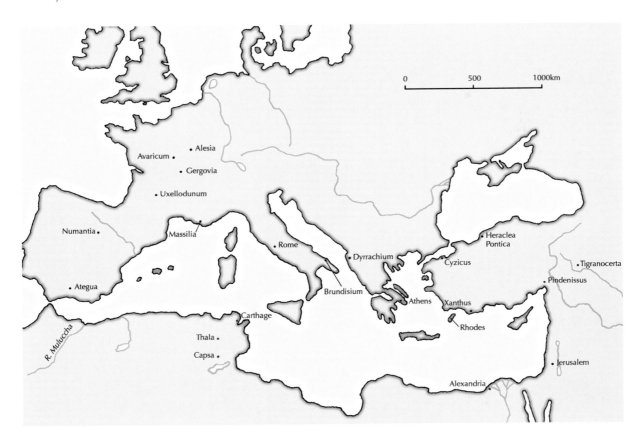

ARTILLERY STONES

Over 200 stone balls came to light at the Hellenistic town of Dora (Tel Dor in Israel), and perhaps belonged to the new fortifications constructed there in the 3rd century. Some of the balls were inscribed with weight markings, following an alphabetic system where E (*epsilon*, the fifth Greek letter) stands for 5 minas, I (*iota*, the tenth Greek letter) stands for 10 minas, and so on. (The mina was a Greek unit of measurement which, at Athens, weighed almost a pound or roughly 436g.) One ball marked IH (*iota ēta* = 10 + 8 minas) weighed 17lb (7.7kg), very nearly its marked weight; another, marked KB (*kappa bēta* = 20 + 2 minas) weighed 21lb (9.5kg). The Dora stones have been convincingly divided into 14 groups, ranging from a tiny 3 minas up to 1 talent (57lb or 26kg).

(Right) The largest of the stone missiles discovered during Schulten's excavations at Numantia (here labelled 1 and 3) have a diameter of 16cm, and weigh around 4kg (approx. 12 Roman lbs). Number 6, found in the town of Numantia, weighs 1.3kg; Schulten suggested that it had been shot from a 4-pound ballista. Numbers 10 and 11, weighing 370g and 225g, were probably intended for throwing by hand. (A. Schulten, Numantia: Die Ergebnisse der Ausgrabungen 1905–1912, vol. III: Die Lager des Scipio, *Munich 1927)*

(Left) Stone balls discovered near the eastern (landward) gate of Tel Dor (Israel). The smooth, carefully dressed stones, ranging from 2lb to 57lb (1kg to 26kg), were clearly designed for use by stone-projecting catapults. Some are inscribed with an approximation of their weight. (© I. Shatzman, by courtesy of Prof. E. Stern and the Tel Dor Project)

Carthage has also produced a quantity of artillery balls, numbering an astonishing 5,600. The dating is uncertain, but they must predate the Roman destruction of the city in 146 BC. Unfortunately, at the time of their discovery, only the bare minimum of detail was recorded, and the stones were each assigned to one of five categories: light (5½lb–10lb or 2.5–4.5kg), medium (11–16½lb or 5–7.5kg), medium-heavy (20–31lb or 9–14kg), heavy (35–57lb or 16–26kg), and super-heavy (63–89lb or 28.5–40.5kg).

In his *Manufacture of missile weapons (Belopoiika)*, Philon of Byzantium lists some standard calibres of stone-projector commonly used in his day; the smallest weight of shot mentioned is 10 minas (9¾lb or 4.4kg). This belonged to a machine with springs as tall as a man; in operation, it probably required clearance of at least 20ft (6m) from front to back, and 10ft (3m) from side to side, and must have weighed well over half a tonne. Of course, it would be a mistake to assume that this sizeable machine was the smallest stone projector in general use. Eighteen of the Dora balls belonged to a 5-mina category, and single 5-mina stones were discovered at Rhodes and Pergamon; some of the 900 'light' stones from Carthage may well have been of this size, too.

Seleucid overlordship. In 163 BC, he besieged the citadel at Jerusalem, the so-called Akra, and expelled the garrison. It is clear that the siegecraft practised by the Jewish forces was fully developed: the historian Josephus reports that Judas 'prepared machinery and raised embankments' (Joseph., AJ 12.363), while an earlier account emphasizes the use of 'artillery emplacements and machines' (1 Macc. 6.20). When the conflict flared up again in the 140s BC, Judas' brother Jonathan 'brought up many siege machines' against the Akra (1 Macc. 11.20), while Simon besieged Beth-Sura, one of the main centres of Seleucid power in Judaea; the rapid construction of embankments and machinery threw the garrison into a panic, and they withdrew under truce (Joseph., AJ 13.156). Later, at the siege of Gazara, Simon 'constructed a *helepolis* and brought it up to the town, battered a tower, and captured it'; the fact that 'the men in the *helepolis* leapt out into the town' (1 Macc. 13.43–4) suggests that it was designed like a siege tower, but the machine clearly incorporated a battering ram.

Jonathan was later killed by the Seleucid pretender Tryphon, who was in turn besieged by the rightful king, Antiochus VII, in the coastal town of Dora (Tel Dor in Israel) in 138 BC. The Seleucid forces encircled the town to prevent any escape, and proceeded to attack the walls with machinery. However, Tryphon did not wait to see the outcome, preferring to flee by ship to Apamea, where he met his end. Excavations at Tel Dor throughout the 1980s unearthed sling bullets, arrowheads and the rounded stone balls used by catapults, as well as larger ones which must have been intended for rolling. Antiochus VII's campaign to reconquer Judaea ultimately brought him to Jerusalem, which he surrounded with two deep, wide ditches, seven camps, and a hundred three-storey towers (Joseph., AJ 13.238–9); the city was starved into submission, despite the defenders' attempt to expel all who could not contribute to the defence.

ROME'S SPANISH CAMPAIGNS, 153–134 BC

All this time, Roman armies were busy in Spain, where the defeat of the Carthaginians had left a vacuum. As early as 195 BC, M. Porcius Cato had achieved great successes in the south, but when he claimed to have captured 400 'towns' (Plut., Cato Mai. 10.3) he perhaps used the term loosely. Similarly, in 181 BC, Q. Fulvius Flaccus was said to have captured 'many forts' there (Livy 40.33.9). At any rate, Roman campaigns among the Celtiberians of the northern highlands succeeded only in stirring up a resentment that would last for

The Chevalier de Folard's engraving of Numantia displays no geographical knowledge of the site and little consideration of Appian's description, but demonstrates how Folard's contemporaries imagined a typical Roman siege. The mistaken belief that Roman armies invariably attempted to blockade their enemies was still common into the 20th century. (Author's collection)

generations. In 153 BC, Q. Fulvius Nobilior, whose father had besieged Ambracia in 189 BC (above, p. 109), attempted to capture the Celtiberian stronghold of Numantia, but failure forced his successor to conclude a peace treaty. In 142 BC, it was the turn of Q. Caecilius Metellus, who had earned the sobriquet 'Macedonicus' from his success against rebels in northern Greece. His term of office is chiefly remembered for events at two Celtiberian towns. First, in the vicinity of Contrebia, Metellus devised the stratagem of marching and counter-marching in a desultory fashion until the townsfolk grew complacent, at which point he descended upon them suddenly and captured the town by surprise (Val. Max. 7.4.5). He insisted upon such secrecy that not even his officers were aware of his intentions, giving rise to the story that, when asked for the next day's orders, Metellus responded, 'if my own tunic could tell, I would burn it' (Frontin., *Str.* 1.1.12).

The second town was Centobriga, and here Metellus deployed siege machinery. The writer Valerius Maximus, who compiled his *Memorable Words and Deeds* for the emperor Tiberius around AD 30, records that the defenders seized the children of a deserter and 'exposed them to the blows of the machine' (Val. Max. 5.1.5). Metellus immediately broke off the assault to spare the boys' lives, whereupon the neighbouring communities bowed to Rome, apparently overawed by Metellus' honour and clemency. Valerius Maximus seems to imply that the Romans were using a battering ram. But Livy's version of the story specifies that 'the people of Centobriga exposed the children of the deserter Rethogenes to the shots of the artillery' (Livy, *Per.* 53). It is true that Valerius Maximus is often criticized for inaccuracy, but it is conceivable that, on this occasion, both he and Livy are correct, if the Roman battering assault was accompanied by an artillery barrage.

Meanwhile, Numantia continued to defy Rome. Admittedly, the hilltop site was difficult to approach, but the historian Velleius Paterculus (a source far superior to his contemporary Valerius Maximus) could not decide whether the Numantine success was due to native courage or Roman incompetence (Vell. Pat. 2.1.4). Metellus' successor, Q. Pompeius, resorted to diverting the town's water supply (App., *Hisp.* 78), but his men were constantly harassed as they worked, and new recruits sent out to replace losses fell ill and died from dysentery. In order to conceal the failure of a campaign marked by defeat and humiliation, Pompeius made a pact with the townsfolk, but almost immediately reneged. It was left to his successor, M. Popillius Laenas, to continue the war in

View from Peña Redonda, looking west towards the hill of Cañal. The figure on the left is seated amongst the ruins of the Roman camp, while on the right, the winding course of the Merdancho can be seen (marked b). The distant hill on the right is Dehesilla. (A. Schulten, Numantia: Die Ergebnisse der Ausgrabungen 1905–1912, vol. III: Die Lager des Scipio, Munich 1927)

138 BC. This time, the Numantines were determined to remain within their fortifications, so Laenas tried escalade. However, it seems that, fearing a trap, he cancelled the assault at the last moment, exposing his retreating troops to attack in the rear and subjecting Rome to yet another humiliating defeat (Frontin., *Str.* 3.17.9). His successor's year of office, 137 BC, was likewise marked by misfortune and defeat. Indeed, matters were so bad that C. Hostilius Mancinus abandoned camp and prepared to withdraw by night, but the Numantines pressed his retreating army so hard that he sued for peace (Plut., *Ti. Gracch.* 5.1–4). The Senate in Rome subsequently refused to ratify such a humiliating pact, and even sent Mancinus back to the Numantines, in symbolic cancellation of the treaty.

Meanwhile, Mancinus' successor, M. Aemilius Lepidus Porcina, turned his attention to the town of Pallantia. However, despite the use of siege machines, operations dragged on so long that the Romans again fell foul of famine and disease, the bane of any army making a lengthy stay on the same spot. Lepidus was forced to adopt Mancinus' reprehensible tactics, and withdrew under cover of darkness, leaving the sick and wounded behind. He was subsequently recalled to Rome and fined (App., *Hisp.* 82–3). His replacement, Q. Calpurnius Piso, avoided Numantia altogether, preferring to take a small amount of plunder from the exhausted Pallantines.

THE SIEGE OF NUMANTIA, 133 BC

Such was the catalogue of disasters facing Scipio Aemilianus, the destroyer of Carthage, when he arrived at Numantia. The friends and clients with whom he travelled perhaps included Polybius; although this historian's work terminated with the events of 146 BC, he was a companion of Scipio, and is widely presumed to have been the ultimate source for Appian's description of the Numantine campaign.

In a move entirely characteristic of Roman warfare, operations began with the siting of a camp some distance from the town, before the troops moved up for the siege (App., *Hisp.* 87). This camp may have been one of the five which the German archaeologist Adolf Schulten found 7km east of Numantia on the hill of Renieblas, but the chronology of the site has never been adequately untangled. Having reconnoitred from afar, Scipio then established two camps outside the town, one under his own command and the other under his brother, Q. Fabius

Maximus (App., *Hisp.* 90). Schulten's intimate knowledge of the site, from excavations conducted in the area between 1905 and 1912, led him to place Scipio at Castillejo, a hill to the north of the town; Maximus he placed to the south, on the hill of Peña Redonda. His conjectures stemmed partly from an appreciation of the topography, and there is no denying that Castillejo occupies the prime strategic position, separated from the town by a kilometre of rolling countryside. But there is no particular reason to place Maximus at Peña Redonda. Its inaccessible location ensured that the archaeological remains survived relatively undisturbed, and the degree of preservation may have clouded Schulten's judgement. The big camp at Dehesilla is a better candidate, commanding an altogether easier approach to Numantia and providing an overview of the western side to complement Castillejo's control of the north and east.

His predecessors had tried every stratagem known to them, so Scipio settled on the construction of an ambitious set of siege-works. Appian describes a sequence comprising the initial two camps, followed by the siting of seven forts around the town; then, because the nearby river Duero could not be bridged, 'he

View towards Peña Redonda from the hill of Numantia, taken in early morning sunshine. The siege wall descends the slope on the left (running from d to e), from the Roman camp down to the river. (A. Schulten, Numantia: Die Ergebnisse der Ausgrabungen 1905–1912, *vol. III:* Die Lager des Scipio, *Munich 1927)*

Plan of Numantia, showing the locations mentioned in the text. (© Author)

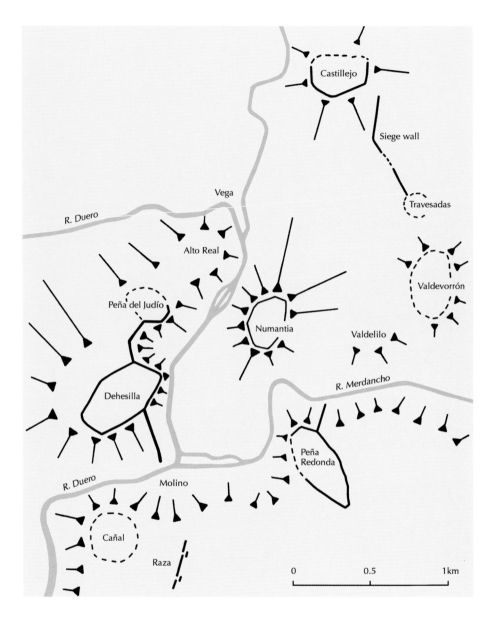

Plan of Numantia, showing the locations mentioned in the text. (© Author)

set two forts alongside it' as the anchor points for floating obstacles (App., *Hisp.* 91). Besides Castillejo, Peña Redonda and Dehesilla, Schulten identified another four, far less well-preserved camps, to arrive at a total of seven, and postulated a further two 'riverbank forts'; this scheme has remained largely uncontested.

There can be little doubt that a 17-acre (7ha) siege camp sat on the hill at Castillejo; besides sporadic remains of limestone foundations, corresponding to barracks and possibly a headquarters building, there were finds of Roman pottery, coins and weaponry. Similarly, at Peña Redonda, the outline of a 27-acre (11ha)

camp is clearly marked by the foundations of a 13ft-thick (4m) stone rampart; extensive remains of barracks and other buildings can still be seen, and the site produced the same kind of finds as at Castillejo. South of Castillejo and about half a kilometre due east of Numantia, Schulten postulated a camp on the low hill of Valdevorrón. Although a perimeter rampart was not located, the site turned up ceramic evidence and some small finds including a Roman coin; the terrain would have permitted a camp of up to 22 acres (9ha). The sizeable gap to the north was closed by a camp at Travesadas, situated on a 10-acre (4ha) plot of low-lying ground. Here, the remains of buildings and sporadic traces of the defences were unearthed, along with pottery and small finds. Schulten also found pottery and traces of stonework on the hill of Valdelilo, but he considered its position dangerously close to Numantia, so he excluded it from consideration.

Schulten believed that Scipio must have placed a garrison at the southern end of Numantia, but all he found on the hill of Raza was a 330yd (300m) stretch of wall with two *titulus*-protected gates. (*Titulus* is the name given to a length of rampart and ditch lying some distance outside a gap in the defences; this was the

View from the north side of Dehesilla (marked c), looking towards Castillejo (a). Schulten discovered the line of Scipio's siege wall as it crosses Peña del Judío (b). (A. Schulten, Die Ergebnisse der Ausgrabungen 1905–1912, vol. III: Die Lager des Scipio, Munich 1927)

One of Schulten's excavation trenches south of Dehesilla, looking downhill towards Molino. Some of the stones forming the foundations of Scipio's siege wall measured almost 1 cubic metre. (A. Schulten, Numantia: Die Ergebnisse der Ausgrabungen 1905–1912, *vol. III:* Die Lager des Scipio, *Munich 1927)*

standard Roman method of protecting an open gateway.) More recent field-work there failed to recover any archaeological material whatsoever, but Spanish researchers have reported ceramic evidence and possible traces of defences on the neighbouring hill of Cañal, which commands views over the entire siege complex. Clearer evidence was found on the riverside at Molino, where the foundations of one or two possible barracks were found, along with pottery and small finds including a Roman dagger. Schulten took these to be evidence of a small fort, and identified a second one further north at Vega, where the remains were far less coherent but the tell-tale pottery pointed to a Roman presence. Curiously, Schulten treated these two 'riverbank forts' separately from his main series of seven camps. Vega, of course, would have been an ideal spot for Scipio's river-blocking measures, at the confluence of the rivers Duero and Tera; a barrier here would have caught any supplies before they drifted down past the town. (In fact, Schulten proposed two river barriers, at Vega and Molino, but Appian's description is ambiguous; he could mean two forts, opposite one another, supporting a single barrier.)

Schulten was confident that a camp lay on Alto Real, a low hill overlooking Vega, but he found only tumbledown walling and, despite small quantities of pottery, it is debatable whether one of Scipio's forts stood here. (Interestingly, Schulten pronounced that the remains were unworthy of Roman workmanship, and could only have been built by Iberian auxiliaries!) By contrast, there can be

A worker stands in one of the post holes which Schulten discovered on the Numantia siege wall south of Dehesilla. The hole is elliptical, 4¼ft (1.3m) long by 2½ft (0.8m) wide and 5¼ft (1.6m) deep. Schulten reasoned that the large dimensions were to allow a thick upright timber to be securely wedged in place. (A. Schulten, Numantia: Die Ergebnisse der Ausgrabungen 1905–1912, vol. III: Die Lager des Scipio, Munich 1927)

no doubt about the remains at Dehesilla; although ploughing had destroyed the interior, Schulten was able to trace the complete perimeter of a 35-acre (14ha) enclosure. Between the two, on the hill of Peña del Judío, he suggested the siting of a tower, but wall foundations were found curving around the hill in a suggestive manner, and the associated pottery scatter holds out the possibility of an enclosure of up to 10 acres (4ha).

Scipio's siege-works consisted of more than just camps and forts. Appian notes that 'here Scipio first, I suppose, enclosed a town which did not refuse open battle' (Hisp. 91). In fact, this was precisely the tactic he had used at Carthage, again as a last resort. (In claiming an innovation at Numantia, Appian is perhaps conscious of the fact that Carthage was not strictly 'enclosed', but cut off; also, unlike the Numantines, her defenders had been in no hurry to take the field against Rome.) Appian relates that Scipio proceeded to surround Numantia with a ditch and palisade, then another ditch not far behind, and finally a wall 8ft wide and 10ft high (2.4 by 3.0m), with towers at intervals of 1 plethron (100ft or 31m). Although Schulten failed to locate any ditch, he found traces of Appian's periteichismos, or walled encirclement, at various spots around Numantia. The short length identified between Castillejo and Travesadas was badly ruined, surviving only as a limestone facing with a metre of rubble backing. However, a substantial length was uncovered on either side of Dehesilla, where it was found to comprise an inner and an outer stone facing, sandwiching a rough, stony infill;

the overall width was approximately 12ft (3.5m). And on the stretch running up to Peña Redonda, an extra layer had been added to the sandwich, resulting in an overall width of 15½ft (4.7m). Schulten reasoned that, from these massive foundations, the wall must have been stepped at the rear, in order to arrive at a 2.4m-wide wallwalk (corresponding to Appian's reported width of 8ft). He calculated that a complete circuit would have measured around 9km; but, as the stretches he uncovered totalled only 1,680m, it may be that other parts were never built in stone. The absence of a ditch he explained by reference to the rivers, proposing that it had only ever existed on the eastern side, where there was no river to screen the siege-works.

Only limited traces of Appian's interval towers were found. First, south of Dehesilla, Schulten thought he could discern a trio of 10ft-wide (3m) guard rooms tacked onto the rear of the siege wall, and spaced at roughly 80ft (25m) intervals. However, the remains are rather ephemeral. Another pair of similar annexes, further south near Molino, was better preserved. But more striking were the massive, stone-revetted post-holes which Schulten found, immediately behind the siege wall, on the same stretch near Dehesilla. He believed them to be sockets for the corner posts of Appian's watch towers, although no clearly defined set of four came to light. Nevertheless, he decided that, on the Dehesilla-Molino stretch, towers with a floor area of around 17ft by 17ft (5m by 5m) were positioned at roughly 26ft (8m) intervals. For their appearance, Schulten favoured a two-storey timber-built design, with the front uprights buried in the siege wall; but the artillery expert, General Erwin Schramm, preferred the safety of a position entirely behind the wall, where he proposed a free-standing three-storey design, with one or two light catapults above wallwalk level and a signalling mast on the upper floor.

Schulten believed that Scipio constructed a full circumvallation, linking seven camps (Castillejo, Travesadas, Valdevorron, Peña Redonda, Raza, Dehesilla and Alto Real) and two 'river forts' (Vega and Molino). A strict reading of Appian requires two camps, seven forts and another two river barrier forts. We have seen that, of Schulten's proposed sites, Raza probably ought to be replaced by Cañal, and Alto Real by Peña del Judío, while Molino should be raised to the status of a fort; the less substantial remains at Vega might have been linked with Scipio's river barrier. If we designate Castillejo and (arguably) Dehesilla as camps, this leaves only six forts, and it may be that Valdelilo was Scipio's seventh. At any rate, it must be admitted that the archaeology does not sit happily with Appian's description.

Siege Warfare in the Age of Marius and Sulla

THE WAR AGAINST JUGURTHA, 111–105 BC

On the death of Micipsa, the philo-Roman ruler of Numidia (north Africa), his adopted son, Jugurtha, challenged the rightful heir, Adherbal, and besieged him in the town of Cirta. The writer Sallust describes how, after an initial assault 'with shelters, towers and machines of all kinds' (*Jug.* 21.3), Jugurtha encircled the town with a ditch and palisade, and erected watch towers. The blockade continued for four months until the townsfolk surrendered, appealing for Roman arbitration. However, Jugurtha took the opportunity to kill his rival and slaughter all the men in the town. Sallust explains that Jugurtha had resorted to blockade 'because its natural strength prevented his taking Cirta by storm' (*Jug.* 23.1). It may be more than coincidental that Jugurtha had served as a Roman ally at Numantia, where he saw Scipio blockade a similarly unassailable town.

When Rome tried to restore order, successive consuls failed to capture Jugurtha, including the nephew of the Metellus who had achieved success in Spain 35 years earlier. (Nevertheless, in the tradition of his family, this Q. Caecilius Metellus took the sobriquet 'Numidicus'.) In 109 BC, he surrounded Zama with pickets of troops and attempted simultaneously to undermine and to scale the walls, under a barrage provided by slingers. But the defence was

The ballista *belonging to the Ermine Street Guard re-enactment group is the optimum size to launch stones weighing around 4 Roman pounds (1.3kg). Even such a lightweight catapult requires considerable space to operate efficiently. (© Ermine Street Guard)*

ferocious: having lined the walls with artillery, the townsfolk rolled down boulders, threw sharpened stakes, and poured a burning mixture of pitch and sulphur onto the Romans. In the following year, at Thala, Metellus surrounded the town with a ditch and palisade, perhaps deliberately emulating Jugurtha's tactic at Cirta. However, he then constructed an embankment to carry battering rams up to the wall and, in the sixth week, broke through the defences. Unfortunately, weeks earlier, Jugurtha had slipped out of the town unnoticed, and the townsfolk, in desperation, burned their valuables and threw themselves onto the bonfire.

Metellus' successor was C. Marius, a 50-year-old soldier of humble origins, who had earlier served with distinction at Numantia. He famously swelled his ranks with the landless poor, placed under the watchful eyes of reliable time-served veterans. After storming several minor towns, just to blood his new troops, he decided to capture the desert town of Capsa, which was 'protected not only by its ramparts and weapons and men, but still more by the difficulty of the surrounding country' (Sall., *Jug.* 89.4). Indeed, the remoteness of some north African towns presented Roman armies with major logistical problems. At Thala, the supply of drinking water had been Metellus' primary concern, until a chance downpour simultaneously solved his difficulties and convinced his troops that they were under divine protection. Similarly, Capsa's inaccessible location demanded special tactics. Marius decided to drive cattle alongside his marching column, so that his troops ate fresh meat for a week and saved the hides to manufacture water skins for their march across the desert. Three days from Capsa, they embarked on a series of night marches with minimal equipment and, when they arrived unexpectedly before the town, they quickly seized the gates. Although the populace promptly surrendered, Marius' troops sacked the place, killing all the adult males. Sallust explains that this was to deny Jugurtha a strong base, and should not be taken to imply greed or brutality on Marius' part (Sall., *Jug.* 91.7).

A second major siege conducted by Marius relied on audacious assault. The target was Jugurtha's treasury, located in an isolated fort on a rocky hill near

Schramm's reconstruction of the famous Ampurias catapult. The original iron spring-frame was discovered in 1912 at the ancient site of Emporion (Spain). It is thought to date from the later 2nd century BC, but similar machines were used from the days of Marius and Sulla right up to the Jewish War. (© D. Baatz)

the Muluccha River. According to Sallust, 'the place was unsuitable for embankments, siege towers, and other machinery' (*Jug.* 92.7), and the only approach road was narrow and precipitous. Hurling stones and fire, the defenders easily destroyed the shelters that concealed Marius' advancing troops. However, by chance, a Ligurian auxiliary collecting snails for his supper stumbled upon a hidden path to the rear of the fort. Immediately realizing the potential for a ruse, Marius sent a small task force of trumpeters and centurions by this alternative route, while he himself launched a full-scale frontal assault under a *testudo* of shields, supported by catapults, archers and slingers. The defenders were so sure of their superiority that they had left the shelter of their walls; but the blasts of the trumpeters, when Marius' task force reached the rear of the fort, sent them into a panic, and they were easily defeated.

ROMAN TACTICS

In siege warfare, Roman armies initially took a rather different tack from their Hellenistic neighbours. They favoured the storming escalade, unsupported by heavy machinery, as shown by their siege of the Samnite town of Silvium in 306 BC (Diod. Sic. 20.80); at the same time, Demetrius Poliorcetes was terrorizing the eastern Mediterranean with his formidable *helepoleis*. No doubt, Roman acquaintance with Carthaginian practice during the Punic Wars of the later 3rd century BC, and with the operations of Philip V of Macedon during the early 2nd century BC, demonstrated the usefulness of the siege tower and the battering ram. Nevertheless, a more pragmatic approach was adopted.

From around 200 BC onwards, Roman besiegers often dealt with uneven terrain and sophisticated outer defences simply by burying them beneath a wide embankment (*agger*). In many cases, this necessitated piling up tonnes of earth and rubble, beginning some distance from the town and gradually moving closer; the larger embankments required timber shoring at the sides. At Avaricum in 52 BC, Caesar was obliged to build an *agger* 80ft (23.7m) high, as the town was situated on high ground amid impassable marshland. The embankment's width of 330ft (97.6m) amply accommodated the two siege towers that gave the men covering fire during the construction phase, but it was primarily designed to facilitate a mass infantry assault on the battlements.

Such large-scale earth-moving operations called for a different type of protection from the Hellenistic ditch-filling tortoises. Gangs of soldiers, passing brushwood and baskets of earth forward, required long covered passageways, and the men working at the front needed to be screened from the defenders on the town wall. The Romans often employed a shelter called the *vinea*, which the late Roman writer Vegetius describes as a light timber structure, open-ended with wickerwork sides, a boarded roof, and a fireproof covering of rawhide (Veg., *Epit. rei mil.* 4.15). Arranged end-to-end to form long corridors, these are perhaps the devices that Caesar calls 'open tunnels' (*cuniculi aperti*: Caes., *BGall.* 7.22).

Men emerging from these corridors required frontal protection, which was probably provided by the *pluteus*, a large convex wicker shield with an arched roof. Vegetius claims that its triangular base sat on three wheels (Veg., *Epit. rei mil.* 4.15), but such a basic device cannot have been heavy and must easily have been manhandled into position. The *vinea* and, to a lesser extent, the *pluteus*, were virtually ubiquitous in Roman siegecraft, owing to the fact that they were so useful in construction work. Other shelters were no doubt improvised out of wicker and rawhide to suit the occasion.

Many Roman sieges involved the use of an earthen ramp to carry men and machines up to battlement level. The workers were protected by lines of sheds. (© Author)

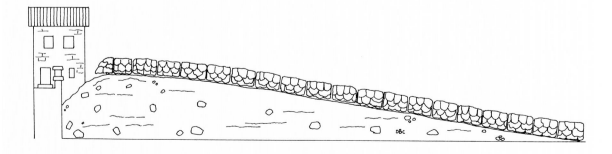

THE SIEGES OF THE ITALIAN WARS, 91–88 AND 83–80 BC

Several towns were besieged during the Social War of the legitimate Roman government against rebel elements in central Italy, who were seeking the rights of Roman citizenship. Unfortunately, there is no detailed account of the uprising, but hints are preserved especially by Appian and Diodorus Siculus. Events began at Asculum, where all the Romans in the town were slaughtered. Thereafter, rebels attacked the Roman colony at Aesernia, and beat off the consular army that attempted to relieve the town. Diodorus Siculus claims that the townsfolk expelled all of their slaves to reduce the number of hungry mouths, a measure which prominent Romans exploited to make their escape. As conditions worsened, the townsfolk resorted to eating dogs, and were finally starved into submission. Venafrum fell to treachery, Nola was betrayed, and the sack of Nuceria persuaded the neighbouring communities to capitulate and provide troops for the rebels.

Meanwhile, another rebel force besieged the colony of Alba Fucens and defeated the consul P. Rutilius Rufus, who was carried back to Rome 'dripping with blood' (Florus 2.6.12). His deputy, Cn. Pompeius Strabo, was besieged in Firmum, until a relieving force arrived and, together, they chased the rebels to Asculum, which in turn came under siege. Another rebel force, led by a native of Asculum, succeeded in breaking into the town, whereupon their commander ostentatiously committed suicide, despairing of his fellow townsmen's performance in the siege. The town fell to Roman forces a year later, in 89 BC.

Around the same time, L. Cornelius Sulla, who had served under Marius (usually ungraciously), marched against the town of Aeclanum. The townsfolk hoped to stall him, but his troops proceeded to pile firewood around the timber fortifications and set them ablaze; the town promptly surrendered, but Sulla looted the place as a punishment. The details of how other towns, such as Canusium and Pompeii, fell to siege in 89/88 BC remain shadowy.

There was more siege warfare in 83 BC, when Sulla, returning from his campaigns in the east (see below), was intercepted by the army of Marius' son (the old man had died in 86 BC, having stirred up Rome against Sulla). Sulla's battle-hardened legions drove the younger Marius' men to take shelter in Praeneste, which they proceeded to invest with a wall and ditch, to prevent any supplies getting through; even worse, as Sulla defeated successive relieving forces, he paraded the heads of their generals around the town to demoralize the besieged. When the townsfolk finally gave in, Marius hid in a tunnel and committed suicide.

SULLA AND MITHRIDATES, 88–85 BC

The north wall of Pompeii, east of the Herculaneum Gate, survives up to 25ft (7m) in height. The pock-marking visible here appears to have been caused by a barrage of missiles ranging from sling bullets to small-calibre ballista balls. These are likely to represent shots that fell short or were accidentally skewed during the siege of 89 BC, as Sulla's men directed their missiles at the timber gate or at the defenders on the battlements. (© American Academy in Rome)

Sulla had been absent from Rome for four years, on account of the First Mithridatic War. In 88 BC, King Mithridates VI of Pontus overran Rome's possessions in Asia Minor; adding insult to injury, he humiliated the Roman commissioner there, M'. Aquillius, by parading him around on an ass before pouring molten gold down his throat to punish Rome's avarice. Mithridates then turned his attention to the wealthy trading city of Rhodes, whose inhabitants immediately strengthened their defences and 'erected war machines everywhere' (App., *Mith.* 24). An epic maritime siege ensued, but Mithridates' secret weapon, a fearsome contraption known as the *sambuca* (see pp. 136–137), proved to be a disappointment when it collapsed under its own weight. It is likely that the fire, reportedly hurled down upon the machine by the goddess Isis, really came from Rhodian incendiary missiles. Meanwhile, the proficiency of the Rhodian fleet kept their Pontic aggressors from entering the harbour, and Mithridates withdrew in exasperation.

Sending his forces over to Greece, the king installed his favourite, Aristion, as despot of Athens, while his general, Archelaus, took charge of the port of Piraeus. By summer 87 BC, Sulla's five legions had arrived to besiege the divided Pontic forces. At Athens, Sulla was content to have his men contain the situation until he could personally capture the strategically important Piraeus; but the ladder parties that he threw at the walls in a lightning assault were repulsed. The artillery scholar Eric Marsden thought it an extremely optimistic attack, but he was perhaps influenced by Appian's exaggerated claim that the walls of Piraeus were 40 cubits (60ft or 18.5m) high (App., *Mith.* 30). At 30 cubits (46ft or 14m), the walls of Teichos, near Dyme, were thought to be unusually strong (Polyb. 4.83.4), and few city walls would have exceeded 30ft (around 10m). In any case, to attempt an escalade was a perfectly respectable tactic; after all, initial attacks on Carthage and Numantia, for example, had been based on escalade, and the Romans had often profited from such a bold approach.

Nevertheless, for a well-defended town to fall required either luck or a full-scale mechanized siege. Sulla decided upon the latter. After prevailing upon the neighbouring Greek towns to provide equipment, including catapults, he set his men the task of constructing siege machines; Plutarch makes the

The strong defences of Ceramus (Turkey), probably constructed in the later 2nd century BC, seem never to have been tested in siege warfare. Sulla gifted the town to neighbouring Stratoniceia in 81 BC. (A. W. McNicoll, Hellenistic Fortifications from the Aegean to the Euphrates, Oxford, 1997. Reprinted by permission of Oxford University Press and Ms T. Winikoff)

THE SAMBUCA

The *sambuca* (or *sambykē*) was 'a Roman device invented by Heraclides of Tarentum' (Ath. 634b), an engineer active around 214 BC. Often mounted between a pair of ships, it resembled a giant laddered drawbridge, and served to transfer marines onto the sea walls of coastal towns. However, the *sambuca* developed by Damios, an otherwise unknown engineer from Kolophon in present-day Turkey, is quite different. First, it was designed for use on land, and second, it utilized an innovative vertical screw to alter the elevation of the ladder. This version of the machine is only known from a description by Biton.

The shape of Damios' machine has engendered a certain amount of controversy. Biton says that the *sambuca* itself, a 60ft (18m) ladder with an assault platform at one end and a counterweight at the other, sat on a 'trestle' (*killibas*); the trestle was fixed to a 27ft-long (8m) undercarriage, equipped with 3ft-high (0.9m) wheels. The vagueness of the description has given scholars ample room to indulge their imaginations, but Marsden's model, consisting of a single horizontal timber supporting a tall upright, would have been far too precarious for practical use. Schramm's wide, rectangular undercarriage would have given more stability, but he mistakenly designed the ladder as a single beam with rungs projecting on either side.

Brian Delf © Osprey Publishing Ltd

Biton's ladder clearly has sidewalls, 'so that the men climbing up will make the ascent confidently' (Biton 59.10–60.1), and a widened jumping-off area at the top. In fact, it probably resembled the shipboard version, described by the historian Polybius in the 2nd century BC. He says that 'a ladder is prepared, 4ft (1.2m) wide, in such a way that it reaches the wall from its position; each side is fenced and covered with a high breastwork … At the top of the ladder is a platform, protected by wickerwork on three sides, on which four men are stationed' (Polyb. 8.4.4). It seems likely that Damios' assault platform had similar protection; with the machine at its action station, the wicker panels were removed and the men rushed out.

Unlike the shipboard version, Damios' ladder had, at the rear, a 6ft-long (1.8m) lead-filled box. Schramm was unsure of its purpose, but Marsden assumed that this counterweight was intended to balance the machine like a seesaw; consequently, he added a horizontal pivot, fixed to the trestle. Drachmann, who pronounced the whole thing 'an armchair invention', highlighted the absurdity of this arrangement, but rather than question Marsden's interpretation, he denounced Biton's work as a sham.

Of course, the ladder was never intended to rock like a seesaw. On the contrary, its movement was regulated by a 15ft (4.5m) vertical screw, running up through the trestle to a component called the 'fastener' (katakleis). Biton is a little vague on the workings of these elements, but the ladder, horizontal at rest, was probably hinged to the rear of the 'fastener'; the screw would then elevate the front of the ladder, fine-tuning the height of the assault-platform. The counterweight played no part in this operation, but was required to preserve the machine's stability. Schramm and Marsden both assumed that the ladder projected by at least 40ft (12m); in that case, the short end would have needed ballast of around 2 tonnes to offset the weight of an assault unit of perhaps eight or ten soldiers on the forward platform.

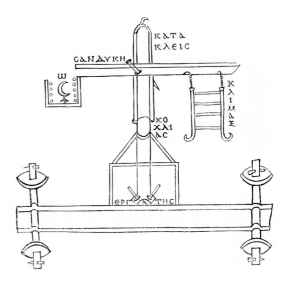

Damios' sambuca. The manuscript illustration, dating to the 11th/12th C., was probably not based on Biton's original diagram, but was a later attempt to make sense of his text. (C. Wescher, Poliorcétique des Grecs, *Paris 1867)*

astonishing claim that ten thousand pairs of mules were in daily service, presumably hauling the raw materials (Plut., *Sulla* 12.2). Meanwhile, Sulla's legionaries threw up an embankment with earth, timber and masonry robbed from the ruined Long Walls that once linked the port to Athens. A story told centuries later, that one of Sulla's men was struck down by a thunderbolt while bringing up earth for the embankment, is perhaps a garbled report of the sling bullets that must have filled the air.

But Archelaus proved a formidable foe. Building up a siege tower opposite the Roman works and sending his men on midnight sorties to burn the Roman equipment, he even managed to undermine the embankment, and when Sulla sent sappers to tunnel their way into the town, they were intercepted underground and beaten back. The siege continued through the winter and into the following year. Finally, constant bombardment by Sulla's artillery disabled Archelaus' tower, and battering rams positioned on the newly repaired embankment broke through; for good measure, the Romans also undermined a length of the town wall. However, although Sulla sent in troops in rotation, the Pontic garrison was still numerous enough to repulse his attacks.

All this time, Sulla had been intercepting supplies sent from Piraeus to relieve the beleaguered garrison of Athens. Consequently, hemmed in by Roman troops who had latterly cut a ditch all around the city, the inhabitants were weak from starvation; their only sustenance came from wild plants and boiled leather, and some had allegedly turned to cannibalism. When a poorly guarded stretch of wall came to Sulla's attention, he ordered a nocturnal escalade and unleashed his frustrated soldiers on the defenceless inhabitants. For this, he earned the disapproval of the later writer Pausanias, who commented that Sulla had been 'more savage than one would expect from a Roman' (Paus. 1.20.4). Pausanias must have known that it was standard practice to kill the males of sword-bearing age, but he perhaps expected the women and children to be sold into slavery, as Mummius had done at Corinth in 146 BC (Paus. 7.16.5). Instead, Sulla ordered a wholesale massacre, which Plutarch could only explain as retribution for the insults and obscenities that had been thrown at Sulla's wife from the walls. Returning to unfinished business at Piraeus, the Romans attacked the walls with such renewed energy that Archelaus was dumbfounded by their persistence, and evacuated the town by sea.

We have no Numantia for this period, no site where archaeology and literature combine to illuminate one another. Many sieges are known only from a brief notice in the sources. Frontinus mentions the capture of a town called Isaura in 75 BC by P. Servilius Vatia, who employed the well-worn stratagem of diverting the town's water supply (Frontin., *Str.* 3.7.1). A fragment from Sallust's *Histories* seems to describe the same event: it tells of townsfolk mounting a nocturnal sortie, in the mistaken belief that the Romans had abandoned their fortification; 'the ditches', writes Sallust, 'were half filled with the bodies of the slain' (Sall., *Hist.* 2 frg. 87). The chance find of an inscription in the wilds of Turkey not only confirmed the location of the town, but preserved the text of a dedication by Servilius, fulfilling a vow made to some deity for the successful outcome of the siege (AE 1977, 816).

LUCULLUS, POMPEY AND MITHRIDATES, 74–71 BC

The two consuls of 74 BC, M. Aurelius Cotta and L. Licinius Lucullus, were keen to resume the war against Mithridates; the former lost no time in beginning naval operations, but was soon bottled up in Chalcedon and had to be rescued by his colleague.

From Chalcedon, Mithridates moved to Cyzicus, nowadays a peninsula but in antiquity an island connected to the mainland by a bridge. Plutarch records that 'Mithridates besieged the people of Cyzicus on both sides: by land, encompassing them with ten camps, and by sea, blocking up with ships the strait that separates the mainland from the town' (Plut., *Luc.* 9.3). Appian adds the detail that, 'as he possessed many soldiers, he pressed on with all the siege-works, walling off the [residential?] quarter with a double wall and surrounding the rest of the town with a ditch' (App., *Mith.* 73); embankments were also raised to carry battering rams. Meanwhile, the Pontic fleet brought siege machinery up to the walls (see illustration overleaf), including a 100-cubit-high (150ft or 46m) wooden tower that carried catapults and missile troops. However, Mithridates was no more successful here than he had been at Rhodes 15 years earlier. All of his machines, 'the marvellous works of Niconides the Thessalian' (Plut., *Luc.* 10.2), were wrecked in a storm, and when poor sanitation brought disease to his siege camps Mithridates was finally persuaded to give up.

Lucullus' strategy of attrition, which Plutarch poetically rendered as 'thumping Mithridates in the belly' (Plut., *Luc.* 11.1), was unpopular with his legionaries, who were thereby denied the opportunity for plunder. Perhaps responding to this disaffection, Lucullus threw his troops enthusiastically at Themyscira; embankments were raised for siege towers, and tunnels were dug 'which were so large that, in them, a multitude could attack one another under the ground' (App., *Mith.* 78). However, the siege appears to have been abandoned when the defenders discovered the tunnels and inserted bears and other wild animals, including swarms of bees. Subsequent operations at wealthy Amisus (present-day Samsun on Turkey's Black Sea coast) took the form of repeated escalade, suggesting that Lucullus' troops had perhaps lost their appetite for digging full-scale siege-works. When a Roman assault finally caught the guards unawares, Callimachus, the king's deputy in Amisus, set fire to the town to cover his own flight, and succeeded in creating the maximum of confusion. Lucullus strove to save the place from destruction while his men

(Continued p.142)

MITHRIDATES VI BESIEGES CYZICUS, 73 BC

During Mithridates' assault on Cyzicus from the sea, pride of place amongst his siege machinery went to the shipborne tower, 'out of which, when they brought it up to the wall, a bridge sprang from under the machine' (App., Mithr. 73); this description calls to mind the *sambuca*, which Mithridates employed 15 years earlier at Rhodes. Fortuitously, the historian Polybius describes in detail the version used by the Romans at Syracuse in 213 BC, perhaps the machine's debut, and we have taken that machine as the centrepiece of the scene.

Appian records that the defenders were driven back, and four of Mithridates' soldiers managed to set foot on the battlements, but they were killed and the attack petered out. Nothing is known of the ancient walls of Cyzicus, and we have suggested a scheme of closed battlements and shuttered windows, as at Heraclea-by-Latmus. Such a fortification would have been difficult to capture by escalade, and might explain Mithridates' failure. (Adam Hook © Osprey Publishing Ltd)

Scene from the Arch of Titus (Rome), showing the plunder from Jerusalem paraded in the triumph of AD 71. Garlanded men can be seen carrying placards (left and centre), probably describing the individual exhibits, and another carries the seven-branched candelabrum, or menorah, looted from the Temple. (© R. Cowan)

rushed to ransack the burning buildings; the next day, he is said to have wept as he surveyed the destruction, just as Scipio had done at Carthage (Plut., *Luc.* 19.4; cf. App., *Pun.* 132).

In the meantime, Cotta was engaged further west at Heraclea Pontica, where 'he devised machines, such as the tortoise, which he thought would be most terrifying to the besieged' (Memnon 34.1). But when his siege equipment failed to achieve results, spitefully he burned it and beheaded the engineers. The subsequent blockade provoked treachery in the starving town, and Mithridates' garrison commander opened the gates to the Romans. However, the victory almost turned sour as the first Roman troops to enter seized the booty, denying a share to their comrades back in the camp; violent disagreement was avoided only by gathering all the valuables into a common pool and dividing them equitably. At Tigranocerta, where Lucullus finally tracked Mithridates down in 69 BC, the town was so rich that, besides whatever trinkets the individual soldiers could gather for themselves, each man received 800 drachmas from the store of booty (Plut., *Luc.* 29.3). And although mutiny in the ranks prevented

Scene from the Arch of Titus (Rome), showing the young Caesar (right) riding in a four-horse chariot, with winged Victory standing behind. On his return from the Jewish War in AD 71, Titus celebrated a joint triumph with his father, the reigning emperor Vespasian, thus emphasizing the dynastic succession. (© R. Cowan)

Lucullus from landing the killer blow on Mithridates, he was permitted a triumph at Rome, embellished with 'the weapons of the enemy, being very numerous, and the royal siege machinery' (Plut., *Luc.* 37.2).

The coup de grâce was left to another of Sulla's protégés, Gnaeus Pompeius (the self-styled 'Pompey the Great'), before he moved on to Judaea to settle a succession crisis in 63 BC. Although the two quarrelling brothers, Aristobulus and Hyrcanus, agreed to abide by Pompey's arbitration, Aristobulus' followers seized Jerusalem and took refuge on the fortress-like Temple platform. Pompey approached from the north, and had an embankment constructed to fill the huge defensive ditch, 6oft deep and 26oft across (18 by 77m). Josephus claims that great progress was made on Sabbaths, when the Jews were forbidden to work and thus could not hinder the Romans (Joseph., *BJ* 1.146). Machines were requisitioned from Tyre to batter the wall and bombard the rebels, and after three months the Romans broke into the sacred Temple. Out of respect for the sanctity of the place, Pompey disallowed his troops from their usual plundering, but he himself could not resist the sacrilege of entering the Holy of Holies.

Siege Warfare in the Late Republic

CAESAR'S GALLIC SIEGES, 57–51 BC

By the time of Caesar, the legions had long been noted for their skills in field engineering, best illustrated by the camp they traditionally entrenched after each day's march. Besieging armies are often mentioned building such a camp, or sometimes a pair of camps as Scipio had done at Numantia. However, the German scholar Willy Liebenam believed that he could discern a particular style of siegecraft that dispensed with all preparations in order to deliver a sudden and unexpected attack. Ironically, his inspiration came from the siege of Gomphi, a town in Greece that Caesar subjected to *repentina oppugnatio* ('violent assault') in 48 BC, when it shut its gates against him. But even here, the legionaries' first act was to build a camp outside the town, and their second was to construct ladders, shelters and screens (Caes., *BCiv.* 3.80); the assault, when it came, was certainly swift, but Caesar's preparations had been thorough. The situation at Cenabum (modern Orléans in France) four years earlier was very similar. Having arrived too late in the day to organize an attack, Caesar's troops settled down and pitched camp. However, when the townsfolk attempted to flee in the dark, the legionaries sprang into action; firing the town gates, no doubt to illuminate the chaotic scene, they set about looting and burning the place (Caes., *BGall.* 7.11).

No fewer than 17 sieges are known to have been prosecuted by Caesar himself, and many involved the constructional skills of his soldiers. Nowhere is this clearer than at Avaricum (modern Bourges), a town almost entirely surrounded by marshes, except to the south, where the only approach route was obstructed by a deep gully. When he besieged the town in 52 BC, Caesar had to construct a great

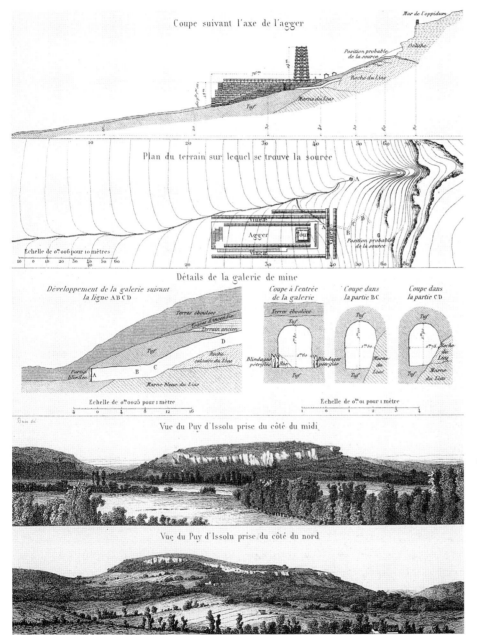

During Caesar's siege of Uxellodunum, the Gauls set fire to barrels filled with pitch, grease and wood-shavings, and rolled them down onto the Roman embankment. Napoléon III's investigations at Puy d'Issolu in 1865 led him to place the scene of this event on the western slopes, where he claimed to have found traces of burning. (Napoléon III, Histoire de Jules César, II: Guerre des Gauls, Paris 1866)

145

Details of Colonel Stoffel's excavations at Gergovie in 1862. Napoléon concluded that 'the communication between the great and little camps was composed of a parapet, formed by the earth thrown out of two adjacent ditches, each four feet in depth [1.2m] and six in breadth [1.78m], so that the breadth of the two together is twelve feet'. (Napoléon III, Histoire de Jules César, II: Guerre des Gauls, Paris 1866)

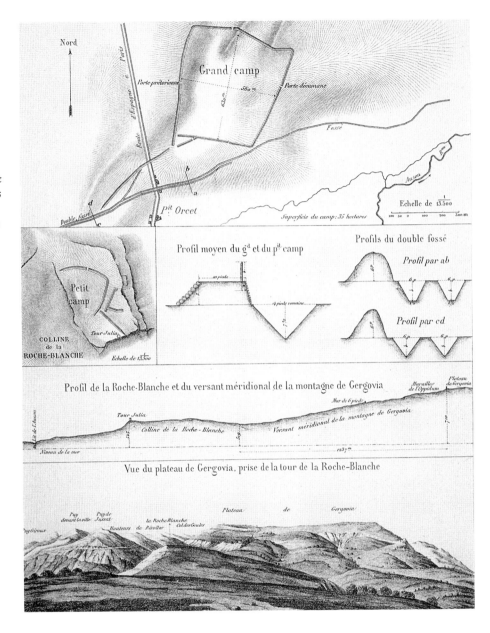

embankment so that he could bring overwhelming numbers of men across the gully and up to the walls; in 25 days, the massive structure, 330ft wide (98m) and 80ft high (24m), was complete. A similarly breathtaking feat of engineering was accomplished in the following year at Uxellodunum (Puy d'Issolu), where Caesar ordered the construction of a 60ft (18m) embankment, from which a ten-storey artillery-armed siege tower could target the fresh water spring that was sustaining the inhabitants and prolonging the siege.

More usually, embankments served as runways along which heavy siege machinery could approach the walls of the besieged town. Sulla's embankment at Piraeus had fulfilled this function, as had Lucullus' at Themyscira and Pompey's at Jerusalem. Caesar's embankment at Noviodunum in 57 BC was of this sort: 'after the shelters were speedily brought up to the town, an embankment thrown up, and towers erected, the Gauls were amazed by the size of the works, whose like they had neither seen nor heard of before, and, perturbed by the speed of the Romans, they sent representatives to Caesar to discuss surrender' (Caes., *BGall.* 2.12). Similarly, 'when [the Atuatuci] saw a siege tower erected in the distance, after shelters had been brought up and an embankment constructed, they at first jeered from their walls and ridiculed why such a machine had been built so far away' (Caes., *BGall.* 2.30); but their scorn turned to alarm when the tower began its steady progress towards their walls, and they promptly sued for peace.

In all of these cases, for the chosen strategy to succeed, certain topographical features, such as the gully at Avaricum, made an embankment essential. Under different circumstances, an assault could be accomplished without one. For example, in 52 BC at Gergovia, atop a formidable hill accessible only from the south, Caesar decided to creep forward across the difficult terrain, consolidating ground as he went. From his initial encampment below and to the east of the hill, he seized the Roche Blanche, a small hill to the west, and 'carried a 12ft double ditch from the larger camp to the smaller, so that even individuals could pass back and forth, safe from a sudden attack by the enemy' (Caes., *BGall.* 7.36). Unfortunately, his plans were botched by the impetuosity of his troops, who were caught on disadvantageous terrain and repulsed; during the fighting withdrawal, no fewer than 46 centurions fell. In 1862, the archaeological remains of Caesar's earthworks were uncovered by Colonel Eugène Stoffel, during a programme of archaeological excavations sponsored by Napoléon III to provide information for his *Histoire de Jules César*. More recent work by the Association pour la recherche sur l'Age du Fer en Auvergne (ARAFA) has confirmed the existence of Caesar's two camps; but, at several points along the presumed course of the double ditch, only a single ditch was found, 5½ft (1.70m) wide and 3¼ft (1m) deep, raising the possibility that the earthwork was not of uniform character over its entire length.

The earthworks at Gergovia were on a fairly small scale, and have more in common with field fortifications (for example, the ditches and artillery positions supporting the battle line at the Aisne in 57 BC; *BGall.* 2.8) than with siege-works. However, Caesar's general readiness to throw a rampart around an enemy town is surprising, for the technique of *periteichismos* practised by Scipio at Numantia had not been used (as far as we know) for 25 years. Its last proponent

North ditch of Caesar's large camp at Gergovia. The classic V-section of the ditch, approximately 3½ft (1.1m) wide and 1½ft (0.5m) deep, is visible in the side of the excavation trench. The hill of Gergovie can be seen in the background. (Y. Deberge; © ARAFA)

had been Sulla, at the siege of Praeneste, when he 'cut off the town at a great distance with a ditch and a wall' (App., *BCiv.* 1.88); four years earlier, at Athens, he had 'commanded the army to surround the town with a ditch, so that no one might secretly escape' (App., *Mith.* 38). The tactic presumably appealed to Caesar in the 50s, as it had to Sulla in the 80s. Perhaps such large-scale earth-moving exercises helped maintain discipline amid the tedium that sometimes accompanied siege warfare. Certainly, Plutarch claims that, when M. Licinius Crassus confined Spartacus' slave army in the toe of Italy in 71 BC by walling off the peninsula, part of his reasoning was 'in order to keep the soldiers busy' (Plut., *Crass.* 10.7).

Equally, experienced soldiers like Sulla and Caesar must have appreciated the demoralizing effect that encirclement had on an enemy. In 52 BC, after Caesar spent two days surrounding Vellaunodunum, 'on the third day, ambassadors were sent from the town to surrender' (Caes., *BGall.* 7.11). If they had not, it is likely that Caesar would have launched an assault. This was certainly the case in the following year at Uxellodunum. Prior to Caesar's arrival, his legate C. Caninius Rebilus planted three camps on the surrounding hills and 'proceeded to carry a rampart around the town' (*BGall.* 8.33); but it was Caesar's attack on their water supply that led to the townsfolk's surrender. Years earlier, in order to keep the Atuatuci within their walls while his embankment was under construction, Caesar had surrounded the town with 'a rampart 15,000 feet [4.4km] in circumference, with closely-spaced forts' (Caes., *BGall.* 2.30). Here, the investment was simply a prelude to an aggressive assault. Caesar's contemporary, the prolific letter-writer Cicero, claimed to have used a similarly aggressive technique when he besieged Pindenissus in 51 BC. Summarizing the whole operation in a letter to his friend M. Porcius Cato, he wrote, 'I surrounded the town with a rampart and ditch; I penned it in with six forts and large camps; I attacked it with embankments, shelters and siege towers' (Cic., *Ad fam.* 15.4.10).

THE SIEGE OF ALESIA, 52 BC

Ironically, rather than Cicero's dynamic assault on Pindenissus, it is Caesar's blockade of Alesia that has often been taken to represent the Roman style of besieging. Topographically, Alesia, situated on the plateau of Mont Auxois, is strikingly similar to Numantia, and Caesar's chosen strategy was virtually identical to Scipio's; by maintaining a close blockade, he starved the defenders into submission. Caesar describes the sequence of events as follows: first, the army was encamped at convenient places; then 23 forts were constructed in a ring, to maintain a watch on the town; finally, siege lines were thrown around the site to complete the blockade. Colonel Stoffel's excavations between 1862 and 1865 were never published in full, as they were simply intended to corroborate Caesar's description of the siege for Napoléon's *Histoire de Jules César*, but parts of the siege-works have now been studied using modern archaeological techniques by a Franco-German team directed by Michel Reddé.

Napoléon decided on a sequence of eight camps, designated A to D, G to I, and K. There were sound archaeological reasons for placing A and B on the Montagne de Flavigny, and C on the Montagne de Bussy; indeed, in the 1860s, the ramparts of Camp B were apparently still standing, and a campaign of air photography between 1986 and 1995 revealed Camp C in amazing detail. However, there is little to recommend Napoléon's placing of Camp D at the foot of Mont Réa. Stoffel could trace only a few disjointed lengths of ditch, but Napoléon conjured visions of the desperate defence of a camp here; he claimed that the hotchpotch of discarded weaponry and domestic refuse, which included pottery and millstones, 'would lead us to suppose that the Romans threw upon the assailants everything that came to hand'. Based on such feeble and circumstantial evidence, Camp D has long been doubted.

None of Napoléon's other camps demonstrates a close relationship with the siege-works. The enclosure on the Plaine de Grésigny, which he labelled Camp G, lies in an exposed position far beyond the siege lines, as do the features on the Plaine des Laumes, which he proposed as Camps H, I and K. Indeed, recent excavations have shown that Camp I was post-Roman in date, a finding that recommends caution in assuming a Caesarian origin for the others.

Napoléon's 23 'redoubts' fare even worse, as even he admitted that only five actually existed, while the others had been pencilled in 'at the most convenient places' in a ring around Mont Auxois. Of the five genuine sites, only Napoléon's no. 10, on the northern slope of the Montagne de Flavigny, is convincing as one of Caesar's *castella*. No. 22, exposed on the heights of Mont Réa, is actually a prehistoric enclosure, and three others, situated on the Montagne de Flavigny (no. 11) and the Montagne de Bussy (nos. 15 and 18), are likely to have been among the camps that Caesar initially established (see map p.152).

Catapult arrowhead (length, 5in/12cm; weight, 3¼oz/ 94g) found in the ditch of Caesar's small camp at Gergovia, during the 1996 excavations. (J. Ward; © ARAFA)

Aerial view of Mont Auxois (ancient Alesia) from the south, with the Montagne de Bussy behind. The course of the Ozerain can be seen in the foreground. (© Archéologie aérienne René Goguey)

Military operations were restricted on three sides of Mont Auxois by river valleys, but the open meadow of the Plaine des Laumes to the west offered a likely route, either for a massed eruption from the town or for the approach of a relieving force. So Caesar secured it with a ditch, allegedly 20ft (6m) wide with perpendicular sides. Stoffel located this feature, running in an arc from river to river, but its dimensions may have been more modest than Caesar claimed; a section cut across it in 1996 revealed a flat-bottomed trench, some 3.1m wide and 1.3m deep.

Caesar described his main siege lines, 11 miles (16km) in circumference, as consisting of two ditches, the inner one filled with water, and a palisaded rampart with turrets every 80ft (24m) (see illustration p. 156). Excavations in the 1990s on the Plaine des Laumes confirmed the broad outline of Caesar's scheme, while emphasizing differences of detail. For example, the width of the innermost ditch, nearest the enemy, varied between 4m and 6.5m, and nowhere was it was found to be deeper than 1.5m; Caesar had specified 15ft wide by 15ft deep (4.5m by 4.5m). Five metres further out from the enemy lay a second ditch, consistently

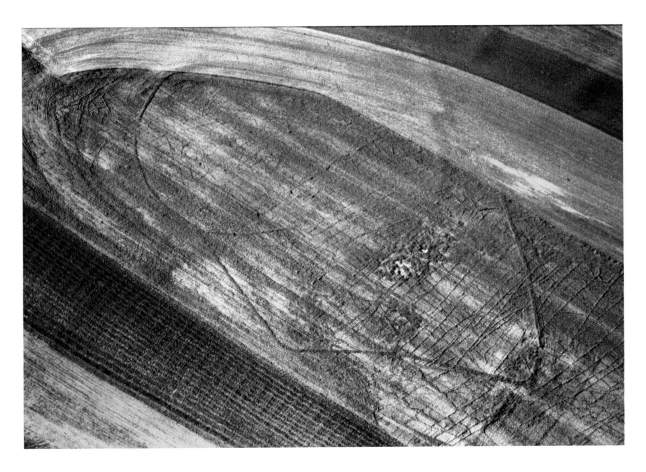

2.7m wide but again never deeper than 1.5m. Surprisingly, 15m behind these, a third ditch was discovered, immediately fronting the rampart; it fluctuated between 1.1m and 3.2m wide and between 0.8 and 1.4m deep. The rampart itself had been furnished with four-posted turrets at roughly 15m intervals. Minor differences of detail were discovered on the Plaine de Grésigny, where no third ditch was found, and traces of a wicker fence appeared in the strip between the first and second ditches.

Caesar claimed to have added further obstacles, 'so that the fortifications could be defended by a smaller number of troops' (*BGall.* 7.73). First, there were rows of five tree trunks with sharpened branches, sunk into 5ft (1.5m) ditches, and named *cippi* ('gravestones') with soldiers' irony. Then came eight rows of sharpened stakes set vertically in 3ft (0.9m) pits, staggered in a quincunx pattern and concealed by brushwood; these were humorously dubbed *lilia* ('lilies'). And in front of these, buried at random, were barbed spikes fixed in foot-long (0.3m) lumps of wood and nicknamed *stimuli* ('spurs'). Archaeological investigations on the Plaine des Laumes turned up subtle variations of these obstacles: six rows of

Aerial view of Camp C at Alesia, viewed from the east. At 19 acres (7.8ha), this is the largest of Caesar's camps. (© Archéologie aérienne René Goguey)

Plan of Alesia, showing features identified archaeologically or from aerial photography. Napoléon III's original scheme, identifying features by letter or number, has been retained for clarity. (© Author)

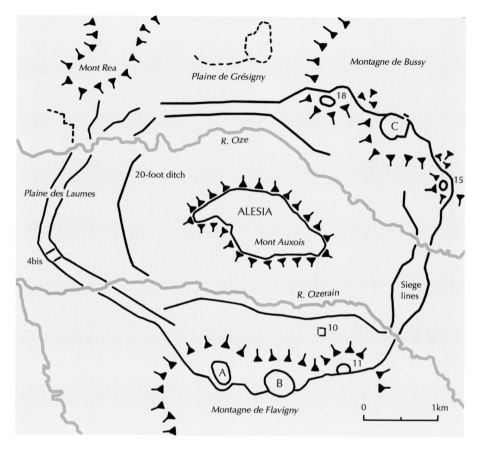

small post-holes, only 1ft (0.3m) in diameter, filled the wide strip between the second and third ditches in a staggered formation, like Caesar's *lilia* but far smaller. And where the line turned around Mont Réa, although the excavators found only a single ditch, it was fronted by six or seven rows of small post-holes, again in the familiar staggered pattern.

Farther east, on the Plaine de Grésigny, the inner ditch was fronted by two parallel slots, 5ft (1.5m) apart. If these are the foundation trenches for *cippi*, as the excavators suggested, then they represent another subtle departure from Caesar's description. Caesar stipulates 'rows of five', but it has never been clear whether he meant five ditches, or five lines of tree trunks per ditch. Napoléon favoured the first interpretation, which has coloured all subsequent reconstructions of the Alesia siege-works, but the classicist Thomas Rice Holmes believed that the second interpretation better suited Caesar's Latin. Unfortunately, the trenches on the Plaine de Grésigny, each around 10in (25cm) wide and 8in (20cm) deep, are too small to have accommodated multiple rows of tree trunks.

Having laid out one line of siege-works, Caesar then constructed another one, comprising 'similar fortifications of the same kind, facing the other way against the enemy outside' (*BGall.* 7.74). The excavations on the Plaine des Laumes found that the outer rampart was fronted by an 11ft-wide ditch (3.5m), a 26ft (8m) gap, and a 19ft-wide (5.7m) ditch. This line, too, incorporated obstacle fields between the ditches and beyond the outer ditch. The researcher and illustrator Peter Connolly has coined the term 'bicircumvallation' for double siege lines, one facing inwards and one facing outwards. Something similar had first appeared at Agrigentum in 262 BC and again at Capua in 212 BC (above, pp. 102–103), and the arrangement was eminently sensible when attack might be expected from without, as well as from within. However, it must stand as testimony to the efficiency of successive Roman armies that they rarely found themselves in this position.

One feature of the siege-works at Alesia remains to be mentioned, namely the fortification discovered within the siege lines on the Plaine des Laumes; it has been named '4 bis', as it lies near the point where Napoléon placed *castellum* 4.

North-east corner of Camp C at Alesia, viewed from the air. The camp ditch presents itself as a thick dark line, broken at the 40ft-wide (12m) gateway. Two parallel lines of defences lie beyond the gateway, protecting it from outside in the manner of a titulus; also, the ditch can faintly be seen curving inwards, covering the gate on the inside. A smaller 'postern' can be seen to the right, where the ditch of the circumvallation meets the corner of the camp. (© Archéologie aérienne René Goguey)

Roman pilum *head found in a shallow ditch within castellum 11 on the Montagne de Flavigny at Alesia. (© M. Joly / Ph. Barral)*

Parallel ramparts were found to have closed off a compartment, roughly 100m square, between the inner and outer lines; each rampart was fronted by a ditch, 3.8m wide by 1.1m deep, and access to the resulting enclosure was via a gate, positioned where each rampart butted against the main siege lines. This seems a prime candidate for one of Caesar's forts, and others perhaps remain to be discovered in similar positions around the siege-works.

THE SIEGES OF THE CIVIL WARS, 49–31 BC

Caesar's conquest of Gaul was substantially complete by 50 BC; alarmed by the increasing hostility of his erstwhile ally Pompey, he resolved to march on Rome. The ensuing struggle between the Caesarian and Pompeian factions spread across the Roman world and resulted in several well-known sieges. Most strikingly, Caesar continued to employ his familiar encircling technique. For

example, arriving before Corfinium in 49 BC, his forces encamped on opposite sides of the town, before surrounding it with a rampart and forts; to prevent any escape, troops were deployed 'in a continuous ring of sentries and pickets, so that they touched each other and filled up the whole fortification' (*BCiv.* 1.21). In the event, the town was betrayed within seven days; much too early for us to decide whether Caesar planned to blockade it, as at Alesia, or take more active measures, as for example at the town of the Atuatuci.

A blockading strategy was certainly preferred on a few occasions. In 49 BC, as Pompey prepared to evacuate his troops from Italy using the port of Brundisium, Caesar attempted to blockade the harbour. Again, his legionaries showed their engineering skills, extending breakwaters from either shore and linking them with a substantial turreted pontoon bridge. But Pompey's heavy transport vessels were able to infiltrate the still-unfinished barrier, and he evacuated his troops just as Caesar entered the town by escalade. In the following year, Caesar caught Pompey on the Adriatic coast, and tried to prevent him from reaching his supply base at Dyrrachium (modern Durrës in Albania) by throwing a ring of earthworks around his position. Pompey's response was to begin his own ring of earthworks inside Caesar's, forcing his enemy to extend

Napoléon III's interpretation of the Alesia siege-works, reconstructed at the Archéodrome near Beaune (France). On the left can be seen the 12ft-high (3.5m) palisaded rampart, with sharpened branches (cervi) projecting from the base of the wickerwork battlements. On the right, beyond the two ditches, Caesar's obstacle field starts with the entanglement of sharpened tree trunks known as cippi. (© Author)

CAESAR'S SIEGE OF ALESIA, 52 BC

Hemmed in by Caesar's siege-works, the Gauls manufactured wickerwork panels, and equipped themselves with ladders and grappling hooks. The panels were for bridging the ditches, along with earth infilling; the ladders were for mounting the rampart, and the hooks for pulling down the Roman parapet. The assault was supported by Gallic slingers and archers. Caesar records that the Romans drove back the Gauls 'with slings throwing 1lb stones, as well as with stakes which had been distributed within the siege-works, and sling bullets', and adds that 'many missiles were discharged from the artillery' (BGall. 7.81). Many who survived the barrage trod on the spikes or stumbled into the lily pits in Caesar's obstacle zone, and the assault finally failed.

The most recent findings have been incorporated to give an accurate picture of Caesar's fortifications on the Plaine des Laumes; note, for example, the closely spaced turrets and the light fences screening parts of the inner ditch. Most interesting of all is the compartment between the two siege lines (known as '4 bis'), which has been reconstructed as a *castellum*, with tented accommodation for around half of a legionary cohort. (Adam Hook © Osprey Publishing Ltd)

the outer line until it stretched for 17 miles (25km). 'This was a new and extraordinary method of making war', writes Caesar, 'as much for the number of forts, as for the extent and size of the fortifications, and the whole manner of the blockade' (*BCiv.* 3.47). After frequent skirmishes, Pompey saw that Caesar was weakest in the south, where he had completed his ring by running twin ramparts, 600ft (175m) apart, down to the sea, but had not yet linked them along the coast. (Once completed, it would have resembled one end of Scipio's works at Carthage, in miniature, and is reminiscent of the compartment at Alesia.) A concerted amphibious assault by Pompey overwhelmed Caesar's fortifications, and he abandoned the operation.

Most interesting of all, though, is the case of Q. Cassius Longinus, Caesar's general in Spain. In 47 BC, having quarrelled with his quaestor, M. Claudius Marcellus, he encamped outside Ulia, hoping to benefit from the town's protection. However, both he and the town were hemmed in by Marcellus, whose siege-works were perhaps conceived as a miniature version of Alesia; certainly, a substantial relief force is said to have been repulsed from the 'outer

The Gallic hillfort of Alesia, viewed from the east. The natural protection afforded by the plateau's steep sides discouraged the Romans from launching a direct assault. (© Archéologie aérienne René Goguey)

De Folard's imaginative reconstruction of the siege of Massilia in 49 BC shows the besiegers' brick tower (left). However, it is clear from Caesar's account that the 60ft-long (18m) gallery should extend from the tower right up to the town wall, giving complete protection to troops moving backwards and forwards. The wheeled shed is De Folard's own addition. (Author's collection)

fortifications' (*BAlex.* 62). Caesar's governor in the province, M. Aemilius Lepidus, duly arrived to arbitrate, and ordered Marcellus to dismantle the siege-works.

Of course, not all sieges of this period were conceived as blockades. Caesar's attack on Ategua in 45 BC, for example, resembles his earlier operations at Vellaunodunum and Uxellodunum. The first stage was to encircle the Pompeian-occupied town with earthworks; this was then followed by the construction of an embankment, although work was hampered by the defenders' incendiary attacks. A section of wall was demolished, no doubt by battering ram (the text of the *Bellum Hispaniense* has been damaged at this point), but skirmishing continued around the siege-works, and Caesar was obliged to throw a ring of soldiers around the town. The siege finally ended, not with a storming assault, but with the surrender of the disheartened Ateguans.

A more spectacular example of aggressive siegecraft is provided by the attack on coastal Massilia by Caesar's deputy, C. Trebonius, in 49 BC. He began to construct two embankments at different points on the landward side, but was severely hindered by the town's *ballistae*, which had allegedly been engineered to

THE ROMAN MUSCULUS

A particular type of shelter known as the *musculus* appears only rarely in ancient writings. Vegetius describes it as a small machine, reminiscent of the Hellenistic ditch-filling tortoise in its role of protecting men as they brought forward building materials (Veg., *Epit. rei mil.* 4.16). However, he is surely mistaken. From Caesar's description of the *musculus* in action during the siege of Massilia in 49 BC, it is clear that it was an enormously robust gallery, constructed when the standard *vineae* and *plutei* failed to stand up to the defenders' formidable artillery; its name, meaning 'little mouse', is surely another example of soldiers' humour.

The extra protection was required by men moving up to the enemy wall for undermining work. In other words, it was the Roman equivalent of the Hellenistic 'digging tortoise'. Caesar's version was 60ft (18m) long, 4ft (1.2m) wide, and 5ft (1.5m) tall, with a pitched roof. It was built out of 2ft-thick (0.6m) timbers, and entirely covered with a fireproof layer of tiles and clay, followed by a waterproof layer of rawhide, to foil any attempts at dissolving the clay (Caes., *BCiv.* 2.10). It was perhaps unusual to mobilize such a structure; at any rate, the defenders were taken by surprise when it was suddenly advanced to the wall on sets of rollers normally used to transport ships. With the *musculus* in place at the wall foot, the defenders were powerless to prevent the Romans from undermining one of the city's towers.

discharge 12ft (3.5m) iron-pointed spears instead of the usual rounded stone balls. The legionaries' standard wickerwork shelters (*vineae*) could not stand up to such punishment, so Trebonius arranged for the workers to be protected by galleries made out of timber 1ft thick (30cm). In addition, he had a 30ft-square (9m) brick refuge built close to the town, so that the workers could shelter within its 5ft-thick (1.5m) walls; but he quickly realized how useful a tower would be in this location, and again exploited the legionaries' engineering skills to raise the structure, under constant threat of enemy missiles, until it had six storeys. This opened up new possibilities, and Trebonius ordered a massive gallery to be built, 60ft (18m) long, stretching from the brick tower to the town wall. Realizing the danger posed by the gallery, the Massiliotes tipped blocks of masonry and blazing barrels of pitch onto it from the battlements above. But they were driven back by the artillery in the brick tower, and their improvised missiles were easily deflected by the gallery's 2ft-thick (60cm) gabled roof, with its coating of padded rawhide over clay. Then, concealed within the gallery, Trebonius' legionaries undermined the town wall, whereupon the townsfolk lost hope and surrendered.

Caesar's murder in 44 BC sparked off a new round of civil war involving his adopted son Octavian (the future emperor Augustus) and his erstwhile lieutenant M. Antonius (Shakespeare's Mark Antony). Again, a full range of siegecraft is in evidence. For example, late in 44 BC, Antony encircled Mutina (now Modena in northern Italy), where one of Caesar's murderers, Decimus Brutus, had taken refuge, but he was increasingly threatened by successive relieving forces and departed in the following spring. Octavian perhaps drew a lesson from Antony's failure. Late in 41 BC, when he trapped Antony's brother Lucius in Perusia (modern Perugia), he built an elaborate system of siege-works 'with two fronts, facing the besieged and any coming from outside' (App., *BCiv.* 5.33); Appian adds that the 10km circuit was studded with wooden towers, and sharpened stakes were added to the ditch. Lucius was forced to surrender, after failing in his desperate attempts to break out. In 40 BC, when Brundisium (modern Brindisi in the heel of Italy) shut its gates against Antony, he cut off the town with a wall and ditch and summoned his siege machinery, but Octavian encamped nearby and the generals finally made peace with one another.

Armies operating in the eastern provinces were more ready to employ the techniques of Hellenistic siegecraft, either because the expertise was available there, or the sophisticated town defences demanded special measures. In 43 BC, another of Caesar's murderers, C. Cassius Longinus, built a wall across the neck of the Laodicea peninsula, trapping the governor of Syria, P. Cornelius Dolabella, in the town there. A naval defeat denied Dolabella an escape like that of Pompey from Brundisium, and Cassius proceeded to threaten the town wall with an embankment; but the town fell to betrayal. In the following year, while Cassius moved on to besiege Rhodes, his co-conspirator, M. Junius Brutus, assaulted Xanthus. The townsfolk had demolished the extramural buildings to deny their use to the besiegers as a source of timber; they took the further precaution of digging a 50ft (15m) defensive ditch, but Brutus' troops worked night and day to level out the terrain, and the Roman siege machinery soon arrived at the walls, where the townsfolk lost no time in setting fire to it. Plutarch claims that a change in the wind blew the flames back on the town, creating a conflagration (Plut., *Brut.* 30–31), but Appian writes that, when the Romans broke into the town, the inhabitants burned themselves and their possessions on bonfires (App., *BCiv.* 4.80). Whichever is true, the destruction of the town distressed Brutus, who had wanted only to extort money and troops.

A full mechanized assault was necessary in 37 BC, when Herod the Great, in alliance with Antony's general, C. Sosius, attempted to recapture Jerusalem from the renegade Antigonus. As in Pompey's siege of 63 BC, embankments were raised for the advance of siege towers and battering rams against the

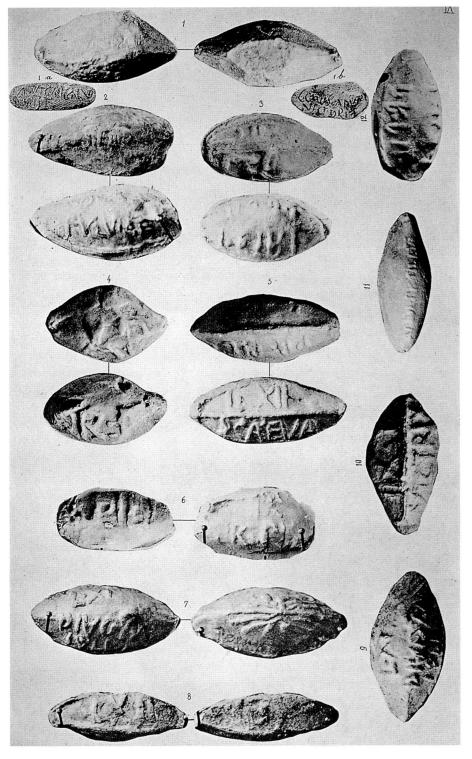

A selection of lead sling bullets from the siege of Perusia, 41/40 BC. The thunderbolt motif, which recurs on many bullets, can be seen on no. 7. Some bullets carry references to legions and personalities, such as no. 5, which names Caesar's redoubtable centurion Scaeva. Others carry insulting obscenities, such as no. 2, which names as its intended target the sexual organs of Antony's wife Fulvia. (C. Zangemeister, Ephemeris Epigraphica 6, Rome & Berlin, 1885)

city's formidable defences, and the fortifications of the Temple platform were taken by escalade. Antony probably planned the same kind of operation when he arrived before the Parthian capital of Praaspa in 36 BC, but his 300 wagon-loads of siege machinery lagged behind and easily fell prey to a Parthian attack. Although he raised siege embankments, perhaps hoping to use them for an infantry assault as Caesar had done at Avaricum, he was eventually forced into an ignominious withdrawal, during which he lost around 20,000 legionaries.

Earthworks and siege machinery capture the imagination, but Roman armies had not lost their appetite for the simple brutality of the frontal assault. For example, in 43 BC, P. Cornelius Dolabella (destined to die months later in Laodicea) took the town of Smyrna in a classic *coup de main* under cover of night; when the general in charge, C. Trebonius, ordered his captors to take him to Dolabella, they replied that their general wished to see only Trebonius' head (App., *BCiv.* 3.26). In 35 BC, Octavian attempted a storming assault at Metulum, a town in present-day Croatia, raising embankments against the walls and throwing four boarding-bridges across; but when three of them broke under the weight of the intense hand-to-hand fighting, the men refused to use the fourth, until Octavian himself ran out onto it. Although this one also broke, the townsfolk were sufficiently intimidated to surrender.

RULES OF SIEGECRAFT?

Some scholars have argued that the Romans were bound by law to spare a town that surrendered, but this is nonsense. It is clear that writers like Sallust and Appian expected an honourable commander to show some degree of mercy, but Marius' treatment of Capsa in 107 BC shows that wider strategic requirements could take precedence (above, p. 130). As a further example, while the Romans were engaged in settling a dynastic dispute in Judaea in 57 BC, the fortresses of Alexandrion, Hyrcania and Machaerus were surrendered, yet their defences were demolished, no doubt to prevent their use by rebels. More usually, the fate of a town rested simply on the mood of the commander, as with Sulla's sack of Aeclanum in 88 BC (above, p. 133). Praeneste provides a more chilling example: Sulla certainly spared any Roman citizens among the population, but he had all the locals and the hated Samnites slaughtered, and plundered the town's wealth.

Another modern myth involves the battering ram as a symbolic initiator of the siege. It has been variously claimed that, once the battering commenced, there was no turning back; or that the option of surrender was rescinded as soon as the battering ram touched the wall. This notion is easily dispelled by reference to Octavian's siege of Metulum, where his initial battering assault was foiled by the construction of a new wall behind the breached wall; when his attempt to reach the new wall by boarding-bridge, though unsuccessful, nevertheless alarmed the townsfolk, he was happy to accept their surrender. (In the event, they later reneged on the peace terms and had to be slaughtered.) But the idea of the battering ram as a point of no return derives from a misunderstanding of Caesar's ultimatum to the Atuatuci. He clearly implies that he will accept their surrender, only if they save him the trouble of bringing up his battering ram; far from obeying a fictional tenet of Roman law, he says that he is doing this 'rather because it is his habit [i.e., to be merciful] than because the Atuatuci might deserve it' (Caes., BGall. 2.32). Scholars have also pointed to Cicero's general plea, that mercy should be shown not only to those who have been conquered, but also to those who have surrendered to avoid conquest, 'however much the ram struck their wall' (Cic., Off. 1.35). This is simply a rhetorical flourish, and should not be taken to prove that there was a rule whereby mercy was never shown to those who surrendered during a battering attack.

Siege Warfare During the Principate

When we turn to the Principate, the period of Roman history that covers the reigns of the emperors down to AD 284, few sieges are known in detail. Although Octavian (known, from 27 BC, as the emperor Augustus) continued to employ encircling tactics, for example at the mountain stronghold known as Mons Medullius, greater emphasis was again given to the storming assault. In AD 9, while campaigning in Dalmatia (an area now encompassing Croatia, Bosnia and Yugoslavia), the armies of Germanicus and the future emperor Tiberius stormed a succession of strongholds. At Splonum, there is the curious case of the cavalryman who terrified the defenders by knocking down a section of parapet with a stone; and at Raetinum, the townsfolk waited for the Romans to break in, before setting fire to the place and fleeing to safety.

A generation later, Cn. Domitius Corbulo, Nero's successful general (so successful that the emperor had him killed), was famous for saying that 'the pickaxe was the means of vanquishing the enemy' (Frontin., *Strat.* 4.7.2). Although he might seem to have been advising the reduction of strongholds by digging siege-works, Corbulo was probably advocating the protection of a campaigning army by carefully entrenching a camp each evening. His dynamic style of siegecraft is typified, not by earthworks, but by the kind of storming assault that he unleashed at Volandum in AD 58. Having set up a long-range barrage from catapults, slingers and stonethrowers, he sent one task force to undermine the defences, protected by a *testudo* shield-formation, while another moved ladders up to the wall; 'the attack was so energetic', writes the historian

Tacitus, 'that within a third of the day the walls were stripped of their defenders, the barricades at the gates were overthrown, the fortifications were scaled and captured, and every adult was butchered' (Tac., *Ann.* 13.39). When his army subsequently arrived outside Artaxata, the townsfolk immediately surrendered, thereby saving their lives, although nothing could stop Corbulo demolishing their town.

THE JEWISH WAR, AD 66–74

The readiness of Roman armies to storm fortifications is again apparent from the events at such towns as Joppa, Gabara, Japha and Gerasa, during Rome's First Jewish War. Typically, once the defences were scaled, all males of sword-bearing age were slaughtered and the legionaries were given free rein to plunder and

Tiberius' siege of Andetrium, AD 9. When the future emperor Tiberius was sent to Dalmatia to put down an uprising, he trapped Bato, the ringleader, in the hilltop fortress. Tiberius ordered an uphill assault, while he watched from a platform. It was a common tactic for the besieged to roll heavy objects downhill. The place was finally captured when a detachment of Romans made a wide detour and surprised the defenders by appearing on their flank. (Adam Hook © Osprey Publishing Ltd)

165

destroy. But these rapid actions have been overshadowed by the detailed accounts of more elaborate operations at Jotapata, Gamala and Jerusalem, and the spectacular archaeological remains at Masada.

At Jotapata in the early summer of AD 67, after the defenders had endured a week of assaults and had beaten each one back, the future emperor Vespasian decided to construct an embankment up to the walls. His intention, like Caesar's at Avaricum, was to enable his legionaries to storm across onto the battlements, but the defenders foiled his plan by heightening the town wall at this point. The historian Josephus, who was present as the defending general, records that Vespasian then brought up a battering ram, under cover of a missile barrage (see illustration pp. 168–69). But, although the wall was finally breached, the Roman attack was repulsed and Vespasian had no option but to increase the scale of the operation, yet again. This time, three 50ft (15m) iron-clad siege towers were constructed to overlook the town walls, while the embankment was again heightened. Finally, writes Josephus, 'on the forty-seventh day, the Roman embankments overtopped the wall' (Joseph., *BJ* 3.316); that night, the legionaries silently crossed over into the town and began the slaughter, sparing only the women and children to be sold into slavery.

The largest ballista used by Roman armies shot stones weighing 80 Roman lbs (1 talent, or 26kg). It was probably a machine of this size that, according to Josephus, smashed the battlements at Jotapata and knocked a man's head cleanly off his shoulders. The experimental machine depicted here was built for BBC Television; it is probably set at too high an angle for optimum shooting. (© A. Wilkins)

Some months later, at Gamala, Vespasian again countered difficult terrain by building an embankment for battering rams. But when the legionaries eagerly burst into the town, they were hindered by the steep, narrow streets, and presented a static target for the missiles of the defenders, huddled high on the hillside. They withdrew as rapidly as possible, but a second attack succeeded, after one of the towers on the town wall was undermined. The legionaries set about their usual business, and according to Josephus (perhaps exaggerating only a little) 'blood, pouring downhill, flooded the whole town' (Joseph., *BJ* 4.72).

The war reached its climax in AD 70 when, yet again, a Roman army arrived outside Jerusalem. Vespasian's son Titus orchestrated a full-scale siege, no doubt fully aware of previous Roman operations here. As Tacitus later commented, 'all the devices for conquering a town, known from the ancients or newly thought up, were assembled' (Tac., *Hist.* 5.13). Three embankments were constructed to carry battering rams against the outer wall, a new defence since the days of Pompey and Herod; a second wall was breached and taken; then two pairs of embankments were thrown up against the Temple platform. When one pair collapsed to undermining, and the other went up in flames, Titus briefly flirted

(Continued p.170)

Aerial view of Yodefat (Israel), ancient Jotapata, looking south. Archaeological investigations on the northern slopes uncovered mortar and rubble which perhaps belonged to Vespasian's siege embankment. Quantities of arrowheads also came to light, along with two hobnails from the sole of a legionary's boot. (© M. Aviam)

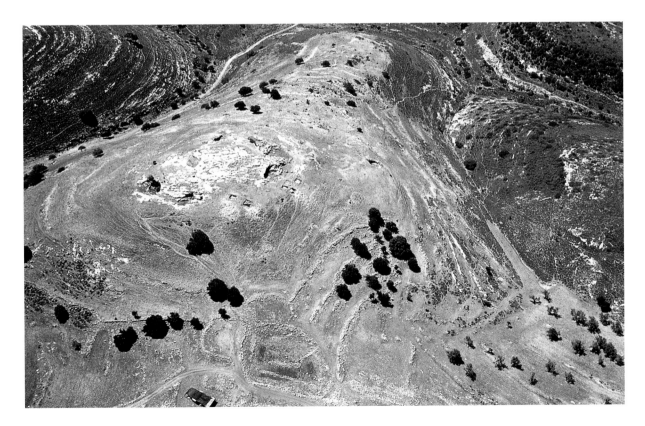

Vespasian's siege of Jotapata, AD 67

The Roman siege embankment at Jotapata was originally intended to elevate the legionaries to parapet level, but when the townsfolk cunningly heightened the wall to 20 cubits (9m), the Romans had no option but to break through, and the embankment became the runway for a battering ram. As Josephus comments, 'the Roman commander resorted to this plan, in his eagerness to take the town by storm' (*BJ* 3.218).

Catapults, archers and slingers maintained a constant barrage, so that the defenders would stay under cover and not interfere with the ramming work. But some, venturing onto the battlements to disrupt the operation, lowered sacks of chaff in front of the ram-head to deaden its blows; others rushed out with firebrands to set the Roman siege-work ablaze. Although one Jew managed to drop a boulder onto the ram and break its head off, the machine was soon repaired and the battering resumed. (Adam Hook © Osprey Publishing Ltd)

The ancient site of Gamala (Israel), a steep-sided hill accessible only from the east, along a narrow neck of land (bottom right). The town wall was breached below the synagogue (bottom left). Over the years, archaeological work has turned up huge quantities of arrowheads and small ballista balls. (© Author)

with the idea of blockading the city, and had his men construct a 40-stade (7km) encircling wall, complete with 13 forts. As usual with major construction projects, the work gangs vied with one another to be first finished; 'the whole thing was built in three days', writes Josephus (*BJ* 5.509); 'for work worthy of months, the speed defied belief' (prompting one translator to comment wryly, 'indeed it does!'). But, as so often in the past, no sooner was the encirclement complete than the assault began again in earnest. A new embankment carried rams up to the formidable Antonia fortress, which sat at the corner of the Temple platform; the demolition of the fortress opened up a broad ascent onto the platform itself, where the Temple was finally destroyed, despite Titus' protestations. In the days and weeks to follow, the looting and slaughter spread down into the city.

(Continued p.174)

Brian Delf © Osprey Publishing Ltd

THE ROMAN SIEGE TOWER

From around 200 BC, Roman armies made increasing use of siege towers. On one of the earliest occasions, however, at the Greek town of Atrax, their inexperience with heavy machinery led to disaster, when a siege tower foundered on a poorly compacted embankment; one wheel became stuck in a rut, causing the machine to list violently, and the whole enterprise was abandoned (above, p. 109). Later operations were conducted more successfully.

Vegetius gives a brief but comprehensive description of the mobile tower, as it might have appeared in the mid-1st century AD (Veg., *Epit. rei mil.* 4.17). He begins by emphasizing that, for stability, different heights of siege tower required different base dimensions, and suggests bases of 30ft (8.9m), 40ft (11.8m), and 50ft (14.8m) square. Unfortunately, he does not mention the corresponding heights, but they would not have been excessive. Although ten-storey siege towers are recorded from the time of Caesar (*BAlex.* 2), the towers constructed during Rome's Jewish War varied from the 50ft (14.8m) examples at Jotapata in AD 67 (Joseph., *BJ* 3.284) to the 50-cubit (22.2m) ones at Jerusalem in AD 70 (Joseph, *BJ* 5.292). In each case, their height was commensurate with their role in protecting the men who were working on the embankment. It is true that the Romans used a 60-cubit (90ft or 26.6m) machine to assault Masada in AD 74 (Joseph., *BJ* 7.309), but this was necessitated by the local topography. By and large, it is clear that, by the mid-1st century AD, the guiding principle of military engineering was functionality, in place of the Hellenistic fascination with awesome size.

Vegetius mentions three distinct levels in his tower, but intermediate stages would have been inserted according to the desired height. At ground level, in an unusual departure from the Hellenistic design but entirely in keeping with Roman pragmatism, it was equipped with a battering ram. In the middle, it carried a boarding-bridge (*exostra*), 'made from two beams and fenced with wickerwork'. And at the top, it incorporated a fighting platform for spearmen and archers, whose task was to provide a covering bombardment. Unfortunately, the undercarriage is not described, but Vegetius' reference to 'many wheels' suggests that there were more than the basic four, though we can only guess at their size and disposition.

As a defence against fire, the entire structure was clad in rawhide and layers of rags; the rags would surely have been inflammable, unless they were stuffed beneath the rawhide to form a cushioned layer. Vegetius advises those opposing a siege tower to strip off the rawhide, whereupon the machine would be vulnerable to burning; if this cannot be accomplished, he says, the defenders must ensure that their incendiary missiles pierce the fireproof layer. It was probably to counter this risk that, during Rome's Jewish War (AD 66–74), the siege towers were clad with iron plates; the weight penalty must have been offset by the benefit of increased protection. Engineers may not always have been mindful of the extra stress that heavy cladding imposed on the framework, judging by the spontaneous collapse of one of the siege towers at Jerusalem in AD 70 (Joseph., *BJ* 5.292-5).

As far as the boarding-bridge is concerned, Vegetius calls it a 'bridge (*pons*) ... which the soldiers fix between the siege tower and the wall, when it is suddenly extended; using it to come out of the machine, they cross over into the town and occupy the walls'. It was evidently pushed forwards, but no construction details exist. Wickerwork fencing no doubt extended along each side, as much to prevent the soldiers from falling off as to give them a modicum of protection. It would have been important for such a bridge to be at the precise height of the enemy battlements, so that the soldiers would not have to negotiate an unfavourable gradient.

Vegetius also mentions the *sambuca* as an alternative form of boarding-bridge. This device, he says, is so named from its similarity to a harp, for 'just as there are strings on a harp, so on a beam which is attached to the siege tower, there are ropes which lower a bridge from above by means of pulleys, so that it descends to the wall, and immediately the soldiers come out of the tower and, using it to cross over, they invade the town walls'. This is similar to the shipboard *sambuca* that differed substantially from Damios' wheeled version (above, pp. 140–141).

Finally, Vegetius briefly describes the unusual stratagem of incorporating within the tower a concealed turret, which could suddenly be hoisted into position using ropes and pulleys, if the defenders managed to heighten their walls. If this is anything more than a flight of fancy, the turret must have been of rather less substantial construction than the parent tower in order to be easily winched into place.

Camp C at Masada, viewed from the west. Schulten interpreted the rows of dry-stone structures inside the camp as barrack blocks, but the British archaeologist Sir Ian Richmond suggested that they were dwarf walls on which the soldiers pitched their tents to obtain cooler accommodation with less effort. (© Author)

Although the fall of Jerusalem signalled the end of the war, rebels still held three of the fortified palaces originally built by Herod. At the first of these, Herodium, we know nothing of the siege. At the second, Machaerus in present-day Jordan, Josephus records that, 'after reconnoitring the vicinity, [the Roman commander Sextus Lucilius Bassus] decided to make his approach by heaping up [an embankment] in the eastern ravine, and set to work, hurrying to raise the embankment swiftly and thereby make the siege easy' (Joseph., *BJ* 7.190). The archaeological remains show that, on the contrary, Bassus planned his assault from the west. It is on this side that the unfinished siege embankment can still be seen, and some way behind it a small camp of 0.44 acre (0.18ha), which might have accommodated 100 or so men within its 9½ ft-thick (2.9m) ramparts. Another nine or ten camps, most of them much smaller, are dotted around the site, linked by the disjointed lengths of a 3km circumvallation. However, it was not by assault that Bassus conquered the place, but by a ruse: having captured one of the rebels trying to attack the Roman lines, Bassus threatened to crucify him, whereupon the defenders surrendered.

THE SIEGE OF MASADA, AD 74

The third of Herod's palaces provided the setting for the most famous siege of the Jewish War, perhaps the best-known siege of all, at Masada; along with Numantia and Alesia, it offers that rarest of opportunities – the combining of historical narrative with archaeology. Bassus had died in office, so a new Roman commander, L. Flavius Silva, was sent out; the evidence of inscriptions suggests that he was given the Judaean command some time in AD 73, and must have arrived late in the year to begin preparations for the siege. Like Scipio at Numantia, he 'immediately seized the whole area by establishing garrisons in the most suitable locations, threw up a wall in a ring around the whole fortress, so that it would not be easy for any of the besieged to escape, and distributed men to keep watch' (Joseph., *BJ* 7.275–6).

Studying aerial photographs of the site in 1929, the British archaeologist Christopher Hawkes believed that Silva had first encamped on the east side in Camp B, before transferring his legion to Camp F in the west. However, recognizing a parallel with Numantia, the German archaeologist Schulten realized that the two positions were complementary. Silva was simply following the standard practice of ensuring maximum visibility of the besieged fortress; in this respect, Camps B and F fulfil the same role as Castillejo and Dehesilla (or Peña Redonda) at Numantia, and Camps A (or B) and C at Alesia. Once the 4.5km siege wall was laid out, Camp C would have provided the manpower to patrol the eastern sector; at just over an acre (0.43ha), it should be classified as a small fort, but lacking the fort's usual administrative buildings, it could have accommodated around 500 men. The similarly sized Camp E probably fulfilled the same role in the west. The smaller encampments, A and D in the east, G and H in the west, perhaps each held 200–300 men. Visitors to the site can still appreciate the observational role of tiny Camp H, whose position perched high on the southern cliffs parallels that of Cañal at Numantia.

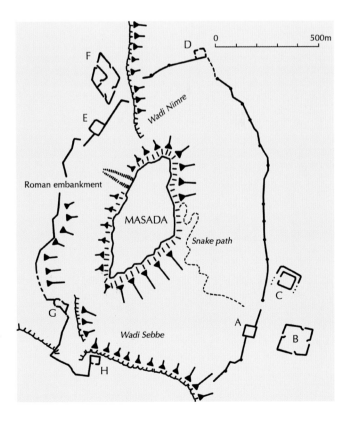

Plan of Masada, showing Flavius Silva's circumvallation with associated camps (labelled B and F) and forts. The security of the exposed eastern stretch was tightened by a series of towers. An earlier camp appears to underlie C, and may have belonged to an advance reconnaissance party. (© Author)

175

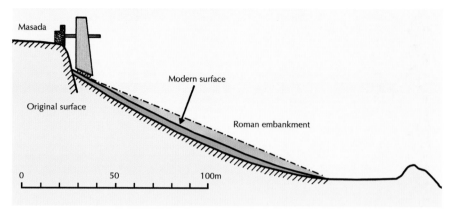

Masada

Modern surface

Original surface

Roman embankment

0   50   100m

General Adolf Lammerer first realized that the Roman siege embankment at Masada was built on an existing geological spur, sloping up to the fortress. His suggested gradient of 19° required up to 60ft (20m) of material to be added (shown here as a dashed line). More recently, Dan Gill has suggested that only about 1m has eroded from the present-day surface. (© Author, after Lammerer)

Having encircled the enemy fortress, Silva began the next phase of assault by constructing an embankment. Again, these were tried and tested tactics, but the logistical feat seems incredible to the present-day visitor. Josephus says that Silva found only one place capable of supporting an embankment, namely Leuke ('the white place'), which he describes as a 'very broad rocky prominence which ran far out, 300 cubits [450ft or 135m] below the height of Masada' (Joseph., *BJ* 7.305). When Schulten explored the site in 1932, he was accompanied by General Adolf Lammerer, who suspected that the Romans had simply built the framework of their embankment onto an existing spur, jutting from the side of Masada. This has now been proven by the geologist Dan Gill, who has estimated that the bulk of the present-day ramp is a natural chalk outcrop, topped by 13–16ft (4–5m) of compacted debris. The striking coloration of the chalk spur suggests that this was Josephus' Leuke (although its base lies 300 feet below the plateau, not 300 cubits). Josephus describes the raising of the embankment:

> Ascending onto it and occupying it, Silva ordered his army to pile up an embankment. Working eagerly and with many hands, the embankment was firmly raised up to 200 cubits [300ft or 90m]. But he thought that it was neither firm enough nor sufficiently large to be a foundation for machinery, so a layer of large stones was fitted together on top, 50 cubits [75ft or 22m] in breadth and height (Joseph., *BJ* 7.306–7).

No vestiges of this extra layer have ever been found. It is sometimes interpreted as a separate platform at the head of the embankment, but Silva's siege tower required a smooth runway right up to the wall. Hawkes' suggestion of a stone causeway running up the crest of the embankment is the most plausible, but Josephus' measurements are problematic, unless his '200 cubits' refers to the original spur, and his '50 cubits' to the material piled on top by the Romans. However, Gill has suggested that, originally, this material averaged only 8m in thickness (6m along the crest, 10m on the sloping flanks), creating a smooth runway which, at its apex, fell 12m short of Masada's summit. Certainly, this would explain the extreme height which Josephus attributes to

Silva's siege tower; at 60 cubits (27m), it was considerably higher than previous Roman towers, but this increase ensured that the top 10m overlooked the fortress battlements.

The iron-clad tower was reportedly equipped with catapults, and probably also held the battering ram that Silva finally deployed against the wall. However, it was well known that rams worked most successfully against stone fortifications, by dislodging individual blocks and shaking the wall apart, so when the Romans breached Masada's wall, the defenders threw up a timber-laced earthwork, against which the ram was powerless. As Josephus says, 'the blows of the machinery were weak from being directed against material which yielded and settled with the battering and became more solid' (Joseph., *BJ* 7.314). Accordingly, Silva resorted to the age-old expedient of setting fire to the woodwork, but the next day, when his troops entered Masada, they found that the defenders had committed mass suicide.

View of Masada from the west. The white mass of the siege embankment, clearly visible climbing the side of the mountain, represents an extraordinary solution to a particular problem. It is likely that a more gentle gradient was usually preferred. (© Author)

The imposing rock of Masada, viewed from the Roman position in Camp H, to the south. Soldiers posted here were ideally placed to monitor any movement in the fortress. (© Author)

Modern scholars often imagine that this period was the high water mark of ancient siege warfare, although no obvious superiority can be discerned over the siegecraft of Sulla or Caesar. Marsden pointed to the 160 artillery pieces that Vespasian deployed at Jotapata as being a decisive factor, and it is true that, apart from their firepower, their psychological effect must have bolstered the army's performance while eroding the defenders' confidence. But the tactics of the period can readily be paralleled from the sieges of earlier times. The massive preparations at Jotapata recall those of Caesar at Avaricum; the desperate street fighting in Gamala can be matched by Caesar's repulse from Gergovia; and at Masada, the circumvallation is a distant echo of Scipio's encirclement of Numantia, while Silva's tactics are the direct descendant of Cicero's at Pindenissus.

SIEGES OF THE 2ND CENTURY AD

Even during the periods of conquest that marked the reigns of emperors like Trajan (r. AD 97–117) and Septimius Severus (r. AD 193–211), reports of sieges are few and far between. This is not to say that no siege warfare occurred; only that the relevant historical reports have not survived. For example, Trajan's Column in Rome shows scenes of Dacian tribesmen attacking Roman fortifications and Romans attacking Dacian hillforts, and the Column of Marcus Aurelius has scenes of legionaries looting German villages. It is particularly unfortunate that we lack a full description of the epic siege that gripped Byzantium between AD 193 and 195, as the defenders strove to repulse Severus' general, L. Marius Maximus.

Hatra, viewed from the north-east. The town is surrounded by a siege wall, which can be seen crossing the photo from left to right and running off into the distance. No associated camps or guard posts have been identified, and it may have been the work of Persian besiegers in AD 240. (© Author)

179

THE SIEGE TOWER OF APOLLODORUS

The siege tower described by Trajan's engineer Apollodorus demonstrates a very basic design, perhaps tailored to particular circumstances where wood was in short supply. His instructions proceed point by point, and were apparently delivered to the emperor by a trained apprentice who was familiar with his master's machines.

Apollodorus begins by recommending that, for safety, the erection of the siege tower be carried out at some distance from the enemy walls. This really goes without saying; it was, after all, the principal reason for furnishing the various machines with wheels, and as such will have been common practice. On the other hand, it was definitely not common practice for a military engineer to restrict himself to short beam-lengths, but Apollodorus' chief concern is the ready supply of materials; he proudly announces that, by following his instructions, 'using few and short timbers, a large tower is raised, equal in height to the wall' (Apoll. 167.8–10).

Indeed, the longest timbers were only 16ft (4.7m) long and 1¼ft (37cm) wide by 1 span (22cm) thick. The four corner uprights of the tower were triple thickness, and converged gradually towards the top. The base consisted of two pairs of parallel joists, with the wheels fixed between each pair. Unfortunately, Apollodorus does not elaborate on this, but there would have been ample space for two wheels per side, around 2⅖ft (74cm) in diameter, each on its own short axle.

Once it was built, the entire structure was boarded over with planks. Apollodorus first suggests that animal hides should be loosely hung all around for protection, 'not fitted to the planks, so that they have room to bunch together and absorb the missiles' (Apoll. 173.15–16); he then recommends that the planks be fastened with broad-headed nails and covered with a thick layer of clay, a method of fireproofing found on other machines. Later, almost as an afterthought, he recommends a primitive fire hose device called the siphōn, consisting of ox intestines attached to leather sacks of water; theoretically, in the event of fire, squeezing the sacks would cause water to spray out.

The top storey remained open to the elements, but was provided with a parapet of boarding. The tower's purpose, as a protected staircase, was achieved by an internal system of ladders leading to a top-storey drawbridge of ingenious design. Hinged at the floor, its side-beams were 20ft (5.9m) long, but the drawbridge itself was solid for only a quarter of that; the remainder was an open frame, like a window. The result was that, while in the upright position, it appeared to be a continuation of the top storey parapet, forming, as Apollodorus says, 'a defence (proteichisma) for the fighters in the tower' (Apoll. 168.9). The drawbridge was operated by ropes running from the corner uprights, similar to Vegetius' sambuca. When these were released, the drawbridge lowered and a system of rush matting, strengthened with rigid crosspieces, was extended across the unboarded section, to create a solid bridge.

Apollodorus' tower probably required only three or four storeys to ensure that the drawbridge lay at wall-height. With its small footprint and compact design, it is quite a different machine from its Macedonian forebears. Apollodorus is perhaps mindful of the machine's stability when he recommends a specially levelled running surface: 'if the ground underneath is not smooth but has hollows, we shall construct a base (hypothēma) for the tower, with a similar arrangement [of beams?] as the tower, which evens out the slope of the ground and makes a level surface, on account of its construction' (Apoll. 173.9–12). This tantalizingly brief sentence may represent Apollodorus' description of the agger, or embankment, which became almost the hallmark of Roman siegecraft.

Siege warfare in the East was overshadowed by three unsuccessful attempts on Hatra in present-day Iraq. First, Trajan attempted to capture the prosperous desert town in AD 117, but was almost shot while reconnoitring; poor weather and the attentions of troublesome insects forced his withdrawal. Then, campaigning in the same area 80 years later, Septimius Severus twice lost his siege machinery to the defenders' incendiary attacks (AD 198/199). On the second attempt, he managed to breach the outer wall, but even 20 days in the stifling heat was too long for his European veterans, who were already resentful after his execution of their favourite officer; Severus, like Trajan, had to acknowledge defeat at Hatra.

THE RAM-TORTOISE OF THE ROMANS

The battering ram remained the standard assault weapon throughout the Roman period. The geographer Pausanias, writing around AD 150, provides the interesting information that walls of mud-brick withstood battering more effectively than stone walls, whose individual blocks tended to shatter or become dislodged (Paus. 8.8.8). The same effect is noted by Apollodorus, who explains that brick walls absorb impact, whereas battering shakes stone walls apart (Apoll. 157.7–158.4). Nevertheless, by Roman times, the most common defences were of stone-faced rubble; demolishing the facing would cause the core to collapse.

Naturally, Apollodorus includes a ram-tortoise in the arsenal of machines that he offers to the emperor Trajan. However, its four key design principles stand in stark contrast to the philosophy of Diades or Hegetor (above, pp. 76 and 88). First, the suspension ropes had to be long to allow the ramming-beam a full range of movement and produce a powerful battering action; second, the tortoise had to be compact and easy to move; third, the sides had to slope steeply so that heavy missiles would glance off without

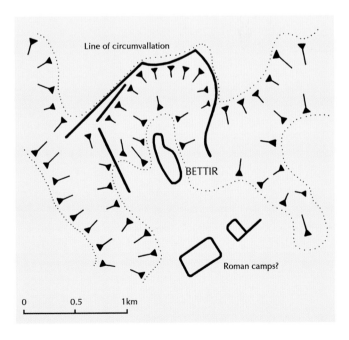

The stronghold of Bettir (Israel) was blockaded by Hadrian's general C. Julius Severus during the Second Jewish War (AD 131–5). The siege-works are known only from field-walking and aerial reconnaissance. The double wall which Schulten detected at the north-west corner may simply be the result of a realignment. (© Author)

A reconstruction of the ram-tortoise described by Apollodorus of Damascus. The outer cladding of timber and wickerwork, covered with a fireproof layer of clay, has been omitted, so that the frame and undercarriage can be seen. (© P. Slisz)

doing damage; and fourth, the ram head had to be protected from above by a projecting roof.

The design of the tortoise was certainly simple enough. Its 12ft-wide (3.5m) undercarriage comprised two pairs of joists, with the wheels located between each pair, just like the siege tower (see p. 180). Along each of the outer joists were four rafters, which rose at a steep angle to support a longitudinal ridge beam. The rafters were braced halfway up by internal uprights, sitting on the inner joists, and the whole structure was strengthened by being boarded over with 4-dactyl thick (3in or 7cm) planks. Apparently, this main shed was supplemented by 'the one behind, of lesser height, for the crew, and two other smaller ones behind, necessary for their safe passage' (Apoll. 155.13–15).

During the ramming, Apollodorus recommends that the undercarriage be raised on wedges, to prevent the machine from rolling back with each blow (Apoll. 157.1–6). The projecting roof was achieved by making the ridge beam longer than the undercarriage beams. Accepting a length of 24ft (7m) for the undercarriage, as proposed by the anonymous Byzantine writer, the ridge beam would then measure perhaps 30ft (9m) or so. This would certainly square with Apollodorus' stated aim of using short timbers to design easily transported machines.

Apollodorus suggests that the ramming-beam was hung so that the front end was longer, with a lead weight attached to the rear end to restore the balance; the result, he claims, was increased power, as if from a heavier beam. Rope binding is mentioned, but only in the context of constructing a composite beam from two or three shorter pieces. In contrast to the likes of Hegetor's ram, the head was slotted into the beam, and fastened by an iron collar to prevent the wood from splitting.

It seems to have been conventional to cast the iron ram head as an effigy of the actual animal's head. Proof of this comes from a brief description of the battering rams used during Rome's Jewish War (AD 66–74):

> This is an immense beam, resembling the mast of a ship; it is capped at the front by a mass of iron, modelled like a ram's head, from which it takes its name. It is hung in the middle by ropes, just like one of the beams in balancing-scales, [and is] supported by firmly based uprights on each side. Pushed back by a crowd of men, and swung forwards by them in a mass, it strikes the wall with the projecting iron (Joseph, *BJ* 3.214–6).

Although Josephus witnessed the machine in action, he had little grasp of its structure, and may never have seen beneath the outer shed; he vaguely alludes to wickerwork panels and rawhides protecting the machine and its crew. His frequent references to the machine as a *helepolis* (e.g., *BJ* 3.230–1) should not mislead us into imagining something along the lines of Vegetius' combined tower and ram (above, pp. 172–173), for there is not the slightest hint that this is anything other than a ram-tortoise.

By good fortune, two ram-tortoises can be seen on one of the sculptured panels of the Arch of Septimius Severus, which was erected in AD 203. Both depict the sloping roof and triangular cross section characteristic of the Roman version of the machine, and Apollodorus' recommendation that a second tortoise should follow behind, to shelter the ramming crew, is illustrated by one of the machines.

SIEGES OF THE 3RD CENTURY AD

Historical sources for warfare in the 3rd century are even more fragmentary than for the 2nd, and modern commentators shy away from discussion. Fortunately, archaeology has come to the rescue with two splendid siege sites, the first at Dura Europos in Syria and the second at Cremna in south-west Turkey.

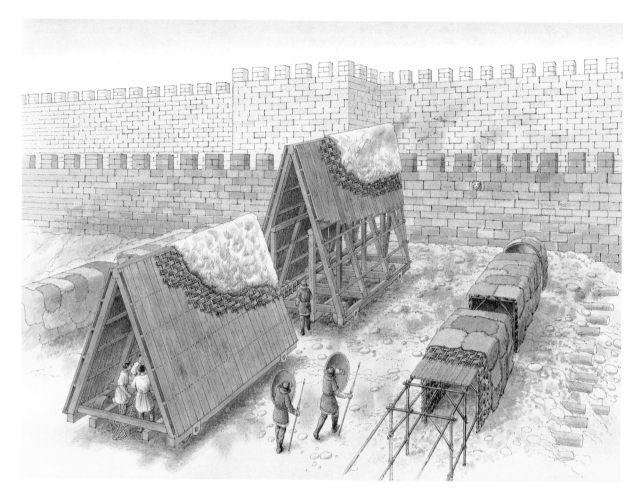

Roman battering ram. Apollodorus' ram-tortoise is completely different from its Hellenistic precursors, with a basically rectangular undercarriage, 11½ft (3.5m) wide, supporting a ridge-beam some 23ft (7m) above the ground. This results in a steeply sloping roof, designed to deflect the projectiles that the enemy habitually dropped from the battlement. (Brian Delf © Osprey Publishing Ltd)

Around AD 256, the Roman garrison occupying the desert town of Dura Europos began preparations to withstand an impending Persian attack. As the town was protected by natural ravines to the north, south and east, only the western side required attention; here, the Romans shored up the wall with great sloping banks of earth in front and behind. This had less to do with keeping siege machinery away from the walls, which could best have been achieved by digging wide ditches, and more to do with tackling undermining; for, if the walls were undermined, the makeshift buttresses would encourage slumping rather than total collapse. And, indeed, when the Persians successfully undermined Tower 19, midway along the town wall, only this emergency shoring preserved the defences. However, the subsequent abandonment of the town suggests that it was finally captured.

In the early 1930s, a Franco-American team of archaeologists discovered a Persian tunnel (Tunnel 1), measuring approximately 4ft (1.20m) wide by 6ft

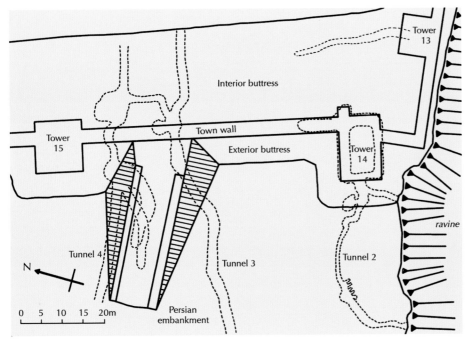

Plan of the Persian siege-
works at Dura Europos. The
convoluted arrangement of
tunnels underneath the siege
embankment would benefit
from further archaeological
investigation. The feature
running north-west from
Tower 13, once thought to
be a Roman countermine,
is probably a natural fissure.
(© Author)

(1.75m) high, passing under the corner of Tower 19 and turning to run beneath the town wall for about 50ft (15m). Following a tried and tested method, the Persian sappers must have shored up their work as they proceeded, so that the tower and adjacent curtain wall sat, not on bedrock, but on timber beams, which would subsequently be fired to bring down the fortifications. Alerted to the Persian mining operations, perhaps by the sound of pickaxes or by the sight of the accumulating debris in the desert to the west, the Roman defenders dug their own countermine, intending to forestall the Persian plan (see illustration p. 188). In the event, the mine was fired, but the Persians must have been dismayed to see that the tower still stood.

It was probably at this stage that they began to construct a siege embankment, some way to the south, beyond Tower 15. However, it seems that their work was hampered by missile fire from Tower 14, the southernmost tower, sitting just where the western desert wall turns and heads east along the brink of the southern ravine. To neutralize this threat, the Persians dug another tunnel (Tunnel 2), entering from the concealment of the ravine and skilfully directing its sinuous course right under the tower. Another smaller tunnel branched off, back to the ravine, perhaps as a ventilation shaft for the main combustion chamber. Again, the massive buttressing of the wall prevented the tower's complete demolition, but its walls came apart as they sank into the mine.

Corpse discovered in Tunnel 1 at Dura Europos. Presumed to have been one of the besiegers, as he was facing the town when he fell on his back, he was perhaps cut down by Roman soldiers, intent on disrupting the Persian siege operations. He wears a chainmail coat, and a Persian-style helmet lay nearby. (© Yale University Art Gallery)

We can only speculate as to the purpose of the curious knot of tunnels which passed underneath the siege embankment. The excavator, the Comte du Mesnil du Buisson, concluded, from his study of the pick-marks in the rock, that the two main tunnels were dug by the Persians. According to his scheme, as Tunnel 4 passed beneath the town wall, it was intercepted by the Romans, who then proceeded to burrow up into the embankment in the hope of destabilizing it. That they succeeded, argued the Comte, is proven by the pronounced shelf which can be seen halfway along the embankment; furthermore, burnt areas exposed during its excavation showed, in the Comte's opinion, that two galleries had been dug and fired. In response, the Persians dug another tunnel (Tunnel 3) which, after passing under the town wall, turned north and broke into a large chamber where the Roman sappers were allegedly gathering. Finally, having neutralized the threat from Tunnel 4, the Persians used Tunnel 3 to invade the town, diverting attention from their colleagues storming up the partly collapsed

embankment outside. Although plausible, the entire scenario rests on archaeological evidence which is capable of more than one interpretation. Only further investigation will clarify the course of events.

The siege of Cremna in AD 278 is more straightforward. The historian Zosimus relates that, when a Roman army arrived in the area to deal with a bandit chieftain named Lydius, the latter took refuge in this well-fortified town, which was defended on three sides by impassable cliffs. His ploy to expel all those who could not bear arms backfired when the refugees were herded back into the town, so he tossed them over the cliffs. Lydius is said to have relied upon one man in particular, 'skilled in the construction of machines and capable of shooting missiles from machines with great accuracy' (Zos. 1.70); when this artilleryman was punished for uncharacteristically missing his aim, he defected to the Romans and used his skill to shoot Lydius as he stood at an open window.

The Persian siege embankment at Dura Europos, viewed from the south-west. Excavations in the 1930s demonstrated that it was piled up between twin banks of mud brick, the right-hand one over 6ft (almost 2m) thick, which perhaps continued above the level of the causeway to form side walls. Tower 15 can be seen on the left. (© M. C. Bishop)

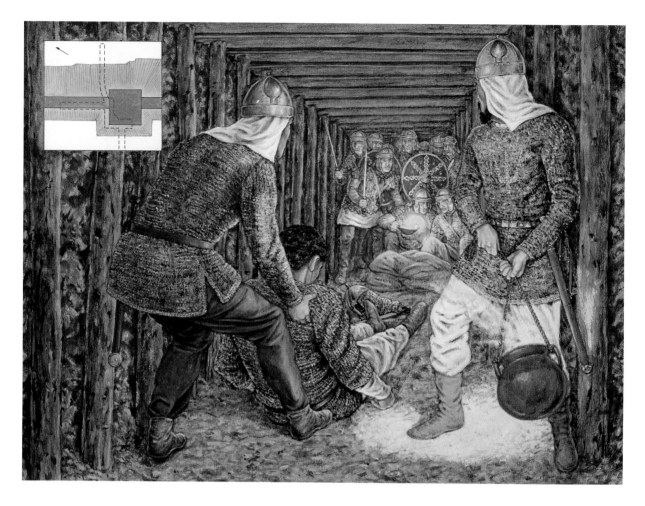

This scene depicts an underground encounter between Romans and Persians, both engaged in mining operations beneath the desert wall of Dura Europos, AD 256. Archaeological evidence suggests that the Persians, having undermined Tower 19, had shored up the foundations ready to be fired, when the Roman defenders broke into their tunnel via a countermine. (Adam Hook © Osprey Publishing Ltd)

Zosimus gives no hint of the siege-works that came to light in the 1980s. Archaeologists found the remains of two parallel walls, roughly 840ft (250m) apart, blocking the only access route to the town; each was equipped with a system of turrets to assist in surveillance. As the only identifiable camp, a tiny 0.42-acre (0.17ha) enclosure, was tacked onto the outside of the outer line, the excavator believed that the siege-works formed a double wall facing the town. However, the orientation of the turrets shows that the western wall faced outwards in the manner of a bicircumvallation. The bulk of the troops would have operated in the area between the walls, like Scipio's army at Carthage (above, p. 114).

In time-honoured fashion, the construction of the siege lines was followed by preparations for assault. The most striking feature at Cremna is a huge artificial mound that spans the valley between the siege lines and the town wall. Although this has been interpreted as an artillery platform to enable a short-range barrage against the defences, it bears all the hallmarks of an unfinished siege embankment. No doubt a battering ram stood by, ready to roll forward when the remaining 20m gap was filled. Certainly, the response of the townsfolk was to thicken the town wall at this point with a 50ft-deep (15m) counter-mound, obviously intended to reinforce the curtain wall against the imminent battering attack. However, the assassination of Lydius must have led to the town's surrender.

THE SIEGE WARFARE OF ROME'S ENEMIES

The story of siege warfare, from the defeat of Carthage in 146 BC down to the 3rd century AD, largely concerns Roman armies besieging non-Romans or other Roman armies. At the start of this period, Rome was the virtual ruler of the Mediterranean, having gradually absorbed the declining Hellenistic kingdoms of the east. Mithridates VI of Pontus was the last eastern potentate with the wealth and sophistication to field a siege train; even Herod the Great required Roman assistance to retake Jerusalem in 37 BC. In AD 51, when another Mithridates, this time the king of Armenia, was attacked by his neighbours from Iberia (present-day Georgia), he took refuge with the Roman garrison of Gorneae. This episode prompted Tacitus' disdainful comment, 'there is nothing of which barbarians are so ignorant as machinery and the craft of besieging, but to us that aspect of warfare is well known' (Tac., *Ann.* 2.45).

It was common knowledge that the Parthians, who had inherited much of the old Seleucid territories in Iran, were equally inept at besieging. During the interminable game they played with Rome, each seeking to exert

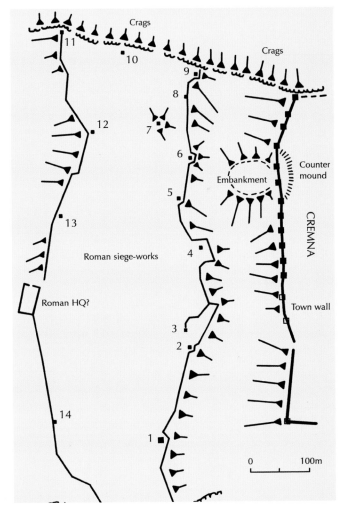

Plan of the siege-works at Cremna. The west wall of the town (right), built in Hellenistic times, faces a double line of siege-works across the broad natural valley that serves as the town's forward defence. (© Author)

Tower 14 at Dura Europos, viewed from within the town. The Persian attackers successfully undermined the four walls, causing the tower to come apart, thus preventing its use as a platform for catapults and archers. The buttress is a modern addition. (© M. C. Bishop)

authority over the other by changing the ruler of Armenia, the emperor Nero propped up his nominee, Tigranes V, with a Roman garrison; the Parthians promptly besieged them in the royal city of Tigranocerta, with the aid of Adiabenian allied troops. However, as Tacitus reports, 'when the Adiabeni began to bring up their ladders and machinery, they were easily driven back, and were soon slain by our men sallying forth' (Tac., *Ann.* 15.4–5). The Roman historian believed that the Parthians lacked the courage for siegecraft. Certainly, their cavalry armies were more suited to the hit-and-run tactics that destroyed Antony's siege train in 36 BC.

The Germanic tribes are also generally charged with incompetence in siegecraft. Although Tacitus knew of two occasions when German had besieged German, they relied on weight of numbers rather than technology or tactics. In AD 69, when a coalition of Germans, stiffened by renegade Batavian auxiliary troops, besieged the legionary camp at Vetera (Xanten in Germany), their makeshift siege machines were easily broken up by the defenders on the

wall, and the arrival of a relieving force was enough to scare them off. Similarly, the Gauls who attacked the camp of Caesar's lieutenant, Q. Cicero, in 54 BC fled at the approach of Caesar's army. Astonishingly, during the preceding weeks, they had imitated the Caesarian practice of circumvallation and had erected a siege tower, under instruction from Roman prisoners. It is a salutary reminder that, even if the Romans had a peculiar affinity with siege warfare, they did not hold a monopoly on the construction and use of machinery; it was perfectly possible for non-Roman craftsmen and workers to achieve this, given proper guidance.

The so-called siege mound at Cremna, viewed from the north. The excavator interpreted it as an artillery platform, while acknowledging that it might eventually have carried a column of storm troops over the town wall. In fact, it bears all the hallmarks of a siege embankment, and was probably intended to bring a battering ram up to the wall. (© S. Mitchell)

The Elements of Roman Siegecraft

THE ENCAMPMENT

It was a matter of routine for a Roman army to fortify a camp after each day's march. Such camps are explicitly mentioned at several sieges, and it seems reasonable to suppose that, in most cases, the besieging general's first act was to provide secure accommodation for his men. Once the army had moved up for the siege, new encampments were required. The historical sources suggest that it was common to establish two camps in complementary positions, thus ensuring complete visual coverage of the enemy town. Often, supplementary guard posts were sited all around to keep a closer watch, in many cases linked by a continuous barrier of some kind. Vegetius explains that 'besiegers make a ditch beyond missile range and furnish it not only with a rampart and palisade but also with turrets, so that they can withstand sorties from the town; they call such a siege-work a *loricula*' (Veg., *Epit. rei mil.* 4.28).

THE CIRCUMVALLATION

The term 'circumvallation' is not found in Latin literature. Ancient authors often use verbs with the prefix *circum* ('around') to indicate the surrounding of a town: for example, *circummunire*, to surround with a wall, or *circumvallare*, to

192

surround with a rampart. But there was no special word to replicate the Greek *periteichismos*. At Alesia, Caesar refers simply to 'the Roman fortifications' (*BGall.* 7.78), and his forts at Dyrrachium were linked by 'continuous fortifications' (Caes., *BCiv.* 3.44). However, in a rare exception to the rule, he refers to the rampart and forts with which he invested Corfinium as a *circummunitio*, which literally means a 'surrounding fortification' (*BCiv.* 1.19). More usually, in order to indicate a circumvallation, writers employed a phrase such as Cicero's description of Pompey at Brundisium, 'penned in with ditch and rampart' (*Ad Att.* 9.12). And the author of the *Bellum Hispaniense* uses a different circumlocution, when he writes that 'Caesar besieged Ategua with fortifications, and began to draw arms around the town' (*BHisp.* 6). (An individual length of wall was often called a *bracchium*, 'arm', or in Greek a *skelos*, 'leg'.) In rare cases like Alesia, with its double siege lines, the second line was quite simply designated 'the outer fortifications' (*BGall.* 7.77).

In the 19th century, Napoléon III confused the issue by referring to Caesar's lines of investment, for example at the town of the Atuatuci, as 'contrevallations'. When he turned to Alesia, he applied the same term to the inner line, and dubbed the outer line the 'circonvallation'. This was the traditional vocabulary used by French military theorists to describe the double lines of earthworks common in 15th- and 16th-century siege warfare. However, Schulten deplored the French terminology, and proposed reversing the two terms used by Napoléon, so that the inner line (indeed the only line, where a single siege wall was used) was the *circumvallatio*, and the far more rarely used outer line was given the modern name of 'contravallation'. French scholars traditionally retain Napoléon's terminology for the site of Alesia, but its use elsewhere should be discouraged.

Interestingly, the author of the *Bellum Alexandrinum* refers to the siege-works at Ulia, which may have been of the bicircumvallation variety (above, pp. 157–158), as both *munitiones* ('fortifications') and *opera* ('works'), in the same sentence (*BAlex.* 63). The latter is another problematic term, as the ancients drew no distinction between the building of earthworks and the building of machinery; both could happily be labelled 'works', and often only the context indicates the author's intention. For example, writing about the siege of Ambracia in 189 BC, Livy draws a distinction between the *munimenta*

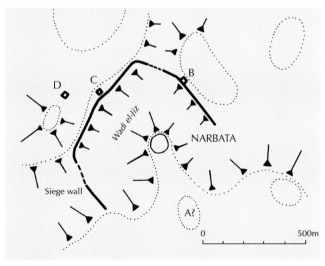

Plan of Narbata (Israel), where a Roman circumvallation has been recognized. The site exhibits several peculiarities, such as the small size of the three camps (marked B, C and D), only one of which is attached to the siege wall. The gaps in the north and south-west sectors may have been created by torrents in the Wadi el-Jiz, but the encirclement perhaps remained open to the south. Camp A is purely speculative. (© Author)

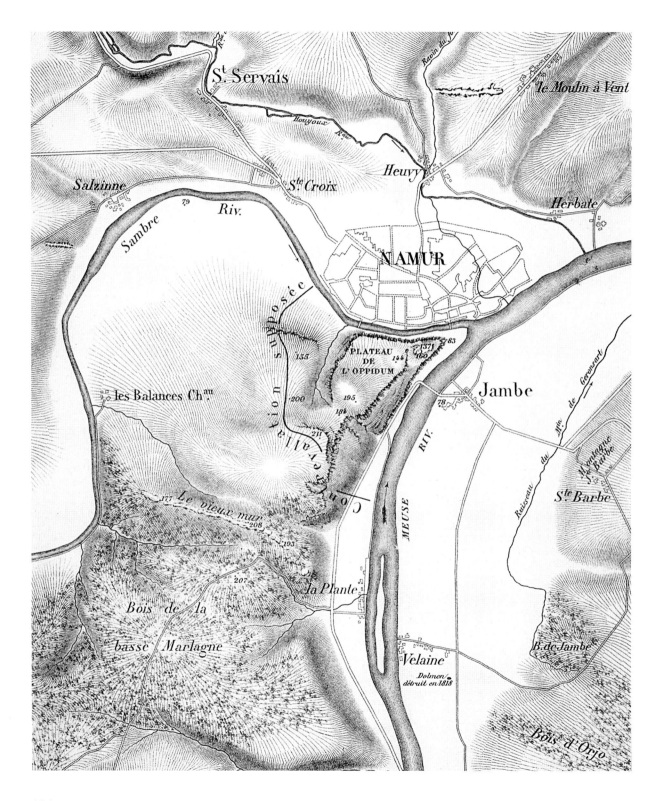

'by which the town was surrounded' and the *opera* 'which the consul prepared to move up to the walls' (Livy 38.5.1); the first are fortifications, and the second are machines. On the other hand, when Hirtius writes that, in 51 BC, Caninius constructed *opera* around Uxellodunum (*BGall*. 8.37), he is referring to the circumvallation.

The ditch and palisade was probably the most common form of barrier. Even when a solitary ditch is mentioned, as at Athens in 86 BC or Tigranocerta in 69 BC, the upcast material perhaps formed a low rampart. Of course, a ditch on its own, even a substantial one, may not seem a particularly secure barrier, but it would have served to apply the psychological pressure of containment. This was surely a major part of the strategy behind circumvallation. However, the Austrian scholar Georg Veith, overly influenced by Numantia and Alesia, concluded that Roman strategists must have favoured the blockade. The maxim attributed to Scipio Aemilianus, that only a reckless general would fight before there was any need, became misinterpreted as meaning that a good general took no risks; this in turn was taken as proof that the Romans preferred to starve an enemy into submission than risk shedding blood. Certainly, Schulten believed that the siege of Numantia (and, by extension, Alesia) embodied the famous strategy of *sedendo et cunctando* ('sitting and waiting'), whereby Q. Fabius Maximus had worn Hannibal down. Unfortunately, this has led many modern scholars to attribute an entirely imaginary policy of 'patient obstinacy and thoroughness' to Roman besiegers. But in doing so, they ignore the many instances of towns taken by sudden and bloody assault.

THE SIEGE EMBANKMENT

As we have seen, there was often a requirement to pile up an embankment against the enemy wall, occasionally to elevate infantry for a massed attack across the battlements, but in most cases to facilitate the advance of wheeled machinery across rough terrain, or where the approach was impeded by ravines or gullies. It seems that all manner of material could be used in its construction; a Byzantine lexicon defines a siege embankment as 'a device of war erected from stones and timbers and heaped-up earth' (Suda A203). The prevalence of wood is confirmed by the many occasions on which defenders attempted to set them alight (for example, Avaricum, Uxellodunum, Massilia, Jotapata, Jerusalem) and wood fragments were found in the embankment at Masada. The poet Lucan describes Trebonius' embankment at Massilia as earth and brushwood compressed by a timber framework at the sides.

(Opposite) Napoléon located the town of the Atuatuci at Namur, and suggested a likely course for Caesar's siege rampart (here labelled 'contrevallation supposée'), but it is considerably shorter than the reported 15,000ft (4.5km). (Napoléon III, Histoire de Jules César, II: Guerre des Gauls, Paris 1866)

Apollodorus' 'ship's prow' tortoise

In the section of Apollodorus' *Poliorkētika* ('Siegecraft') discussing how to deal with defenders who command the high ground, the author mentions a specialized type of shed. Tree trunks, heavily laden wagons, and weighted barrels were often rolled downhill to disrupt the ranks of the besiegers. Apollodorus suggests intercepting these and channelling them away by means of oblique ditches and reinforced palisades. Furthermore, he recommends that assault troops should crowd inside a specially designed shed for protection:

> The tortoise shaped like the prow of a ship (embolon), carried by heavy infantry, is

brought forward on rectangular foot-thick [0.30m] beams, its surface being smooth, or on iron wheels attached to the base, so that when it is set in position it is fixed in the ground and is not shifted by collision (i.e., with the objects rolled downhill against it). It will also have a slanting beam in the front, propping it up against capsizing (Apoll. 140.9–14).

Its triangular shape, with heavily reinforced apex facing uphill, was designed to deflect rolling objects. Apparently roofless, it was light enough for the soldiers to slide along like a sledge, and was wedged in position by a stout prop. By good fortune, this scenario is illustrated on Trajan's Column, in a scene that has been consistently misunderstood, owing to the

Brian Delf © Osprey Publishing Ltd

Scene of a siege from Trajan's Column (Rome). The defenders roll barrels and tree trunks downhill (top right), but these are intercepted by three peculiar machines. The German scholar Otto Lendle made the astute observation that these are likely to represent Apollodorus' 'ship's prow tortoises'. (C. Cichorius, Die Reliefs der Traianssäule, Berlin 1900)

juxtaposition of the sheds with the defenders' tree trunks and barrels.

This concern with hilltop fortifications adds weight to the general suspicion that Apollodorus was writing at the time of the emperor Trajan's Second Dacian War (AD 105/6), which appears to have ended with the storming of native strongholds. Certainly, he was responsible for building the famous Danube bridge for this campaign, and he writes of having previously served at the emperor's side, perhaps during the First Dacian War (AD 101/2).

Liebenam believed that, as a general rule, the siege embankment advanced, layer by layer, until it reached the top of the enemy wall. However, individual designs varied. At Avaricum, Caesar's troops still had to scale the wall, probably using ladders, whereas at Jotapata Vespasian was aiming for the battlements, before the defenders heightened the wall; having modified his tactics to allow a battering attack, Vespasian returned to his original plan and the embankment was again raised to overtop the walls. The topography at Gamala called for a different approach; here, the embankment simply evened out the rough and broken terrain so that machinery could be brought up to the wall. We read of defenders attempting to undermine embankments, which suggests that they could be substantial structures, even if they did not rise to battlement level. For example, at Piraeus, the walls stood on a 7ft (2m) plinth of enormous squared blocks, so it is fair to assume that Sulla's embankment was intended to carry battering rams above this layer.

Liebenam's layer-by-layer approach is probably also mistaken. Stoffel's alternative suggestion is more attractive, that the work proceeded in huge steps, each gaining its maximum height before the next was begun. In this way, an unfinished embankment would not resemble Liebenam's low platform, which had achieved its desired length but not yet its target height; on the contrary, it would resemble Stoffel's mound, rising up in steps to its intended height, but still some way from the enemy wall. This is exactly what we find at Machaerus, where the steadily rising embankment was halted 170ft (50m) short of its goal. Equally, the embankment at Cremna stops 65ft (20m) short of the wall; its excessive width must have been caused by the spreading of the constituent earth and stones down into the valley.

During a visit to Masada in 1932, Schulten's companion, General Adolf Lammerer, realized that timbers protruding from the south side of the siege embankment must have belonged to the Roman structure's framework. Timber-work is still visible today. (© D. Gill)

THE SIEGECRAFT EXPERTS

There was a long tradition of writing instructions for besiegers and the besieged, particularly concerning the construction of machinery. Under the patronage of the emperor Augustus, the architect-engineer Vitruvius devoted Book 10 of his *De architectura* ('On Architecture') to machines of various sorts, some of which 'were invented as a protection against danger and a necessity for safety' (*De arch.* 10.10.1). Much the same ground was covered by Athenaeus, who wrote his *Peri mēchanēmatōn* ('On Machinery') for Augustus' nephew and son-in-law, Marcellus. But their texts concentrate on Hellenistic siege machines, and it is unclear how relevant these descriptions would have been to Augustan warfare. Certainly, the philosopher Onasander, whose *Stratēgikos* ('The General') was addressed to Q. Veranius, one of the consuls of AD 49, recommended that the siege commander should be familiar with a range of equipment, so that he could make an informed choice; but his own inclination seems to have been for the storming assault, delivered in waves, preferably where it would be least expected

Aerial view of Machaerus, looking north. The remains of a siege embankment appear as an elongated hump on the left. (© D. L. Kennedy. APA98 / 29.37 / 17 May 1998)

(e.g., Onas., *Strat.* 42.7–13). Similarly, in his *Strategemata* ('Stratagems'), the high-ranking general and administrator Frontinus (a three-time consul, latterly as the emperor Trajan's colleague) entirely disregarded siege-works and machinery, in the belief that 'their invention was long since completed, and I see no substance for further perfection' (Frontin., *Str.* 3.*praef.*).

Frontinus' judgement was premature. Besides the radical overhaul of artillery construction, generally dated to the period around AD 100, we have the work of Apollodorus of Damascus, Trajan's architect and military engineer, who was evidently invited to produce designs for new siege machines. His text, entitled *Poliorkētika* ('Siegecraft'), assumes that a tribal hillfort is the focus of the siege, rather than a fortified town. First, he warns the reader against objects rolled downhill, a scenario that recalls the siege of Andetrium (see illustration p. 165); but where Tiberius was prepared to persevere with a storming assault, Apollodorus recommends a system of banks and ditches to divert the hazardous boulders, tree trunks and wagons, along with sheds specially designed to deflect them. Then he describes the sheds that will be needed, either to protect the legionaries during undermining work, or to carry the battering rams against a tower, a gate or the wall itself. The next section concerns the construction of a siege tower, followed by a novel system of interlocking ladders. He ends with a description of a battlemented raft for assaulting across a river. Some of the incidental elaborations are a little far-fetched, such as the addition of a torsion-powered truncheon to the end of a battering ram; many of these are thought to have been added later by an enthusiastic editor, but the core of Apollodorus' text provides a selection of machines which are 'effective, protective and safe, and that as far as possible are constructed out of easily obtained materials' (Apoll. 137.8–9).

Conclusion

Siege warfare in the 4th century

In AD 356, the future emperor Julian was wintering in a Gallic town with a small entourage when the Germanic Alamanni attacked, but they were unable to get through the locked gates. Ammianus Marcellinus, a participant in the military affairs of the day and a first-rate historian, says that 'after forty days, the barbarians departed, grumbling that it had been futile and foolish to consider the siege of a town' (16.4.2). The Germans' continuing lack of success in siege warfare perhaps had more to do with their temperament than with any technological inferiority. A rebellious unit of Gothic auxiliaries, expelled from Hadrianopolis (present-day Edirne in Turkey) in AD 376, threatened to besiege the town, but were driven off by the defenders' arrows and sling stones. Two years later, following the disastrous battle in the neighbourhood, a Gothic horde again attempted a siege, but were entirely unable to make any headway (see illustration p. 204).

Only with the rise of the Sassanian Persians did Rome encounter an enemy equally skilled in siegecraft. The scourge of the eastern provinces during the later 3rd century, when they captured Dura Europos, Nisibis and even Antioch, they continued to be a thorn in Rome's side. Ammianus describes the Persian siege of Amida in AD 359. The aggressors apparently used artillery and machines captured from the Roman garrison at Singara, and began piling up embankments under the protection of iron-clad siege towers. The fighting continued day after day, without either side gaining the advantage, until a huge earthen buttress which the defenders had built to strengthen their wall shifted forwards, breaching the defences and creating a bridge with the Persian embankment outside. Ammianus describes the horrific sequel, as the Persians sacked the town: 'armed and unarmed, irrespective of gender, were slaughtered like cattle' (19.8.4).

The Persians enjoyed similar success in the following year at Singara and Bezabde with the same range of siege machinery and artillery. When the inhabitants of Singara, in present-day Iraq, refused to surrender, 'a flame-coloured flag was raised as a sign, and the town was attacked on all sides; some carried ladders, others fixed machines together, and a great many tried to find a way, under the protection of shelters and screens, to destroy the

The Arch of Constantine, erected in Rome in AD 312, depicts troops attacking a town wall. Earlier in the year, Constantine had attacked Verona, held by his rival Maxentius' praetorian prefect, Ruricius Pompeianus. Rather than stand siege, Pompeianus decided to take his chances on the battlefield and was killed. (© R. Cowan)

foundations of the walls' (Amm. Marc. 20.6.3). Eventually, the Persians brought up a powerful battering ram and breached a newly repaired tower, whereupon the invaders surged into the town; the dismayed inhabitants were taken prisoner. Moving on to Bezabde, a town in present-day Turkey, the Persian king, Sapor, was subjected to 'the fierce stings of the ballistas and arrows' (Amm. Marc. 20.7.2) from the town walls; only the presence of his shield-bearers kept him from harm. The enraged king unleashed a full-scale assault, and his battering rams were met by showers of arrows and hand-hurled stones; 'nor were the ballistas and scorpions idle, the former whirling out darts, the latter volleys of stones' (Amm. Marc. 20.7.10). Again, a tower was brought down by a huge battering ram, and the Persians ran amok in the town.

The Romans, too, could deploy the full range of siege machinery familiar to earlier generations of besiegers. For example, in AD 324, having trapped his rival Licinius in Byzantium, Constantine (later known as 'the Great') erected siege towers to overlook the walls and protect his men as they constructed an embankment; when the battering rams were ready to advance, Licinius fled and the townsfolk surrendered. Of course, availability of equipment was no guarantee of success. In AD 360, Constantius II, one of Constantine's sons, mounted a full-scale attack on Persian-occupied Bezabde. However, the Persians put up a more spirited defence than Constantine had met at Byzantium. First, Constantius' hopes of undermining the walls were crushed when the defenders dropped huge jars, millstones and column drums down onto the sappers' shelters. Then, after the Romans had thrown up an embankment and brought a giant battering ram up to the wall, the Persians unleashed a hail of fire-arrows; although the machine's fireproof coating kept it undamaged, it was effectively paralysed when the ram head became ensnared in a lasso. It was only with great difficulty that the Romans salvaged it, after the Persians had doused it in boiling pitch and pelted it with iron baskets of flaming brushwood. Finally, when the Persians surreptitiously set fire to the Roman embankment with hot coals, Constantius abandoned the enterprise in frustration.

AMMIANUS' SIEGE MACHINES

The soldier and writer Ammianus Marcellinus had first-hand experience of the Roman army at war, gained in the eastern theatre of the AD 360s. In a well-known digression, he attempts to describe the siege machinery and artillery of his own day, but with varying success, because his language is non-technical and often confused.

After their victory in battle nearby, the barbarian Goths attacked the city of Hadrianopolis in AD 378, intent on looting the imperial treasure that they imagined lay within. The townsfolk joined the garrison in their efforts to repel the attackers. Large onagers hurled stones into the Gothic horde with terrifying effect. (Adam Hook © Osprey Publishing Ltd)

For the battering ram, he explains, 'A tall fir or mountain ash is selected, to the end of which is fixed a long, hard [lump of] iron, manufactured in prominent likeness of a ram, a shape which gives its name to this machine' (Amm. Marc. 23.4.8). Earlier in his work, he had painted a detailed picture of the Persian countermeasures against the enormous Roman battering ram at Bezabde: 'they skilfully ensnared the projecting iron head ... with very long cords on both sides, so that it could not gain momentum by drawing back to strike the walls with frequent blows, and they also poured down boiling hot pitch' (Amm. Marc. 20.11.15). After 800 years, the same techniques used by the besieged Plataeans (above, p. 40) were still effective.

Ammianus' *helepolis*, which follows on from his discussion of the battering ram, is clearly a confused description of a ram-tortoise and far too muddled to

THE STONE-PROJECTING ONAGER

Ammianus' remarks on the one-armed stone-projector are fairly clear, though still vague enough to have spawned three different reconstructions. In short, a single torsion-spring was mounted transversely in a recumbent timber frame. A single, wooden arm was slotted into the spring halfway along, so that it stood upright and travelled in a vertical arc; a sling attached to its free end released a stone when the arm reached the top of the arc. Ammianus claims that the machine was called the *onager*, or wild ass, because it kicked up stones; previously, it had been known as the *scorpio*, no doubt because of the resemblance between the upright arm and the scorpion's tail. (It is clear that, across the centuries, artillery terminology gradually changed, for in Vitruvius' day the *scorpio* was a light-calibre arrow-shooter.)

In the absence of a bow-string, which arrested the arm movement in the traditional two-armed catapult, this machine required a padded buffer to stop the arm. Ammianus writes that 'in front of the wooden structure [i.e., the *onager*], a huge buffer is spread out: namely, a sack stuffed with fine chaff, secured with strong binding, and located on heaped up turves or piles of bricks'. Marsden, the artillery scholar, was misled by the philologist Rudolf Schneider into believing that the entire machine sat on a pile of turf or bricks; it seems, however, that Ammianus meant the buffer alone was raised up in this way. This perhaps applied only to the larger machines, such as the one that famously misfired at Maozamalcha in AD 363, crushing the chief artilleryman with its stone.

A turf buffer would have been a liability whenever the *onager* had to be moved. Yet, Ammianus mentions no such upheaval in connection with the nocturnal redeployment of four machines at Amida in AD 359. In fact, for lighter models, the design proposed by Napoléon III's general, Verchère de Reffye, would have been quite suitable; by incorporating a separate timber-framed buffer, this design reduced the overall weight of the *onager* and increased its manoeuvrability.

In practical tests using miniature models, Michael Lewis demonstrated the superiority of a forward-sloping buffer over the more familiar vertical one. He was also able to establish that the length of the sling had a real bearing on the range of the missile, and that, far from simply lobbing stones in a high arc, the sling could be set to release its missile in a flat, direct trajectory. Modern commentators often assume that the *onager* represented a decline in ancient artillery, but they are confusing simplicity with clumsiness. In fact, it seems to have been an efficient and easily operated machine, and the single torsion-spring removed the need, intrinsic to two-armed catapults, for fine-tuning and balancing a pair of springs.

form the basis of a reconstruction, and although his description of the *ballista* is incomprehensible, he makes a decent attempt at the *onager*, the favoured stone-projecting catapult of the 4th century AD.

A THOUSAND YEARS OF SIEGE WARFARE

Modern commentators often hold up the 1st century AD as a golden age of siege warfare, claiming that it declined thereafter. The belief is prevalent that later armies were less skilled in the besieging art, having forgotten how to construct an embankment or design a siege tower. The British scholar Eric Marsden injudiciously wrote about 'the almost total lack of fighting men who really knew what engines of war could do for them and who knew how to make full use of them'. This is patently false. In the 4th century, Roman and Persian armies alike utilized the same arsenal of weapons, developed in the Greek world from the time of Dionysius I onwards, and achieved the same degree of sophistication as the armies of Caesar and Vespasian.

Having been largely standardized in Macedonian times, the same basic range of siege machines remained in use throughout the Roman period, although it is often claimed, on spurious grounds, that standards declined. On the contrary, the siege machinery observed on the eastern frontier in the AD 360s by Ammianus Marcellinus would have been recognized and appreciated by Julius Caesar four centuries before; indeed, very little of it would have been completely alien to Sennacherib, a thousand years earlier. Battering rams were still used to shake walls; siege towers were still used to elevate missile troops; and defenders still relied on fire as their main ally.

Even the use of the siege embankment, which at first sight seems to be a Roman innovation, goes back through the centuries. Initial Roman trials with this type of structure during the Second Punic War marked a major divergence with earlier Hellenistic siegecraft, removing the need for the gigantic towers of the Macedonians. But there was an earlier tradition, which the Spartans perhaps drew upon at Plataea in 429 BC; their use of the siege embankment there was not the isolated incident that many modern scholars assume, but was rooted in the practice of the Persians and their Assyrian forebears. There are remarkable similarities to be drawn between the siege-works constructed at Lachish in 701 BC, and those at Cremna, dating from nearly a millennium later.

The Romans placed a different emphasis on siege machinery, initially relegating it to a supporting role in their frequent and bloody infantry assaults. The more fanciful devices, such as the *sambuca*, were used only infrequently; some, like the *terebra*, we never see in action at all. At the same time, it is apparent that a more functional range of sheds and shelters was adopted, not least to accommodate the battering rams. But although the Hellenistic engineers had favoured gigantic size to overawe their opponents, it is striking how the same basic arsenal of machines was employed throughout antiquity to try to neutralize or circumvent enemy fortifications. The major exception is, of course, the catapult. Despite the attempts of modern scholars to transfer this weapon back to the time of the Persians, and even of the Assyrians, it seems certain that it only came into being around 400 BC.

The first of the Sassanian kings, Ardashir, attempted to capture Hatra around AD 227, but it was his son, Sapor, who finally succeeded in AD 240, after a two-year siege. The city was so thoroughly sacked that, when Ammianus Marcellinus passed by in AD 363, it lay in ruins. (© Author)

Just as there was no noticeable superiority in the siege warfare of the Roman Principate, so the late empire brought no particular decline in competence. Although the conduct of a siege was theoretically influenced by the commander, it depended largely on the defensive capability of the town and the measures employed by its defenders. Artillery notwithstanding, in a period that saw no major technological innovation, Julian's conduct at Maiozamalcha (AD 363), for example, where he raised embankments, deployed artillery and battered down the wall with rams, would have been quite familiar to Scipio, Sulla and Caesar. Likewise, three years earlier, when Sassanian troops besieged Virtha using 'embankments ... and machines' (Amm. Marc. 20.7.18), the strategy would have been entirely comprehensible to Shapur's Achaemenid forebears. Indeed, disregarding the presence of catapults (if these were amongst the 'machines' that Ammianus mentions here), the Sassanian siege was probably broadly similar to Sennacherib's siege of Lachish, a thousand years earlier.

GLOSSARY

Agger
'heap' (Latin; pl. *aggeres*): siege embankment, usually constructed by piling up rubble, brushwood and earth, and often buttressed by a timber framework (Greek, *chōma*)

Ballista
'throwing machine' (Latin; pl. *ballistae*): originally the stone-projecting catapult of the Greeks and Romans; the same basic design was utilized, from around AD 100, for the new iron-framed arrow-shooting catapult

Belostasis
'missile weapon position' (Greek; pl. *belostaseis*): catapult battery, or position occupied by catapults (Athenaeus uses the alternative *belostasia*)

Catapulta
'catapult' (Latin; pl. *catapultae*): any artillery weapon, but usually an arrow-shooter

Circumvallation
modern term indicating an earthwork encirclement, in the manner of the Greek *periteichismos* (q.v.)

Embolon
'point' (Greek; pl. *emboloi*): the ramming prow of a ship, used to describe the beam of a battering ram (also *embolē*)

Escharion
'grid-iron' (Greek; pl. *escharia*): the undercarriage of many siege machines, particularly the *helepolis*, incorporating a grid of criss-crossing beams

Gastraphetēs
'belly bow' (Greek; pl. *gastraphetai*): precursor of the torsion catapult, consisting of a powerful composite bow mounted transversally on a stock to resemble the later crossbow

Helepolis
'city taker' (Greek; pl. *helepoleis*): usually applied to the massive siege towers of Hellenistic times, but also more loosely applied to any particularly impressive siege machine

Katapeltēs
'catapult' (Greek; pl. *katapeltai*): any artillery weapon, but usually an arrow-shooter (cf. *catapulta*)

Musculus
'little mouse' (Latin; pl. *musculi*): a type of shed used in undermining work

Detail of a battering ram from a relief from the palace of Nimrud. (R. Sheridan / Ancient Art & Architecture Collection Ltd)

Onager

'wild ass' (Latin; pl. *onagri*): one-armed stone-projecting catapult which found widespread use in the late Roman period; also known as a *scorpio* (q.v.)

Periteichismos

'walling around' (Greek; pl. *periteichismoi*): term indicating the surrounding of a town with earthworks, often translated as circumvallation (q.v.)

Petrobolos

'stone thrower' (Greek; pl. *petroboloi*): (a) soldier trained to throw stones by hand; (b) the stone-projecting catapult of the Greeks and Romans, like the *ballista* (q.v.), and often specified as *katapeltēs petrobolos* ('stone-projecting catapult') to avoid confusion with (a)

Pluteus

'partition' (Latin; pl. *plutei*): (a) a convex wicker shield with an arched roof, which ran on three rollers; (b) any wickerwork screen or cladding on military structures (Greek, *gerra*)

Sambuca	'harp' (Latin; pl. *sambucae*): a type of siege machine incorporating a mechanically raised assault-ladder (Greek, *sambykē*)
Scorpio	'scorpion' (Latin; pl. *scorpiones*): (a) originally a small-calibre arrow-shooter; (b) the word is later used for the one-armed stone-projecting *onager* (q.v.)
Terebra	'borer' (Latin; pl. *terebrae*): a siege machine for piercing walls using a pointed beam; also *trypanon* (q.v.)
Testudo	'tortoise' (Latin; pl. *testudines*): (a) siege shed of variable design, usually equipped with wheels (Greek, *chelōnē*); (b) the Roman tactic whereby a unit of soldiers interlock their shields to produce a protective roof
Tolleno	'swing beam' (Latin; pl. *tollenones*): a type of siege device incorporating a horizontal boom, pivoting on an upright post
Trypanon	'borer' (Greek; pl. *trypana*): a siege machine for piercing walls using a pointed beam; also *terebra* (q.v.)
Vinea	'vineyard' (Latin; pl. *vineae*): a type of shelter, consisting of a light timber structure with wickerwork sides and a flat boarded roof, entirely covered with raw hides (Greek, *ampelos*)

FURTHER READING

There are few general works on ancient siege warfare. Paul Bentley Kern's *Ancient Siege Warfare* (Souvenir Press, London, 1999) concentrates on the treatment of captured cities from earliest times down to AD 70. Peter Connolly's *Greece and Rome at War* (2nd edn, Greenhill Books, London, 1998) has an appendix on 'Fortifications and siege warfare', discussing a handful of well-known Greek and Roman examples with good illustrations. The fundamental study of Greek siegecraft is Yvon Garlan's *Recherches de poliorcétique grecque* (Boccard, Paris, 1974), although it covers only the 5th and 4th centuries BC; there is no comparable study of later centuries.

English translations of the main historical sources are available in the Loeb Classical Library. For the technical sources, Aeneas Tacticus has been translated, with commentary, by D. Whitehead (*Aineias the Tactician. How to survive under siege*, Oxford, Clarendon Press, 1990), and much of Philon's *Poliorkētika* has been translated by A. W. Lawrence (*Greek Aims in Fortification*, Oxford, Clarendon Press, 1979). For Athenaeus, there is a translation with excellent commentary by D. Whitehead and P. H. Blyth (*Athenaeus Mechanicus, On Machines*, Stuttgart, Franz Steiner Verlag, 2004), but there is no comprehensive edition of Apollodorus. Vegetius is most easily accessible in N. P. Milner's translation (*Vegetius, Epitome of Military Science*, Liverpool University Press, 1993), and Vitruvius in I. D. Rowland's translation (I. D. Rowland and T. N. Howe, *Vitruvius, Ten Books on Architecture*, Cambridge University Press, 1999). Finally, the serious student of siege machinery cannot ignore Lendle's selections, translated into German with the author's detailed commentary. I have periodically mentioned his and other scholars' opinions, and I append a list of their original publications.

BIBLIOGRAPHY

Adcock, F. E., *The Greek and Macedonian Art of War*, University of California Press, Berkeley (1957)

Baatz, D., *Bauten und Katapulte des römischen Heeres*, Franz Steiner Verlag, Stuttgart (1994)

Berlin, A. M. & Overman, J. A. (eds.), *The First Jewish Revolt. Archaeology, History, and Ideology*, Routledge, London (2002), pp. 121–33 on Yodefat; 134–53 on Gamla

Blyth, P. H., 'Apollodorus of Damascus and the *Poliorcetica*', in *Greek, Roman & Byzantine Studies* 33 (1992), pp. 127–58

Briant, P., 'A propos du boulet de Phocée', in *Revue des Études Anciennes* 96 (1994), pp. 111–14

Callebat L. & Fleury, P., *Vitruve, De l'architecture, livre X*, Paris, Société d'édition 'Les Belles Lettres' (1986)

Campbell, D. B., 'The Roman siege of Burnswark', in *Britannia* 34 (2003), pp. 19–33

Connolly, P., *The Holy Land*, Oxford University Press, Oxford (1999)

Deberge, Y. & Guichard, V., 'Nouvelles recherches sur les travaux césariens devant Gergovie (1995–1999)', in *Revue Archéologique du Centre de la France* 39 (2000), pp. 83–111

Drachmann, A. G., *The Mechanical Technology of Greek and Roman Antiquity*, International Booksellers and Publishers Ltd., Copenhagen (1963)

Erdmann, E., *Nordosttor und Persische Belagerungsrampe in Alt-Paphos. I. Waffen und Kleinfunde*, Universitätsverlag, Konstanz (1977)

Gill, D., 'Masada ramp was not a Roman engineering miracle', in *Biblical Archaeology Review* (Sept/Oct, 2001), pp. 22–31 and 56–7

Greenewalt, C. H., Jr., 'When a mighty empire was destroyed, the common man at the fall of Sardis, ca. 546 BC', in *Proceedings of the American Philosophical Society* 136 (1992), pp. 247–71

Grundy, G. B., *Thucydides and the History of His Age*, J. Murray, London (1911)

Hart V. G. & Lewis, M. J. T., 'Mechanics of the onager', in *Journal of Engineering Mathematics* 20 (1986), pp. 345–65

Hawkes, C. F. C., 'The Roman siege of Masada', in *Antiquity* 3 (1929), pp. 195–213

Jimeno Martínez, A., 'Numancia, campamentos romanos y cerco de Escipión', in *Archivo Español de Arqueologia* 75 (2002), pp. 159–76

Kenyon, K. M., *The Bible and Recent Archaeology*, British Museum Publications, London (1978)

Lendle, O., *Schildkröten. Antike Kriegsmaschinen in poliorketischen Texten*, Franz Steiner Verlag GmbH, Wiesbaden (1975)

— , *Texte und Untersuchungen zum technischen Bereich der antiken Poliorketik*, Franz Steiner Verlag GmbH, Wiesbaden (1983)

Lewis, M. J. T., 'When was Biton?' in *Mnemosyne* 52 (1999), pp. 159–68

Liebenam, W., 'Festungskrieg (2)', in *Paulys Realencyclopädie* 6.2 (1909), pp. 2236–55

Maier, F. G., 'Ausgrabungen in Alt-Paphos, Stadtmauer und Belagerungswerke', in *Archäologischer Anzeiger* 1967, pp. 303–30

—, 'Ausgrabungen in Alt-Paphos. Sechster vorläufiger Bericht', in *Archäologischer Anzeiger* 1974, pp. 28–48

Marsden, E. W., *Greek and Roman Artillery. Historical Development*, Clarendon Press, Oxford (1969)

—, *Greek and Roman Artillery. Technical Treatises*, Clarendon Press, Oxford (1971)

—, 'Macedonian military machinery and its designers under Philip and Alexander', in *Ancient Macedonia* 2 (1977), pp. 211–23

Mesnil du Buisson, R. du, 'Les ouvrages du siège à Doura Europos', in *Mémoires de la Société Nationale des Antiquaires de France* 81 (1944), pp. 5–60

Mitchell, S., *Cremna in Pisidia. An Ancient City in Peace and in War*, Duckworth, London (1995)

Ober, J., 'Hoplites and obstacles', in V. D. Hanson (ed.), *Hoplites. The Classical Greek Battle Experience*, Routledge, London (1991), pp. 173–96

—, 'Towards a typology of Greek artillery towers: the first and second generations (c. 375–275 B. C.)', in, S. van de Maele & J. Fossey (eds.), *Fortificationes Antiquae*, Gieben, Amsterdam (1992), pp. 147–69

Özyiğit, Ö., 'The city walls of Phokaia', in *Revue des Études Anciennes* 96 (1994), pp. 77–109

Pritchett, W. K., *The Greek State at War, Part 5*, University of California Press, Berkeley (1991)

Reddé, M., *et al.*, 'Fouilles et recherches nouvelles sur les travaux de César devant Alésia (1991–1994)', in *Bericht der Römisch-Germanischen Kommission* 76 (1995), pp. 73–157

Sackur, W., *Vitruv und die Poliorketiker: Bautechnisches aus der Literatur des Altertums*, Wilhelm Ernst & Sohn, Berlin (1925)

Schramm, E., *Die antiken Geschütze der Saalburg*, Weidmannsche Buchhandlung, Berlin (1918) (repr. Saalburgmuseum, 1980)

—, 'Poliorketik', in J. Kromayer and G. Veith, *Heerwesen und Kriegführung der Griechen und Römer*, C. H. Beck'sche Verlagsbuchhandlung, Munich (1928), pp. 209–45

Schulten, A., 'Masada. Die Burg des Herodes und die römischen Lager', in *Zeitschrift des Deutschen Palästina-Vereins* 56 (1933), pp. 1–185

Strobel, A., 'Das römische Belagerungswerk Machärus', in *Zeitschrift des Deutschen Palästina-Vereins* 90 (1974), pp. 128–84

Tarn, W. W., *Hellenistic Military & Naval Developments*, Cambridge University Press, Cambridge (1930)

Ussishkin, D., 'The Assyrian attack on Lachish', in *Tel Aviv* 17 (1990), pp. 53–86

Veith, G., 'Die Zeit des Militzheeres', in J. Kromayer and G. Veith, *Heerwesen und Kriegführung der Griechen und Römer*, C. H. Beck'sche Verlagsbuchhandlung, Munich (1928), pp. 167–99

Winter, F., *Greek Fortifications*, Routledge, London (1971)

INDEX